THE
MAKING
OF A
COP

THE
MAKING
OF A
COP

Harvey Rachlin

POCKET BOOKS

New York   London   Toronto   Sydney   Tokyo   Singapore

POCKET BOOKS, a division of Simon & Schuster
1230 Avenue of the Americas, New York, NY 10020

Rachlin, Harvey.
    The making of a cop / Harvey Rachlin.
        p.   cm.
    ISBN 0-671-66525-1 : $19.95
        1. Police training—New York (N.Y.)   I. Title.
    HV8148.N52R33   1991
    363.2'071'5—dc20   90-45853
                                                        CIP
First Pocket Books hardcover printing March 1991

10   9   8   7   6   5   4   3   2   1

FOR MY SON, GLENN

ACKNOWLEDGMENTS

I am profoundly grateful to Elaine Pfefferblit, who believed in this project from the start, giving me the opportunity to pursue a dream.

Michael Sanders provided editorial input of the highest caliber and shaped the manuscript into its final form. He never let me off easy in his guidance and he cannot imagine the high esteem in which I hold him.

Helping me launch this project were my agents Glen Hartley and Lynn Chu. Their consummate professionalism and treasured friendship have expanded my career and made it infinitely more pleasurable.

My dear friend Judith Stein read the manuscript and provided sagacious counsel for improving it. She is wonderful, and I cannot thank her enough.

Practically everybody I met at the New York Police Academy was friendly and helpful. I am grateful to all, particularly the following individuals who so generously assisted me:

Deputy Chief Robert F. Burke set everything in motion for me from the first day. Captain Charles D. DeRienzo gave me free rein and was always available to help if needed. Lieutenant Antonio Diaz, modest but great, was there every step of the way, facilitating many things that enabled me to get my story.

Several instructors at the academy were magnanimous in helping me understand the curriculum and police work in general. They spent countless hours with me, on their own time, and provided invaluable insight. They are Frank Dwyer, Michael Wilson, Gary Lombardo, and John Battista.

I am indebted to many at the academy, listed below by department or unit. Many have since gone on to different units or to precincts, or have been promoted or have retired:

Police Science Department: Lieutenant Pedro J. Pineiro, Sergeant George Anderson, Sergeant Sean Doran, and Sergeant Thomas Sandseth.

Social Science Department: Lieutenant Gertrude LaForgia, Sergeant Steven Kaufman, Police Officer William Keeler, and Police Officer Philip Carter.

Law Department: Sergeant Raymond K. DuFresne and Police Officer Raymond Berge.

Physical Education Department: Sergeant Alberto Gotay, Police Officer James Smith, Police Officer Arthur Perry, Police Officer Lillian Rodriguez, and Police Officer Frank Gandini.

Firearms and Tactics Section: Captain John C. Cerar (to whom I am especially grateful), Sergeant Noel Negron, Sergeant John O'Sullivan, Detective Frank D'Mario, Police Officer Salvatore Manna, Police Officer Lawrence Ursitti, Police Officer Eugene Maloney, and Police Officer Tom Barbagallo.

Driver Education and Training Unit: Lieutenant Joseph Lubomski, Sergeant Patrick Boyle, and Detective Edward Unz.

Scheduling Unit: Sergeant Steven J. Adler.

Testing Unit: Lieutenant John F. Madigan, Police Officer Richard Fornuto, and Police Officer Claire Normandeau.

Transit Instructional Services Unit Coordinator Joseph D. Cannon and Housing Liaison Supervisor Rudolph Curatolo.

Dr. Jess Maghan, director of training.

Office Associate Marie Grabec, Police Administrative Aide Maria Rodriguez, and museum curator John Podracky.

Assistant district attorneys David F. Everett and Carol L. Moran.

Detective William Abromaitis, Transit recruits Veronica Vazquez and Kevin Hanley, Richard Hartman of the Patrolmen's Benevolent Association of the city of New York, and Detective Richard Pastorella.

Transit Police Chief Vincent Del Castillo and the following at the Transit Academy: Captain Denis O'Keefe, Sergeant Robert J. Servidio,

Acknowledgments

Sergeant Gary Scirica, Police Officer Donald McHugh, Police Officer Ray McCormack, Police Officer Franklin Rivera, Police Officer Al Geraldi, Lieutenant Michael Ruotolo, and Police Officer Joe Asti.

Paulette Kloepfer did a superb job of typing this manuscript, often having to wade through a sea of indecipherable handwriting.

I would like to thank my parents, Philip and Mazie Rachlin, for always believing in me, encouraging me, and telling me there is no goal that cannot be reached if you're determined and persistent enough.

Finally, thanks to my wife, Marla Rachlin. She endured the loneliness and anguish that accompany a spouse's complete immersion in a project, and throughout was loving and wonderful and unflaggingly supportive of this book.

INTRODUCTION

This book was born out of a lifelong fascination with cops. From the youth who froze in awe at the steely command of the man in uniform to the adult who still thinks of cops as romantic adventurers, I have always known they were a special breed.

The work of a cop is dramatically different from the jobs of ordinary people. In what other profession does a person deal with the totality of society as both savior and penalizer? What other occupation requires one to interact with deranged killers, violent drug dealers, desperate addicts, hysterical accident victims, family members in furious conflict, women about to give birth, teenage runaways, irate drivers who get traffic tickets, and hostile crowds—often several in a single day? Cops must deal with every element of society, from respectable businessmen and harried homemakers to derelicts and psychopaths. The police are at once protectors, hunters, medical technicians, lawyers, psychologists, social workers, diplomats, and even scientists.

The sight of a cop in action has always intrigued me. To see a police car speeding off with its dome lights flashing and its siren proclaiming the arrival of the cavalry makes me simultaneously curious and envious: curious to find out what local tragedy is playing itself out around the corner, and envious of the cops dashing off to adventure while I'm left standing pop-eyed in the middle of my mundane existence.

The presence of a cop on the street always draws my attention. They have such an air of confidence; they exude polish; their bearing communicates order and strength. They are always immaculate, with clean, pressed uniforms and shiny coal-black shoes. With their guns dangling conspicuously from their belts and their shields glittering in the sun, they strike me as modern-day cowboys.

And the world cops inhabit has always been mysterious to me too. How do they solve crimes so quickly? Bring chaos to order so efficiently? Execute daring rescues and defuse volatile situations with such panache? They seem capable of handling anything, and they do it with such apparent ease. Ask them *how* they do it and they'll say, "Hard work." Hard work, sure, but they must have a bit of magic on their side too. And mystery—try getting close to a cop, and a wall goes up. Police officers seem to inhabit a closed universe impenetrable by outsiders.

Who are these people? How does a run-of-the-mill civilian walk into the academy and emerge a few months later a staunch purveyor of law and order, intrepid, self-assured, and righteous, with a superb command of both police tactics and the law?

Over time, my interest grew into an obsession. For a writer, of course, often the best way to deal with an obsession is to write about it.

In researching a book about police training, I would be able to witness the metamorphosis the recruits undergo, see what happens to them emotionally and psychologically during the arduous course of instruction. I would learn to "frisk a perp," handle a .38, settle a domestic dispute—all the things they learn that enable them to deal effectively with the deadly confrontations and uncertainties of life on the street.

As recruits, they would soon be both hunters and prey; there are people who wouldn't think twice about pumping their bodies full of lead. How would they handle it? What made them want to pursue a job that carries such risks?

I imagined that during training the recruits' perceptions would change. They would learn to cast a suspicious eye, even to be a little paranoid. They would hear and see the world differently, size people up by more subtle standards, notice things that the rest of us would miss. I wanted to know what they go through which makes them such astute observers. I wanted to see, too, what toll it would take on them—psychologically, emotionally, physically. I wanted to chronicle the making of a cop.

How was I to approach this project? I could go through the training as if I were going to become a police officer myself, but at thirty-six years of age I was too old, not to mention too out of shape. Even if these limitations didn't exist, what I really wanted was to tell the story as a journalist rather than relate a first-person account as a subject. I wanted a smorgasbord of the experience. I decided the best method was to go through training as a civilian observer.

From the beginning, my choice of police academies could be only New York City's. To keep the peace in Gotham, an expansive, mysterious, and sinister terrain home to virtually every ethnic, racial, religious, and social group, the New York City Police Department surely has to turn out first-class cops.

I called the police academy for permission. Such requests, I was told, were handled by the deputy commissioner of public information. So I wrote to the DCPI. My request was summarily rejected by a high-ranking officer. It was not policy, he informed me in a phone call, to let anyone attend classes at the academy or spend time with its officers during patrol. He added that he personally objected to anyone exploiting the police for financial gain.

I called to his attention two instances I knew of in which journalists had been granted permission for this kind of access. He told me the writer of the more recent article had originally been refused, just as I had been, but that appeals made by executives of the reporter's influential publication to the "highest levels of the police administration" had been successful in reversing the decision. If I had the "clout" to reach and convince top police brass, he said, perhaps I could achieve the same result.

This seemed to me patently unfair. My attendance should not hinge on my "clout," I protested. The officer replied brusquely that without "clout," the only way I'd be able to get in was over his dead body.

Without any personal or political connections, I took the only recourse left to me. I wrote a letter to the New York City police commissioner explaining in detail what I wanted to do. Shortly thereafter, I received a call from DCPI telling me I had been given the green light.

Elated, I began to work out my modus operandi. I wanted to follow a few recruits through training and recount their transformation from civilians to police officers. How many recruits should I "follow," and how would I choose them? I considered following just one recruit and making this book his or her personal story, but what if the recruit dropped out or flunked or turned out to be a poor choice for other reasons? The risks were too great. I decided to cover at least three students to be sure of getting a story and to have a representative cross-section of the class.

Would the academy, I asked, recommend some students who appeared to be good candidates for becoming police officers? No. DCPI not only prohibited this, but barred me from initiating contact with prospective recruits on academy grounds;

this meant I had to approach students before or after classes or during lunch away from the academy. The academy required that each recruit I selected report to an executive officer, who would explain that mine was an independent project and that their participation was strictly voluntary. Not very auspicious conditions under which to recruit a recruit, I thought, but at least I had clearance.

A week before the program was to begin I had a meeting with Deputy Chief Robert F. Burke, commanding officer of the police academy. A large man with a resonant voice and an overpowering presence, he wore civilian clothes with a gun in a shoulder harness; I felt a little intimidated talking to him. But he was very friendly, offering me a brief tour of the photos and mementos in his regal office.

He listened attentively as I explained my game plan. I intended to go to classes, observe my target recruits, and interview them throughout the term. This was acceptable, he told me, but I would not be allowed to use a tape recorder. He established a few other ground rules, and we shook hands.

With training to commence in a few days, I was nervous. How would I be accepted? Would the students consider me a nuisance? Would the instructors resent my presence, or accept it only grudgingly? Would I be taken into people's confidences, or would I be viewed as an unwelcome intruder?

On the last Tuesday in January 1988, I awoke at five A.M., very excited and terribly anxious. In a few hours I was to begin the New York City Police Academy training program that would thrust me into the cops' private world and satisfy once and for all my curiosity about the miraculous transformation of civilians into police officers. Out there were several unsuspecting souls who were about to become the subjects of my investigation.

THE

MAKING

OF A

COP

1
ORIENTATION

Fort Greene, Brooklyn: an upwardly mobile community of expensive brownstones set back from tree-lined avenues and streets bustling with the construction of co-ops and condos, a place where glitzy boutiques and trendy specialty stores sit next to ethnic restaurants and bakeries, and factories from a fading era lie like withered flowers in a newly cultivated garden. It is one hour past dawn in January, and the sun shines dimly, obscured by an ice-gray blanket of clouds that casts an ominous pall over the streets below. The neighborhood is winter-still, sporadically disturbed by the idling of a cold engine, the crackling of tires over ice, the thump of a front door slamming.

Outside Brooklyn Technical High School, a massive monolithic structure that occupies nearly an entire city block, stand more than 650 aspiring police officers. Marshaled into rows of four, they are dressed in business suits. They seem impervious to the bone-piercing wind, but an occasional shiver and a certain blueness around the lips betray a nervous excitement only heightened by the cold. They are the fresh blood, the

1

latest class of recruits selected to begin a training program that will prepare them to become New York City cops.

In joining the New York Police Department, the recruits will become members of a 28,000-unit municipal law enforcement agency that is larger than the combined armed forces of all but 82 nations, ranking just behind Denmark and Bolivia. The recruits will be assuming membership in an organization charged with the momentous responsibility of keeping the peace, aiding the needy, rescuing the unfortunate, unraveling the bizarre, and tracking down the barbaric in America's largest city.

New York is an urban metropolis not unlike others—except for its size; everything here, it seems, is bigger or better. There's more wealth, danger, excitement, glamour, hustle, energy, drama, poverty, squalor. And crime. In 1988 there were 1,915 murders and manslaughters (10 percent of the U.S. total, and more than Great Britain and West Germany combined), 45,824 felonious assaults, 3,412 forcible rapes, 86,578 robberies, 128,626 burglaries, 110,717 grand larcenies, 119,659 grand larceny car thefts, and 43,434 other felonies involving drugs, forgery, arson, prostitution, gambling, and kidnaping.

What unknown fate the city has in store for them is the question looming in the minds of most of the young men and women lined up here, many so recently ensconced in placid jobs where the future was as safe as the work was predictable. What they know about police work they've heard from friends and relatives, gleaned from TV, read in books and newspapers. But they don't really know what the job's about. Will they like it? Will they stick it out? Will it live up to their expectations? Is it as dangerous as they've heard? As boring?

By 8:20 A.M. the recruits have been ushered into the school and are settled in assigned seats in the auditorium; the atmosphere is sober, expectant. A cadre of uniformed police officers—instructors—monitor the proceedings from their sta-

2

tions around the cavernous room. Ten minutes later Lieutenant Frank Geysen mounts the stage.

"On behalf of Chief Burke and Inspector Farrell, I'd like to welcome you to the New York Police Academy."

Lieutenant Geysen, the fifty-year-old commanding officer of recruit operations, has the demeanor of a marine drill instructor. With his six-foot-two-inch frame, military haircut, and penetrating voice, he is an imposing presence.

In rapid-fire delivery, Lieutenant Geysen spells out some of the more important rules of the academy. Lateness. Sick procedure. Inspection. When and how to stand at attention. How to address superior officers. He tells the student officers that the next five and a half months will be demanding, that their life-styles will change drastically. A few recruits grimace; it sounds like he's trying to talk them out of becoming cops.

This is a typical training class, a heterogeneous group that mirrors the melting pot it will protect. There are whites and blacks. Irish, Italians, Hispanics, Orientals, Germans, Jamaicans, and Poles. Catholics, Protestants, and Jews. The recruits are youthful and robust men and women, ranging in size from towering to petite.

Less than twenty years ago the New York Police Academy's training classes were composed predominantly of young men just out of the military. But the sociological revolution of the late sixties and early seventies inspired the city of New York to design affirmative action recruitment programs that led to large numbers of women and minorities joining the police department. Litigation also forced the elimination of minimum height and weight requirements; diminutive cops may now patrol the streets, which some old-liners as well as young officers see as a catalyst to crime.

A glance at these recruits' applications would reveal that they have worked as truck drivers, construction workers, postal clerks, bank tellers, computer technicians, stockbrokers, porters, carpenters, and chefs. Some are veterans of the armed forces, and a handful are college graduates. The one thing they have in common is their desire to become cops.

Andy Varga, a stalky six-foot-three-inch twenty-four-year-old with blue eyes, blond hair, and boyish good looks, is sitting sixteen rows from the stage in the middle section of the room, wondering what his new career will be like. Since he was a kid, cops have been Andy's quintessential role models, stalwart figures with poise and pride who dealt effectively with everyone from neighborhood wiseguys to little old ladies. They had a mystique, a "coolness" about them. The impressive array of equipment they wore on their gun belts made them intimidating; they commanded respect, lived an adventurous life, glowed with confidence. Romantic notions, perhaps, but this was the image Andy had of cops, and this was the kind of person he wanted to be.

Andy knows that cops get injured or killed in the line of duty, but this has not discouraged him or his family. His brother is a cop in Queens, and the Vargas accept the potential danger as an inevitable part of a gratifying and necessary career. Andy has waited more than five years for this day. He is thrilled to be joining the ranks of what he considers to be the finest police force in the nation. He can't wait to start.

Stefanie Hirschhorn, an auburn-haired woman seated ten rows in front of Andy, has always been a maverick among her contemporaries. She feels every bit as different today. Unlike most others here, Stefanie has not harbored a long-time ambition to become a cop. In fact, her presence is more the result of serendipity. To pay for her college education, Stefanie worked as a waitress in a bar where cops hung out. Because of her spiked hair and outspokenness, her law-enforcement friends dubbed her "the East Village liberal." She dated a couple of cops and had a serious relationship with one. As a joke, he brought her an application to take the police civil service

4

test. She called his bluff and took the test, surprising herself as much as him when she did well on it.

When she was hired, it stopped being a joke. She was beginning to realize that becoming a cop was exactly what she wanted to do. She was reluctant to drop out of college, however, and her family and friends protested strenuously. Her fiancé said he could not marry a cop, and Stefanie agonized. A few months later her father died, and Stefanie spent a period of mourning reflecting seriously on her needs and goals. Nobody who loved her, she finally decided, would stop her from pursuing something she really wanted. She accepted the job, and her fiancé broke their engagement.

Tomas Ramos, whose impressive athletic physique makes him appear much larger than his five feet ten inches, is seated in the right front section. From a Puerto Rican family, he is the first of five siblings to be born in the continental United States. Growing up in Brooklyn, Tomas had never been outside New York City but felt a driving need to get off the streets and change his life. The air force was his ticket out, and he served seven years on bases in the U.S. and Panama before enrolling in college as a journalism major. He worked part-time to help pay expenses but eventually got tired of relying on his family for money.

At his brother-in-law's urging Tomas took the police civil service test although he had never considered law enforcement a prestigious career. A man with education, he thought, should not be a police officer, and one day he would certainly finish college. In the two years between the test and today, he had researched law enforcement and found it was the kind of career he was looking for: challenging, unique, and exciting. Now he is amused by the irony that he is to undergo training that will return him to the streets. But this time he will be in a position of authority.

The seats occupied by Andy, Stefanie, Tomas, and the rest

of the class are coveted ones. The New York City police civil service test is usually taken by 30,000 to 50,000 people each time it is given, and those who score high enough must then undergo the department's meticulous background investigation, including a review of academic transcripts, tax returns, and military and employment records.

Background checks are made with the Department of Motor Vehicles, and the candidate's fingerprints are run through the FBI and New York State central fingerprint registries. Neighbors are interviewed. There are medical exams. Prospective recruits may be eliminated for such diagnosed conditions as heart murmurs, high blood pressure, back problems, and impaired hearing and vision. (Or they may be put on medical review, which gives them a chance to consult another doctor to verify or discredit a diagnosis.) There are written and oral psychological evaluations. The paperwork is endless and tedious, as is waiting to be called.

Take Andy Varga. When he was nineteen, he took the police exam. He passed, but he expected a long wait; there were 22,280 candidates ahead of him on the list. Figuring it would take three years before he was called, he joined the navy. While he was in boot camp in Orlando, Florida, the NYPD's Applicant Investigation Unit began a background search.

Andy met the initial requirements of the position—he was a high-school graduate, a resident of New York City or the surrounding counties of Nassau, Suffolk, Westchester, Orange, Putnam, or Rockland, and was between twenty and twenty-nine years old. (Exceptions to the age limit are made if one has military experience.)

Four years went by during which Andy served as a radioman on ships out of Norfolk, Virginia, and San Diego. Finally, one week after his discharge, Andy passed an agility test at the police academy, then submitted to the brief medical exam. The following week he took a four-hour psychological exam. Then he was summoned for an interview with a psychologist.

A few weeks later his unit investigator let him know he had passed each test. Then came the full medical exam, which, a month later, he was again told he had passed. Exactly five years and one month from the time he took the police civil service test, he received a letter informing him he had been accepted.

He learned, happily, that he had been assigned to the NYPD. The city police department is composed of three agencies— NYPD, Transit, and Housing—and the city decides where a recruit is to be placed. Like most of the others who take the police test, his first choice was the NYPD.

A letter requesting Andy to report to Brooklyn Tech for orientation and processing, however, also had a warning: Don't quit your job. Budget cutbacks might postpone the class. Not until their arrival here today could any of the recruits be completely sure they would begin their new career.

The three days of orientation are consumed with filling out forms and listening to guest speakers. The recruits are required to sign an oath: "I do solemnly swear that I will support the Constitution of the United States and the Constitution of the State of New York, and that I will faithfully discharge the duties of the office of Officer in the Police Department of the City of New York according to the best of my ability."

The students are technically probationary police officers now, and they may be terminated for any reason whatsoever during their time at the academy, the five and a half months of field training that follow, and their first year on the job after that. Everyone addresses them as "officer" although they will have to wait twenty-three weeks to get their guns and shields.

Until the early 1970s, guns and shields were issued just a few days into the academy. Background investigations were not extensive then, and those at the academy old enough to remember report wild episodes: students frisking one another in the halls with their weapons drawn, revolvers being cocked in bathroom stalls. A couple of recruits even held up a bank. One instructor who was a student then says, "You had a better chance of getting killed in the academy than you did in the street."

There were no casualties in the academy, but students tragically killed and were killed. In one incident, around 1960, a recruit was coming home with his girlfriend after midnight. Suddenly he heard a garbage can falling and glass breaking, followed by a woman's screams. Out of the corner of his eye he spotted someone running away. He called for the person to stop, but the figure in the dark kept running. He drew his revolver and fired. It was determined later that some teenagers had knocked a trash can into a woman's window, and the woman had responded angrily. The recruit's shots unfortunately took a teenage boy's life.

Another mishap occurred several years later, when revolvers were no longer distributed at orientation but shields were. A few nights after orientation a student officer was in a bar in Bay Ridge, Brooklyn, when a melee erupted outside. He ran out to break up the fight with his shield in his outstretched hand, shouting "Police!" He was grabbed and beaten by a small group of hooligans. As he lay on the ground gasping and begging for mercy, the hooligans stomped on him, injuring him fatally. If the recruit had finished his training, the incident never would have happened. Now the student officers have to wait until graduation to get their guns and shields.

By the end of the first day, the student officers are on the payroll. The starting pay is $26,000. For some, particularly recent high-school graduates, this is a good sum of money. For others it may be a salary cut. Anthony Mascia is twenty-nine years old and has been a city bus driver for ten years. Last year, with overtime, he earned $44,000. He is willing to take an $18,000 cut in pay to fulfill his dream of becoming a cop. He may never earn as much money as he did as a bus driver: After twenty years on the job, a New York City cop's base salary increases only to a maximum of about $37,000, though overtime pay can push this up from $40,000 to $48,000.

All in all, however, the rewards of a career as a police officer are surpassed by few others. This point is made by many who address the recruits during orientation, officers who speak of "enjoying every minute" of their careers.

Persons from various units of the NYPD and the academy speak to the student officers, telling them of the services their departments offer—they are eager to provide assistance in any way needed—but also issuing several warnings.

On abuse of power: "You're not the judge or the executioner. Your job as a police officer is to enforce the law and put together the best case possible to send to the D.A. Abuse of authority can get you indicted." —*Sergeant Raymond DuFresne, Law Department*

About stress: "This job creates a lot of stress. If there's an accident, the crowd that gathers expects the cop to handle it. That will be you now. You're it. You're not going to have the opportunity *not* to do it. And you'll take that accident home with you. . . . Your emotional level is likely to bounce up and down. After a tour of duty, you may need to go to a watering hole to cool off. There are some gruesome and depressing times. If you're not prepared for the downside of this job, it's not for you." —*Officer Bob McClellan, NYPD Counseling Services*

About changing attitudes of peers: "Don't be surprised to hear your friends say, 'Here comes Johnny the Cop. What are you going to do now, arrest me?' " —*Sergeant Robert Woerner, Social Science Department*

On drug use: "There will be no recreational drug use. We don't 'smoke marijuana occasionally' in the New York City

9

Police Department. We don't smoke it *ever*. You can't even carry a prescription drug without also carrying a prescription." —*Deputy Chief Robert F. Burke*

"If they find you putting anything up your nose that's not medicine, you'll lose your job." —*Officer McClellan*

On machismo: "Don't adjust your holster and shades John Wayne–style when approaching a car you've pulled over. If you want to play cop, stay home." —*Sergeant George Anderson, Police Science Department*

About individuality: "The learning process is different from anything you've had before, unless you have had military experience. In education, you're taught to be different. In training, you're taught to be the same." —*Dr. Jess Maghan, Director of Training*

On fitness: "A few years after the academy, cops tend to develop 'radio car spread.' Every week your hours will change with your different tours. You may get out of shape. You won't want to work out, you'll want to eat. You have to take care of yourself because you're going to have to help the man in the street. After all, he's paying your salary." —*Officer Peter Venezia, Physical Education Unit*

On discrimination: "The department will not tolerate racial discrimination. If there's a problem, you have thirty days to solve it informally. If it isn't resolved in that time, the deputy commissioner orders an investigation." —*Deputy Commissioner George Sanchez, Equal Employment Opportunity Office*

About use of authority while at the academy: "Do not get involved in any altercations you encounter. Dial 911 and tell the operator you're a probationary police officer." —*Lieutenant Geysen*

About behavior: "It's unacceptable to have a few drinks and get pulled over, create a disturbance, come in late, or fight with your spouse. Probationary officers are never off duty." —*Officer McClellan*

On the morning of the third and last day of orientation, Lieutenant Geysen announces that three people have already resigned; after hearing descriptions of life as a city cop, they have decided the job isn't for them. By the end, the class will lose more than ten percent of its initial number.

On this day, Housing and Transit recruits join NYPD, and the class size swells to 863. This is a far cry from the record-high January 1982 class, which had 3,000 recruits. The size and frequency of classes vary, depending on city budget, and, some say, political considerations. The size of the present class is about half that of several recent classes.

In this new group is Transit student officer Lissette Sierra-Solis, a twenty-three-year-old Hispanic woman with an expressive face, dark, fiery eyes, and a trim but powerful build. Lissette resolutely surmounted the violence and squalor of the Bronx neighborhood where she grew up to graduate as valedictorian of her high-school class.

Born in Puerto Rico, Lissette moved with her family to New York when she was four. Graduating from Roosevelt High School, Lissette obtained her B.A. in psychology at New York University, then worked as a social worker for a city agency. She had become disillusioned by the system when her husband of seven months, a police officer, encouraged her to take the police test. She passed and hopes one day to work in a sex crimes unit.

The class is broken down into A Squad and B Squad, each

with sixteen companies of about twenty-seven student officers each. The companies are mixed by race, gender, and zip code to give the recruits experience in dealing with the many kinds of people they will come in contact with in the city.

The companies are spread out now in different sections of the auditorium. An Official Company Instructor (OCI) is assigned to each company. The instructors select recruits with military experience to be company sergeants and assistant sergeants; their job will be to move the companies to various locations, do administrative work, take roll call, and ready the students for inspection. Andy Varga and Tomas Ramos become company sergeants.

The OCIs give brief pep talks to their companies. Officer John Eterno of the Police Science Department speaks to his company about academics: "No one who has been accepted as a recruit is incapable of getting through. It may be difficult, but you'll all make it. Just study your lessons. Every cop on the street has done it; you can too."

Officer Eterno is referring to the three academic courses at the academy: Law, Police Science, and Social Science. There are also, in addition to numerous special classes, a daily two-hour physical education class and special field training in firearms and tactics and in driving a radio motor patrol car.

In the afternoon the recruits are addressed by Rabbi Alvin Kass. One of eight clergymen with the New York City Police Department, Rabbi Kass has served twenty-two years in his capacity.

"This is the most exciting and magnificent career anyone could ever enter upon," he tells the recruits. "There's nothing in the world as meaningful as what you are doing. It's a job that has complications and problems, however. That's why there are chaplains. The chaplain can be a pivotal person in your life. Chaplains are the only persons in the police department with whom you can speak in complete confidentiality. The chaplain is the only person who does not have to operate within the bureaucracy. Chaplains can talk to the commissioner without going through red tape."

The students are listening intently. Lissette Sierra-Solis does not know exactly what kind of situation would lead her to see a police chaplain, but she hopes she will never have reason to.

"Police work is indispensable, but the policeman pays a terrible price," continues the rabbi. "The police officer has one great enemy: cynicism. It's an attitude of apathy and indifference to the world from seeing so much of its troubles. You're going to see an awful lot over the course of your career . . . murder, incest, rape, brutality, perversion. It won't be long before you see your first dead body. All this can make a human being cold, callous, bitter."

The rabbi is sweeping the recruits in the front with his eyes, as if he is having a private audience with each one for a fleeting but critical moment. Those seated in the back strain for every word.

"Faith is indispensable to keep things in proper perspective, to keep your judgments wholesome. If you're down or blue, it's part of your job to see a chaplain.

"You may have to use deadly force, perhaps even kill someone in your career. Sometimes, of course, it's kill or be killed, but using a gun should never come easily; it should always hurt you. A police officer should have a humanity that makes hurting someone else tear his insides. Huge men have come to me weeping because having to use their guns was the worst experience of their lives.

"Temptation is always a challenge. Some people will try to make it worthwhile for you to shut your eyes and go away. Most recruits are idealists with honest intentions, but some will yield to the temptation of a bribe. Why? Stress, boredom, need of money . . . It takes faith to reject temptation.

"The police department is the essence of democracy. This department goes out of its way to recruit people from every sector of society. Your life may depend on your partner, so you must develop trust. You will see people from all different walks of life. But underneath all our differences, we're the same. We all get sick, we all hurt if someone punctures us, we all die, we all lose people. There is so much that brings us all together. But there's nothing like what you're doing. Where the action is, the police are. Without you, the law of the jungle prevails.

"Now that you are a police officer, your life will never be the same." Rabbi Kass pauses, then smiles. "It will be better."

The class, inspired, responds with loud applause. For the first time the recruits are experiencing a sense of unity.

With the academy only a day away and all the preliminary formalities out of the way, anxiety descends on the recruits. Real life as a student officer is about to begin, the drama merely hinted at by so many in the past few days about to unfold.

—2—
ZERO DAY

On Friday, the fourth day of training, initial recruit equipment is distributed to the B Squad. At 7:07 A.M., several B Squad companies line up outside the NYPD's headquarters at One Police Plaza in Lower Manhattan. An instructor approaches the sergeant of one group.

"Officer, what company is this and what is your name?"

"Company twenty, sir. Probationary Police Officer Varga."

Andy is a bit uncomfortable with the formalities; it has been a while since he was in a military environment, and he is a little diffident. In fact, although law enforcement is the career he has always aimed for, second thoughts are in his mind. He's thinking that if it's not what he wants, now would be the most opportune time to back out.

"Did you take attendance?"

"Yes, sir."

"May I see the roll call?"

The instructor checks the list and hands it back to Andy with a nod.

"Attention!" The instructor faces the recruits and raises his voice. "We are now going to proceed inside to the equipment section. Take what is handed to you and continue through the section. I expect no problems. Once you've picked up all your equipment, report back outside here, in formation, and you'll stand by waiting for further instruction. Are there any questions?"

The recruits are silent.

"Are there any questions?"

"No, sir!" the student officers shout in unison.

"Left face!" The recruits turn and proceed to the equipment section. Andy hands over his $209 money order and is issued the following: two pairs of dark blue trousers with black stripes down the sides, blue tie, gold tie clasp, dark blue cap, white cotton gloves, dark blue waist-length jacket, reflective belt, green and gold police academy cap device, nameplate holder, two nightstick straps (thongs), whistle, whistle holder, baton, baton holder, rubber billy, two belts, handcuffs, handcuff case, gun cleaning kit and cloth, CPR skill sheet, CPR trainee mask, pen and pencil holder, memo-book cover, first aid book, infant and child CPR book, adult CPR book, triangle bandage, two speedloader cases, and an academy canvas duffel bag to carry it all in.

Their arms full, the student officers of Company 20 exit the building and fall back into formation in front. With one other company, they board a city transit bus that takes them uptown to the police academy.

It is crowded in the bus. Equipment spills out of the bags; batons rap people in the legs as the bus bounces over potholes. Some recruits, in an attempt to lighten the atmosphere, crack bad jokes, and the others laugh nervously. Andy thinks, "Here we go, everybody!"

On 20th Street near Second Avenue, the bus turns left into an enclosed area, called the Campus Deck, where the students alight and fall into formation. It is their first visit to the New York Police Academy since becoming probationary police officers.

The academy is an eight-story granite building with a gym annexed to its west border, a building whose classrooms, laboratories, offices, and facilities the recruits will come to know intimately. There is a pool, a gym, a cafeteria, even a museum of the New York Police Department.

The museum contains historical mementos: antique firearms, shields, and uniforms, an old precinct switchboard, yellowing photographs, and antediluvian fingerprint paraphernalia. Its most infamous exhibit is a trio of weapons—a Thompson machine gun (with its serial number filed off), a .45-caliber automatic pistol, and a sawed-off shotgun—all of which Al Capone gave to his henchmen to execute Frankie Yale, a mobster who tried to bamboozle Capone, his boss, by hijacking his liquor shipments and claiming others did it.

The sixth floor houses a library but is more noteworthy to the recruits for two other reasons: Rooms 627 and 610. In the former are the offices of the academy's commanding officer, Chief Burke, and its second-in-command, Inspector Farrell. The latter is Recruit Administration, where student officers will have to report if they're late, don't follow instructions for sick leave properly, or for other problems that may arise, such as moving to New York from out of state to take the job but not having registered their car in New York State as they're supposed to. Reporting to 610 is like going to the school principal except here, with a nettled police lieutenant or sergeant doing the reprimanding and a career at stake, it's more disconcerting. Indeed, the recruits will come to loathe reporting to Room 610.

During orientation, the recruits were issued two Student Training Activity Report (Star) Cards, which they must carry during tours of duty at the academy. If there is a minor violation or problem, such as a student not doing his homework or forgetting an accessory to his uniform, instructors or supervisors will pull one, and this will be noted on the recruit's final evaluation. Seven pulled Star Cards or a more serious violation of rules results in a Command Discipline (CD), a formal hearing with penalties or termination as possible consequences.

It is zero day, the first academic day, but one without formal instruction. Today the instructors will acquaint the student officers with their courses and with what to expect at the academy during the term.

Company 20 is seated in Room 415 waiting for the Police Science instructor. Soon the officer who supervised the group at One Police Plaza walks into the classroom. He picks up a piece of chalk and writes on the board:

P.O. Battista
Police Science
Day 0

Like most of the other instructors at the academy, Battista is young—twenty-seven years old. In fact, many instructors have less than seven years of patrol experience. But in New York, where there is more action on the streets in one year than most cops elsewhere see in a lifetime, that patrol experience enables the instructors to bring a wealth of knowledge to the classroom. The instructors at the New York Police Academy are bright, articulate, energetic, and enthusiastic. Most important for the recruits, Battista, like all the instructors, is one of them—a street soldier who has come "inside" to train the troops.

The instructors at the academy are hand picked and must have a college degree. Street cops who are interested apply and go through a series of interviews. Unlike college professors, they are videotaped so their teaching potential can be evaluated. They may express a preference for a particular discipline, but the decision is the academy's. While teaching, they wear their police uniforms and carry their guns.

18

Teaching at the academy is considered a good assignment, particularly for those planning to take a promotional exam. It's a good place to study and to learn about revisions of the *Patrol Guide*; it looks good on a résumé, and the tours don't fluctuate as much as a street cop's. The downside is that while patrol officers are awarded two points for every year on the street—accumulated points determining eligibility for special units, choice of precinct, and opening other career opportunities within the department—academy instructors get no points for teaching. This may have no negative effect on cops who have been on the street for ten years, but it could be a detriment to the younger instructors who want to transfer into a special unit.

Growing up in Queens, John Battista was fascinated by the world of cops, by the police cars racing through the streets with their red lights flashing and their sirens wailing. Where were they going? What had happened? His curiosity was tremendous. The authority, challenge, and excitement of the job appealed to him, as well as the opportunity to help people. Only months after graduating from Manhattan College with a degree in accounting, he entered the police academy. He had assignments in Bedford-Stuyvesant and Manhattan for five years before returning to the academy to fulfill another longtime aspiration: teaching.

"Good morning. My name is Police Officer Battista, and I will be your Police Science instructor for the next five months.

"Police Science. What is it?" Officer Battista asks rhetorically. "Police Science is how to become a cop; what to do in every situation you can think of out in the street—whether it's making a simple arrest, writing a summons, delivering a baby, saving someone's life who's about to jump from a bridge. It's how to investigate problems that arise while you're on patrol, how to negotiate situations that develop while you're walking your footpost.

"We'll talk about them all, but before we do, let's get down to some basic rules for my class. First of all, three days ago everyone sitting here was a civilian. You raised your right hand and signed an oath, and people said you were now a police officer. With that you were given more responsibility than you can imagine."

Responsibility is something Andy Varga had plenty of for four years in the service, to the point where he felt his life was too controlled. There were restrictions that impinged upon his freedom and ideals he had to live up to. For a moment, he wonders whether he is losing his freedom all over again.

"Now that you're a police officer," Battista continues, "the first thing you have to do is get rid of any prejudices you might have acquired when you were growing up." He walks through the aisles with slow, deliberate strides, staring each student officer straight in the eyes.

"How many people in this class are prejudiced?"

No one raises a hand. The students sit still, their faces blank.

"Well, I've got news for you," asserts Officer Battista sternly. "Each and every one of you in this class is prejudiced toward someone or something, whether you like it or not." He pauses, observing that several of the recruits are looking uncomfortable. "So what are we going to do about this?" He returns to the front of the room.

"As a police officer, you are a public servant. That means you will help anybody who needs help or assistance. You will protect the life and property of everyone and anyone in this city. So if you do have prejudices—whether it's toward males, females, blacks, whites, Hispanics, Chinese—you'd better keep them to yourself, not only in this classroom, but when you're out there working."

Andy is pretty sure he doesn't have a prejudice toward any single group. He may dislike a specific person for a specific reason, but that feeling is not toward any one particular race or class of people. He wonders whether anyone will turn out to be prejudiced against *him*.

"There are some twenty-odd people in this class," Officer Battista says, "who are going to be a company for the next six months. Not everyone is going to like everyone else. But whether you like a person or not, you had better respect them, show them the same respect you want them to show you. Because one day when you're out on the street, your life may be in danger, and that person you dislike may be the one to show up. So respect them. We're a company, a team, and we're going to be the best in this academy. And remember, we're all one color: blue." Officer Battista allows a quick smile to warm his features. Then he becomes stern again.

"I have four rules." He turns to the chalkboard and writes: "One. Be on time. Two. Do your work. Three. Keep your mouth shut. Four. Always look sharp."

Andy's mind drifts back to the navy. In boot camp, the servicemen were kept up every night until ten or eleven o'clock, and then were awakened at four o'clock the next morning. If anyone fell asleep in class, he would have to do twenty-five push-ups in the aisle. Compared to boot camp, these rules seem simple.

"Follow these rules and you won't have a problem with me, in this academy, or throughout your career," Officer Battista says. "And if anyone feels they can't abide by these rules, they can resign in Room 610 immediately. Does anyone have any questions?"

There is no response.

"I'll repeat. Does anyone have any questions?"

Two words come roaring back: "No, sir!"

"This is a paramilitary organization, and when you speak to someone, you're at attention. Use 'Yes, sir,' 'No, sir,' 'Yes, ma'am,' 'No, ma'am.' One of the hardest things you're going to learn is to take orders and not question them. When you're out on the street, you'll be giving orders. And people don't like to be told what to do. So remember how you feel, because that's how they're going to feel when you give them an order." He pauses to let this sink in.

"How many people in this class are twenty years of age? Raise your hand."

Five hands go up, about twenty percent of the class.

Officer Battista picks out one twenty-year-old.

"How old do you have to be to drink in a bar in New York State?"

"Twenty-one."

"Then don't get caught drinking in a bar. If you do, you can lose your job. Our job is to enforce the law, not just for other people but for ourselves also. Suppose you're in a bar, and somebody says something you don't like to your girlfriend. Before, you'd have been able to 'settle it like a man.' But as a police officer, you don't raise your hand to anyone, and no one raises their hand toward you."

When Officer Battista warns against using profanity in class or when working, Andy becomes a little uneasy. In a difficult situation, the first words out of his mouth would probably be "Oh, shit!" He looks at Rule No. 3 again: "Keep your mouth shut." That one could turn out to be the most difficult of all.

"As a police officer, everything you do will be evaluated from the time you enter this academy until the day you retire," Officer Battista points out. "Your reputation starts now. Anything you say or do is considered public information."

Officer Battista picks up a sheaf of papers and starts handing them out. "A great deal of that information will find its way onto evaluation forms like these."

The Recruit Evaluation Form is where academy instructors record their assessments of student officers at the end of training. Patrol officers are similarly evaluated periodically by their superiors at the precincts.

All of these records are extremely important in evaluating

requests for transfer from patrol to a specialized unit or detail. Andy would like to go to the Emergency Service Unit one day, and he is thinking he'd better apply himself assiduously to his studies throughout training.

"In Police Science, there are seventy-five lessons. We will do one lesson per day. I expect you to go home and do that lesson the night before. When you come into my class every day, know that lesson. Be able to teach it to me. My job is to clear up any problems that you might have. It's not to spoon-feed you the information.

"We have college-level training here, and if you complete the academy successfully, you can earn up to twenty-eight college credits. You are getting paid approximately twenty-six thousand dollars per year to go to school for six months and to train in the field for an equal period. So you'd better be doing the work." Winding up his speech, Officer Battista surveys the rows of faces.

"So what is Police Science? Learning the rules and regulations of this department as well as patrol service duties and responsibilities. My advice is: Remember the four rules, and you'll have no problem."

The students sit quietly, their faces downcast, looking as if they didn't know what hit them. Like many others, Andy is thinking, "What have I gotten myself into?"

Meanwhile, other instructors are impressing upon the recruits what it's like to be a police officer from the perspective of their individual academic departments. As one officer puts it, zero day is when each instructor becomes Lou Gossett, the tough sergeant in the film *An Officer and a Gentleman*. The harangues aren't as tough, but the messages are just as imperative.

Officer Michael Wilson of the Social Science Department tells his class he wants them to start thinking like police officers.

"How does a police officer think?" one student asks.

"I want you to be aware of things you weren't previously." Officer Wilson illustrates his point with specific examples. Subways. In New York's subterranean stations, there are blue lights in tunnels and numbers on stairwells. What do these mean? Blue lights denote where power may be shut off, and numbers are used by cops to report specific locations in calling for assistance.

License plates. What does it mean if the plate begins with a T and ends with a C? That it is registered to the Taxi and Limousine Commission. If a plate begins with an L, it is a livery car; with a Z, a rented vehicle. People. Officer Wilson suggests the recruits develop their powers of observation with an exercise: look at a person on the street, then look away and describe that person in detail. Making astute observations is something a person isn't born with; it must be learned and practiced.

Behavior on patrol is important. If a cop on a footpost walks up and down a block like clockwork and is being observed by two people waiting to commit a crime, knowing the pattern of the cop's patrol will enable them to strike at the most opportune moment. Vary the pattern—deter the crime. On patrol, cops should observe people who look out of the ordinary for a given setting—their dress or color, for example. This doesn't mean they're guilty of anything, but perhaps closer attention should be paid to them.

Officer Wilson implores the student officers to think: "What doesn't fit in this situation?" A spotless brand-new car with dirty license plates. That doesn't make sense. Were the plates stolen and put on the car?

In a subway station, where along the platform should you stand? In the middle? No, someone could come up behind you and push. A safer position would be in front of a column where no one can approach from behind, and observations can be made simply by looking to the right or left.

"What's wrong with my carrying keys on my gun belt?" he asks. They will jingle and alert a suspect being trailed. Watches that make sounds have the same effect, and Wilson tells a story. A plainclothes officer in Brooklyn followed a perpetrator into a dark, abandoned building. The watch alarm went off, and the perp fired in the direction of the sound, hitting the cop. "Maybe you'll never be in that situation," says Officer Wilson, "but we learn by it. Learn from his experience."

William Keeler introduces himself as the Social Science instructor of Company 32, to which Tomas Ramos and Stefanie Hirschhorn are assigned. During his time on patrol, Officer Keeler was with the Organized Crime Control Bureau, where he worked undercover in Harlem buying narcotics and then making arrests. He also worked plainclothes in the Street Crime Unit, where he was involved in decoy operations. Dressed like a tourist with a bag hung over his shoulder, he would stroll around midtown Manhattan and window-shop during the early evening when the streets were crowded. He developed what he calls a "sixth sense"—he could tell when he was being staked out. He would look at reflections in store windows to keep track of the situation, never making eye contact with the robbers-in-waiting, and avoid getting too close to people, particularly the elderly, so no one would get hurt. Eventually one or two robbers would approach, give a shove, and grab the shoulder bag. At that point the backups would come in to make the arrests. Six months earlier he decided he'd like a change; he wanted to teach others the skills he had acquired over the years.

Bill Keeler was happy to be assigned to teach Social Science. Social Science is about communication, about how the police officer uses proper communication skills to deal effectively with the public. The officer must be familiar with the many different ethnic groups in New York City; know how to interact with emotionally disturbed people, the handicapped, juveniles, and the elderly; know how to defuse potentially volatile situations and deal with victims of crime and children or spouses who have been abused. He must also learn to deal with himself. Police have certain powers, and these must be used properly. Social Science provides rules of ethics and integrity to guide the officer's behavior.

Among other things, Keeler explains the city's policy on sexual harassment. Some men may have a machismo image of themselves as police officers, and improper conduct stemming from this image could result in some form of punishment. Sexual harassment ranges from off-color jokes to outright sexual advances, and it is based, Keeler emphasizes, on the perception of the person being harassed. If someone feels uncomfortable in a working environment because of sexual innuendos, it could constitute sexual harassment. He reiterates the city's policy: no sexual harassment will be tolerated. If any student feels he or she is in some way the recipient of sexual harassment, the first course of action is to explain to the person who is making the victim feel uncomfortable that such behavior is not appreciated. In some instances the person simply may not realize how his or her actions are affecting someone else. If the person is made aware of this and the behavior ceases, the case is closed. If the harassment persists, the victim's options include filing a complaint with the Human Resources Administration or the Equal Employment Opportunity Commission.

Frank Dwyer is the Law instructor for Lissette Sierra-Solis's group, Company 19. His soft blond hair and baby face make him look even younger than his twenty-six years. His youth and innocent appearance, however, hide a tough officer with a firm command of the law curriculum.

Though the son of a retired police officer, Frank Dwyer III did not aspire to follow in his father's footsteps. At seventeen he took the police civil service exam more or less to humor his father. Even though he received a perfect score, Frank III headed for college, earning a degree in English and Comparative Literature from Cathedral College in Queens. It was not until his senior year that he decided to become a cop.

Officer Dwyer was at the 102nd precinct in Queens when he saw a department bulletin about openings at the police academy. After the required interviews and a videotaped teaching evaluation as well as a review of his college transcript, he was hired. The assistant chairman of the Law Department asked, "Do you object to teaching Law?"

Of all the academic disciplines, Law is the most difficult. It is the most technical; its concepts are hardest to grasp. There is more to memorize, and the statutes are constantly changing. When a student fails the academy for academic reasons, it's usually because of Law.

"You've moved into a complex discipline," Officer Dwyer begins.

"Lawyers are men of thought, and judges are ultimately men of thought. You, as police officers, will be called upon to be something they never are, which is men and women of thought and action at the same time. Many times you'll be involved in issues that are so legally complex that there won't necessarily be a right or a wrong answer, because the courts have never decided the matter exactly as you encounter it. All you can do is take the rules and guidelines we give you and make the best judgment you can.

"Sometimes the judgment may be to call a patrol sergeant, or the Legal Bureau, or a district attorney. But at other times circumstances will dictate that you act immediately. And then all you can do is take action consistent with your best understanding of the law."

Officer Dwyer's eyes narrow. "You have a grave responsibility to understand that you are no longer an ordinary citizen, and that anything you do or any action you take will reflect not merely on you but on the whole police department. A week ago, if you were arrested, the world would not care, unless it were for some particularly egregious offense. But now you are a police officer. If you are arrested for even a minor offense or become involved in even a minor incident, the event is press-worthy. And you do not want to bring embarrassment on your-self, the department, or your family.

"If you take drugs and I catch you, I'll lock you up. If I suspect you're taking them, I'll have you tested. If you *are* taking them, you'll be fired. Any of you caught in a bar after it closes will be suspended.

"Some of you may have to change your friends.

"You no longer have the right to walk away from an incident you become involved in. You are police officers. You're re-quired to take whatever steps another police officer would take. At this point, however, what that means is to call 911 and get the *real* police there!"

By the end of the tour, the student officers, after all the caveats, are anxious about whether either their conduct or their academic performance, or both, will exclude them from a ca-reer of law enforcement. But there is little time to worry. There is homework—chapters to read in each subject and questions to answer.

The first Law chapter gives an introduction to civil and criminal law; questions at the end of the chapter test the stu-dents' understanding of whether certain acts are violations of civil or criminal law.

Often the street cop responds to disputes where a party claims he has been wronged but where the offense is of a noncriminal nature. These are civil matters decided in civil courts; they pertain to violations of individual rights. From a legal perspective, the cop's job in these instances is simple. He should stabilize the situation, calm the parties down, pre-vent anyone from getting hurt, and make a meaningful referral to the appropriate court or agency. If a claim is under $2,000 in the state of New York, for example, the plaintiff can file in small claims court without hiring an attorney. In what instances would a cop take no legal action and instead make such a referral? There are many: a car owner claims unnecessary repairs were made to his vehicle and refuses to pay the bill but is then unable to get his car back from the shop; an angry customer is rebuffed after demanding a refund for defective merchandise; a singer claims a bar owner didn't pay her an amount previously agreed on for an evening's performance.

Police enforce criminal laws. Criminal acts such as robbery, burglary, arson, and rape violate the rights of individuals and the sanctity of society and are punishable by prison terms. In enforcing the law, a police officer must act within it. As events happen quickly, this usually requires split-second decisions. A scenario in the *Law Guide* reveals the kind of judgments the recruits will be expected to make:

> You're walking your post one day when a druggist runs out of his store and tells you that he was "just robbed by a man with a gun." He then points to a man running down the street and says, "That's him, Officer!" You run after the suspected robber, but he's had a head start, and you realize that you can't overtake him. You also realize that if you don't apprehend him, you may be permitting a dangerous criminal to escape. Can you lawfully use your gun to stop him? Should you use it? What if you could catch the suspect, but before you actually overtake him, he runs into a private home? Can you pursue him inside? If you do enter the home, can you search the interior until you find the suspect? What rights does the suspect have? What is your authority?
>
> These are the questions that you as a police officer must know the answers to. Seldom do you have the luxury of being able to look up the answer. Usually you must act swiftly—often under stress during an emergency or in the

presence of danger. Your decision and later actions have serious consequences—both for you as well as others. Your action may mean the difference between life and death, between freedom and imprisonment. Your actions must be responsible and intelligent and must be based upon a thorough knowledge of the law.

Officer Keeler's Social Science students have to write an essay, "Who Am I?" This, Officer Keeler feels, will give him insight into the students' academic abilities and levels of maturity. One former student, in discussing who she was, wrote about her favorite rock groups, and this set him to wondering whether she was really cop material.

The Police Science homework focuses on observation skills. As future patrol officers, to protect life and property and to apprehend criminals, the recruits will have to make careful observations of the environment—buildings, doorways, windows, streets, vehicles, shops—and people. They'll learn to regard with suspicion conditions that most of us would not be aware of: money being exchanged on the street; a store open beyond its usual closing time; a person who doesn't seem to belong in the neighborhood. A police officer must be able to make assumptions, to look beyond the obvious; such vigilance must be tempered with judgment to avoid descending into paranoia.

Becoming acutely aware of physical appearances is important. In a stressful situation, noticing slight differences in appearance may determine whether the officer takes aim at a perpetrator five feet ten inches tall with a light-brown complexion, an afro, a beard, a jogging outfit, moccasins, and a ski cap—or an undercover police officer six feet tall with a dark complexion, short kinky hair, a mustache, a sweatshirt and jeans, loafers, and a beret.

In observing people, cops have to pay attention to a myriad of details: height, weight, build, age, race, complexion, hair, eye shape and color; the presence of a mustache, beard, scars, tattoos, moles, blemishes, birthmarks, or deformities; peculiarities with respect to eyes, nose, teeth, ears, arms, lips, and walking; colors, kinds, and styles of clothing; accessories, footwear, and headgear.

When Andy gets home and takes out his textbook, he finds that the last Police Science homework question will evaluate how observant he has been in his first day at the academy: "Supply a description of your Police Science instructor."

–3–
LAW

Late one evening, a police officer riding through a plush residential neighborhood spots a scraggly-looking man in a beat-up old car. The car is parked on a dark, dead-end street. The officer's suspicions are aroused, but what may he do?

A bag lady approaches a police officer and accuses a well-dressed businessman across the street of taking her money. What action may the officer take?

A cop orders a teenager, whom he observes looking in car windows and trying the doors, to stop, but the teenager walks away. How may the cop respond?

A college student is pulled over for passing a stop sign. He is nervous because inside his jacket pocket are ten glassine envelopes of cocaine. May the officer, sensing this unease, search the student or his car?

These scenarios illustrate the questions of what police officers legally may do, what they are legally prohibited from doing, and what rights individuals have in possible criminal circumstances. It is the police officer's job to enforce the law—to issue summonses and to arrest criminal offenders, but at the same time interfere with citizens' rights as little as possible. Every police department has procedures for its officers to follow in various situations, but it is laws and court decisions that really define police conduct. In Law class, using case examples like those above, and discussion and debate of criminal law and how it is applied, the recruits slowly acquire the basic knowledge they will need on the streets.

First, a cop must be legally justified in taking an action. He must be well educated and informed because he will have to act quickly. On the street, crimes are often committed in seconds, and there is little time to consider the legal ramifications of an action. May the officer stop a suspicious person? Use force? Ask questions? Conduct a frisk? Search a glove compartment? Open a locked briefcase? Draw a gun? Shoot? All these are actions whose justification might seem obvious to the public in a given set of circumstances but which for the police officer require prudent but instantaneous evaluation and decision-making.

Of course, a cop's entire tour of duty is not spent arresting perpetrators or handing out summonses; in fact, most of the calls police respond to are service-related—taking charge at accidents, handling family arguments, rendering assistance of some sort.

Civil disputes, where criminal activity is absent, are important to cops in that such situations ultimately have an impact on how the police are perceived by the public. Such day-to-day interactions bring police in contact with the people of the city. Derring-do police action may not be called for, but courtesy, compassion, and being a good listener can go a long way to create a positive police image.

It is in handling criminal matters that the police fill their role as society's defenders, guardians of law and order. But cops are only people, after all, and their decisions may sometimes be clouded by a variety of human failings common to us all; and whether they're making an arrest, searching someone, or trying to obtain a confession, cops are bound by laws too.

The legal issues involved in approaching suspicious people on the street or in deciding exactly when to make an arrest are complex. Various police actions may be taken only when certain levels of proof are present to justify them. Acting in haste or improperly can result in a criminal going free and a cop looking stupid. Unfortunately, that happens not so much because of concrete mistakes, but rather, often as a result of making a wrong judgment call. It may take a cop years to come to know exactly what to do and at what point to do it as he's observing someone go from intending to commit a crime to its actual commission.

Covered in several Law lessons, the levels of proof are tied together by instructor Frank Dwyer, using as an example an incident he was recently involved in.

It was the middle of October, ten o'clock in the evening, and unseasonably warm—almost seventy degrees—a nice night for a walk. That was just how he decided he would spend his meal break as he walked out of the 20th Street police academy entrance and across the Campus Deck toward the street. First he'd grab an ice cream.

Dwyer wasn't in uniform. He was wearing blue pants, a white shirt, blue tie, and a gray button-down cardigan sweater. In his waistband was his off-duty revolver, a .38-caliber Smith and Wesson Chief with a two-inch barrel. Dwyer isn't afraid to walk any street in New York City, but there are some, he admits, where, with or without a gun, he feels unsafe. Being a cop and carrying a gun doesn't make you a superman. In some places, he knows, other people have guns too, and they're probably a lot more willing to use them.

The neighborhood around the police academy is considered safe—safe, perhaps, because the academy is there as well as the 13th Precinct, directly behind the academy on 21st Street. When politicians have suggested that the academy be moved to other parts of the city where a police presence is more strongly needed, such as the South Bronx, the community swells into an uproar. The residents and merchants want the academy to stay put, keeping a good area safe.

In his civilian clothes, Frank Dwyer doesn't look like a cop. With his short light hair, serious demeanor, and wire-rimmed glasses, he looks more like a gentle, mild-mannered graduate student.

Walking down 20th Street to Third Avenue, Frank Dwyer didn't have much on his mind. In his midtwenties, his interests ran from paddleball and tennis to literature, art, and women. Then, he was trying to forget the search and seizure material he'd been rewriting for the student *Law Guide* and just enjoy his one-hour respite.

New York City has an aural personality all its own—a pervasive blend of traffic, sirens, and other noises that to a resident are as unobtrusive as background music in a movie. On a warm evening, the heavy air seems to heighten this a bit, as does the putrid odor of garbage rotting along too many side streets. Dwyer was used to it all, walking and watching, alert to his environment without singling out any particular aspect for his attention.

When he got to Third Avenue, Dwyer turned right. He passed a stationery store, a pizza parlor, a bar, and a few smutty storefronts before reaching a Baskin-Robbins. Inside, an Asian girl gave him a cup of vanilla ice cream, and then he headed toward Gramercy Park.

Gramercy Park is only about half a city block long, between 20th and 21st streets and Third and Lexington avenues. It's not open to the general public; only residents of the area who have a key can get in. Dwyer circled the park once, then started heading back toward the academy. Walking down Irving Place, he noticed a young man, a Hispanic, emerge from a car. Dwyer

35

was immediately struck by the jarring contrast of a ragged man alighting from a sumptuous car. There was plenty of light, so he got a good look at the guy—about five feet six, medium build, black hair, and wearing worn-out gray pants, a tattered short-sleeve pullover shirt, and sneakers. "I'll lay down money," Dwyer thought, "that that guy broke into that car." But this was only a hunch; Dwyer had no tangible proof that the man committed a crime or was about to commit a crime. The man moved forward, seemingly disoriented.

A hunch or gut feeling is called *mere suspicion* according to the legal standards of proof. A *standard of proof* is behavior observed or facts ascertained by a police officer that justify official actions. There are several levels of proof, each providing legal authority for certain kinds of police action.

Mere suspicion is the lowest standard of proof because it is nothing more than a hunch, even if it proves correct. Perhaps the disheveled man did own the expensive car, or had borrowed it from a friend, or was using the boss's car to run an errand. Who knows? Legally, what action could Officer Dwyer take? Could he point his gun at the man and holler "Police—don't move! Put your hands up"? No, that wouldn't be reasonable under the circumstances. What he had was just a man who didn't seem to belong to a car. That is not so strange or unreasonable.

Officer Dwyer could continue observing, or he could make what's called a *common-law right of inquiry*. This is a right that courts have granted the police when they harbor a hunch but have few facts to back up their suspicions. They are permitted to ask simple, general questions. In this case, Officer Dwyer may approach the man, identify himself as a police officer (since he's out of uniform), and say something like, "Excuse me, sir, are you okay? You seem confused. Is there anything I can do to help?" The man is not obligated to answer, however, and may walk away. If he does walk away, Officer

Dwyer may not restrain him, block him, or use force to stop him.

The man's evident disorientation made Officer Dwyer suspect he was high on drugs, but if Dwyer were to frisk the man and find drugs or a gun, a New York court of law would probably suppress the evidence. The search is unlawful because a level of proof higher than mere suspicion is required to justify it. Officer Dwyer hadn't seen the man doing anything criminal, so the frisk would be regarded as an unwarranted intrusion.

In the police academy, the Law instructors liken the standards of proof to temperatures on a thermometer, with mere suspicion at the bottom. As the temperature becomes warmer, more police action may be taken. Just above mere suspicion is *reasonable suspicion*.

As Dwyer watched the man wander away from the car, he decided that there was no rush to take any action. He'd just continue observing. The man turned east onto 19th Street, and from the sidewalk approached the passenger windows of a number of cars, holding his hand over his eyes to deflect the light as he gazed in before trying the door handles.

Dwyer was now standing about fifty feet away behind a car, beginning to roll into that high gear cops feel when action is imminent—a racing heart, adrenaline pumping, alert to every sight and sound. The "what-ifs" were also running through his mind. What if the situation escalated and he had to become directly involved? He'd been off the streets for a year and a half. A police officer who would never shirk his duties, he was still not in a good position, alone and out of uniform. If he had to use his gun and other cops came, would he be mistaken for the perp? He'd hate to have to use his gun in a situation like this, but the man could be high. Things could get very rough very fast.

Dwyer was pretty sure the man was about to rip off a car or something inside one. It was now more than a hunch: the man moved from car to car, looking in windows and trying door handles, trying to stay out of sight. It was late at night, and the man wasn't holding his keys in his hand as if looking for his car. The area is also one where auto theft and burglary are very common. If he was not burglarizing the cars, what sort of logical argument could the man make for his actions?

What could Dwyer do now? One legal option is the concept of *stop, question, and frisk*. In a stop, question, and frisk, unlike a common-law right of inquiry, a suspect is not free to leave at whim. If a suspect refuses an order to stop, necessary physical force may be used. A gun may be displayed, but it can be used only in a life-or-death situation when the cop is defending himself or another person. Stop, question, and frisk may be done for all felonies and Penal Law misdemeanors.

Dwyer would have been justified in stopping and questioning the man because of the elements just mentioned. But he wanted to arrest the guy, and thought, "Should I grab him now? No, give him some rope, let him hang himself. I haven't got enough evidence yet. It wouldn't hold up in court."

The suspect suddenly turned and headed back to Irving Place. His attention was diverted by a garbage can in his path, and he rummaged through its contents. "What have I got?" Dwyer asked himself. "A nut?"

Back on Irving, down to 18th Street. When the man crossed 18th Street, he spotted a Jeep, went up to it, and looked in the passenger window. Then he pulled out a screwdriver and wedged open the vent window. Reaching into the car, he popped the lock and let himself in.

At that moment, Officer Dwyer had *probable cause* to believe a crime was being committed, and could arrest the man. Probable cause is a level of proof in which the facts of evidence would lead a police officer to believe that a crime was committed or is being committed by a person, and for which the person who committed the crime may be arrested.

For a conviction, a district attorney must convince a judge

or jury *beyond a reasonable doubt* that the suspect committed or was attempting to commit an offense. Dwyer believed he now had enough evidence for the D.A. to successfully prosecute the case.

With the suspect inside the Jeep, Dwyer contemplated what action to take. Because he was not in uniform and was not assigned to patrol duty, it would be better to have the precinct cops make the arrest. He dashed into a restaurant and, with his shield in his right hand, identified himself as a police officer to the maître d', and asked him to call 911. He told the maître d' what happened and asked him also to give the operator Dwyer's description.

Out on the street again, Dwyer watched the man move around inside the Jeep. Thinking fast, he ran through all the possibilities, wanting to be sure of the man's intent. "Could he possibly just be looking for a place to sleep?" he wondered hopefully. Probably not—the man's hands were busy, and he appeared to be searching for something.

Dwyer started to sweat profusely. Was he trying to steal the Jeep?

Now the man was fiddling with the radio, attempting unsuccessfully to pry it loose. Dwyer relaxed a little. The guy was just looking for something to rip off.

Giving up, the man started to get out of the Jeep. "I've got to do something right now," Dwyer decided, "or he's going to get away before the precinct cops show up." He walked slowly over with his shield held up in his left hand and his gun in his right.

"Police, don't move. Stay in there." The perp didn't seem surprised or even seem to care. His face was blank, confused.

He was still holding the screwdriver, Dwyer saw, a potentially lethal weapon.

"Drop it!"

The man just stared at him.

"I said, drop it!"

No response.

Dwyer took another step toward him, mustering all his authority, and shouted, "Drop the screwdriver. Right now!"

The man's hand opened limply, and the screwdriver clattered to the floor of the car.

Relieved, Dwyer took a deep breath, and almost didn't react fast enough when the man suddenly lunged at him. But his reflexes took over, and as the two grappled, he managed to pull his gun just out of reach of his attacker's desperate grasp.

With his right arm held high to keep the gun away from the man, Dwyer felt his own chest exposed to the man's wild swings. "If he lands a solid punch," Dwyer thought, "I'm gonna drop the gun." And if the man got his gun . . . Dwyer's life was in danger, and without another thought he brought the gun down hard on the man's head. The man merely grunted, blood spurting from his skull.

Oddly, the blow didn't have much effect. An instant later the man threw himself at Dwyer again. A second whack on the head with the gun didn't faze him, and instead he appeared to have gained strength. With a burst of superhuman energy, the man suddenly grabbed the cylinder of the gun.

It was a deadly tug-of-war, and Dwyer's breath came in gasps as he struggled to keep the gun away from him. His arm was tiring. The man's blood was streaking Dwyer's face, in his eyes. From deep within he drew a surge of power and wrenched the man to the sidewalk. As they wrestled, he managed several more blows to the man's head, but to no effect.

The situation was desperate. "Should I shoot him?" Dwyer wondered, exhausted, fighting the man's drug-induced strength. Something held Dwyer back, and he raised his eyes for an instant, catching a brief glimpse of faces, people suddenly materialized in a circle around him, watching the struggle. Their expressions were tense, frightened, uncertain.

"I'm a police officer," Dwyer yelled. "Call the police. I need help!"

After a brief hesitation, one of the watchers pressed forward and grabbed one of the perp's arms. Dwyer got his left hand free and unlocked his adversary's grip on his gun. The Good Samaritan, catching sight of the gun, dropped the attacker's arm and melted into the darkness. But Dwyer was on top, holding his gun high above the perp, who continued to swing and kick with all his might. Just as Dwyer felt he was about to pass out from the effort, he heard the sweet sound of sirens coming rapidly closer.

A few seconds later an unmarked car screeched to a halt beside them, and two plainclothes cops burst out.

"Will they know I'm a cop?" Dwyer thought, panicked. He was in civilian clothes, his shield out of sight in his pocket, and he had a gun. Fortunately, his rescuers sized up the situation accurately, pouncing on the perp, shouting at Dwyer to stand aside. "The maître d' must have given them my description after all," Dwyer realized with a great rush of gratitude and relief. He slumped against the Jeep, winded, and watched as the plainclothes cops subdued the still-struggling perp.

A patrol car pulled up, discharging a sergeant and a patrolman. The patrolman, seeing the blood-splattered ground and Dwyer still holding his gun, took Dwyer's arm and whispered compassionately, "Don't worry. We got a PBA delegate working." He had assumed Dwyer shot the perp; it's standard operating procedure for a cop who has shot someone to have the Patrolmen's Benevolent Association arrange for an attorney to protect his rights. Dwyer was too exhausted for the moment to correct the patrolman's mistake.

The patrol sergeant drew Dwyer out of the way as his men cuffed the perp. Dwyer was thankful to be taken out of the action; he was starting to feel a little dizzy and knew he was in shock.

He moved across the street as several radio cars streamed in and the man was taken into custody. As he watched, a young waitress came out of a restaurant, joining Dwyer and a small crowd watching the police. Without his uniform, the woman didn't recognize Dwyer as a cop. She looked over at the bleeding man being handcuffed by the police, and then glanced at Officer Dwyer. "Isn't it terrible?" she said.

"What?"

"That every time the police catch somebody, they beat them up." Infuriated, Officer Dwyer explained what happened. "Well, I hope so," she said sarcastically, clearly skeptical, then walked away. How quickly the public jumps to a conclusion of police brutality without knowing the facts! The woman could see only that the man was bleeding when he was taken into police custody. The man broke into a Jeep and had fought viciously to take Dwyer's gun to use against him. Dwyer was tired and angry, but there was still much to be done.

After the perp was taken into custody, Dwyer asked the anticrime officers to check the cars on 19th Street where the perp had tried the doors, and to get the license plate of the first vehicle, the Mercedes-Benz, that the perp had emerged from, and to leave a note for the owner. Without the license plates, there'd be no case.

Back at the 13th Precinct, Dwyer immediately headed for the men's room to wash his hands. He was a little concerned because the perp was obviously a drug user, and he had small cuts on his hand. He noticed strands of the perp's hair on his gun too, and that the trigger guard was bent.

Formal charges were brought against the perp: unauthorized use of a vehicle (he went into the Jeep without permission of the owner); criminal mischief (he damaged the window); attempted robbery (for trying to take Dwyer's gun); criminal possession of a gun (for possessing the gun for a time).

When the patrol officers brought the perp to the station house, the cops standing around caught sight of his bloody head and gasped. "Holy shit!" said one. "You did a good job," another officer told Dwyer. The perp was taken to Bellevue, where he would stay for eighteen hours before going directly to Central Booking in downtown Manhattan.

Central Booking, the recruits learn, is a police facility in each borough of New York City where defendants are processed for arrest. Here, prisoners are photographed, frisked, fingerprinted, and put into cells; the arresting officer also submits paperwork to a desk officer there. Central Booking is where perps enter the criminal justice system.

Since the perp wasn't interrogated at the station house, Miranda warnings were not given.

As anyone who has ever watched a cop show knows, after an arrest and before an interrogation a prisoner must be read Miranda warnings. Based on the famous case decided by the U.S. Supreme Court in 1966, a prisoner must be told that he has the right to remain silent and not answer questions, that anything he says may be used against him in a court of law, that he has the right to consult an attorney before talking with police and to have one present during any questioning, and that if he cannot afford an attorney, one will be provided without cost.

But Miranda doesn't have to be read unless there is, as the police academy's equation goes, custody plus interrogation— a questioning session that seeks to incriminate the prisoner. Miranda is so ubiquitous on TV cop shows that the general public thinks every person taken into custody must immediately receive Miranda warnings. Cops find this amusing. Frank Dwyer tells the recruits about people arrested by patrol officers who would immediately complain to a sergeant or lieutenant that they were never read their rights. The boss would tell them, "We don't have to read you your rights," and the people would be confused. Cops may ask pedigree information— name, address, date of birth—but don't need to read Miranda to a prisoner unless guilt-seeking questions are asked. Miranda is supposed to ensure that the prisoner knows he doesn't have to answer those questions unless he consents voluntarily.

Could a police officer or detective ask guilt-seeking questions to someone not under arrest? Suppose all a cop has is mere suspicion, and he goes to a person's home, knocks on the door, and asks if he may come in and talk. May he ask if the person murdered anyone, held up a store, burglarized a home, raped a woman, stole a car? Yes. But the moment the cop has enough evidence to make an arrest and take the suspect into custody, questioning must stop, and Miranda warnings must be read.

Consider a situation where a woman is shot on the street and falls to the ground. A crowd forms around her. A police officer runs over and, not seeing anyone with a gun, starts to give first aid. Then the officer looks up at the crowd and asks, "Who shot her?" "I shot her," a voice responds. Is that person free to leave? No. He will be taken into custody unless he flees, in which case he may be pursued and apprehended for questioning.

Would the officer's question "Who shot her?" be admitted in court? Yes. Would the response "I shot her" be allowed? Yes, again, because when the officer asked the question, even though it was guilt-seeking, it was a general inquiry. The person who answered was not in custody, nor was anyone else, and he gave what's called a *spontaneous* or *excited utterance*. Obviously, at this point, the person who admitted to the shooting would be arrested and then given Miranda warnings before any interrogation began.

Since Dwyer's perp didn't have any identification on him, he was written up in the police reports as John Doe. Dwyer completed an arrest report; a stop, question, and frisk report; and two complaint reports.

At Central Booking, the perp's fingerprints were run to Albany and Washington, D.C. His rap sheet came back, and it turned out that he was wanted on a warrant for skipping bail by not showing up for a previous court date.

Officer Dwyer met with the assistant district attorney, who

wrote up the complaint. Initially, the A.D.A. intended to prosecute the case as a felony, charging the defendant with two
counts of larceny and criminal possession of a weapon. Three
days later, feeling it would be difficult to prosecute as a felony,
the A.D.A. eliminated the felony charge, leaving all misdemeanors. The A.D.A. said he didn't feel a robbery charge would
hold when the perp grabbed Dwyer's gun, because it might be
argued that the defendant was not trying to steal it but get it
away from his pursuer, who was threatening him. The criminal
possession of a gun felony charge might not hold up either
because the gun had been bent, and it wasn't known if that
happened when Dwyer hit the perp with it or when they fell
to the ground. The perp could have possessed a gun that was
not functional, in which case the charge would be a misdemeanor, not a felony. The $1,000 bail was lowered to $100
when the felony charges were dropped to misdemeanors, but
the defendant couldn't make the reduced bail and was sent to
Rikers Island.

The standards of proof, as Officer Dwyer's Law class sees,
can change quickly. But beyond that, Dwyer's experience hits
home, narrowing the gulf between theory and reality, the classroom and the real world. While the students know abstractly
that their instructors are police officers, there is a sense that
they are cops temporarily out of commission because they're
not on the streets making collars, helping people in distress,
living dangerously. So it was with excitement that the recruits
listened to the story; Officer Dwyer is not only someone who
can teach recruits to become cops, he can aptly handle the job
as well.

The incident also makes them uncomfortably aware of the
risk every cop runs every day out on the beat. It's like seat
belts, one recruit says later. You don't take safety seriously
because you don't think "it" will happen to you. But when a
cop close to you gets hurt or is involved in a serious altercation,

reality sets in. Any of us, he laments, can get shot at any time. Any of us can end up fighting for our guns or our lives at any time.

The student officers' other concerns are many: Was Dwyer allowed to have his gun drawn? Could he have legally shot the perp? If so, why didn't he?

Dwyer explains that a police officer may draw his gun or shoot when he fears for his safety, the latter, of course, requiring greater danger potential. Many recruits can't believe that a civilian would not only not listen to a cop but would fight one, no less one with a gun drawn and pointed at him. They are surprised at how long Dwyer was in Central Booking—twenty-four hours—for a relatively simple case. The Hollywood version of cops shooting a criminal one day and out on the street hunting more the next day has no basis in reality. "You're going to have to get used to it," Dwyer tells them. "That's how backed up the cases are. You'll be in Central Booking a long time."

A number of students also question why Dwyer didn't arrest the man the first time he tried a car handle.

"Why? What's the rush?" He explains why it is sometimes better to gather as much evidence as possible for the D.A.

"Just because a guy has a screwdriver in his hand, and he's by some cars, that doesn't give you enough to arrest him. You want something solid."

"Couldn't you arrest him for trying door handles?"

"Perhaps, but are you comfortable with that? Sometimes it's tricky when to arrest someone. It's often a judgment call when to make an arrest. Wait for more if you can. It's like watching kids dilly-dally around a candy counter for minutes," Officer Dwyer says. "You know they're going to steal candy, but you have to wait before you move in. You'll see guys standing on a corner for eight hours of a day. You'll know they're dealing drugs, but you just can't arrest them without tangible proof."

As for the arrested perp, like most other cops, Dwyer followed the case up to a point. Then, disillusioned, he lost interest. The man was in Rikers Island awaiting trial. To follow the case, Dwyer would have to call the A.D.A. to find out the latest status. But caught up in the daily rigors of life, the cop who was so emotionally involved in the case, whose life was at one point in danger, becomes removed from it. Dwyer explains, "You lock somebody up for doing A, and they get convicted of doing C. And you're sort of annoyed and disgusted with the whole thing. So why the hell should you follow the case? To see your good work go down the drain?"

What started out as a relatively decent case probably dwindled down, Dwyer feels. "I just became a cog in the criminal-justice-system wheel."

"Inevitably," he continues, "the defendant's court-appointed attorney plea-bargained a deal with the A.D.A." Dwyer was never called as a witness in the man's trial and has no idea what the plea was. He says he doesn't think the jail time could have been more than six months.

One message the students learn is that, as police officers, they had better never lose a fight. If they do, they might lose their lives while the killer may only get arrested and may plea-bargain later on. As they see the bad state the criminal justice system is in, they become disillusioned, experiencing their first doubts that their ideals of making the streets safe will be met in the face of cold reality.

—4—
POLICE SCIENCE
AND
SOCIAL SCIENCE

Stefanie Hirschhorn is sitting in a Police Science class listening to yet another lesson on the modus operandi of the NYPD. The lesson is straightforward and academic, no problem to grasp. But she's cautiously aware that once she leaves the academy, the material will take on new meaning. Radio codes will no longer be just numbers to be translated into English, but will be shorthand for real-life crises she'll be rushing off to. Ranks will no longer be mere designations with assigned responsibilities, but flesh-and-blood cops with a variety of personalities she'll be dealing with every day. The many units of the department will no longer be faceless divisions, but highly specialized units that may take over for her in critical situations.

Stefanie's mind drifts from the classroom as the instructor details numerous contingencies that may arise on patrol. Police Science prepares the student officers for these, painting scenarios and telling them how to respond to each. Stefanie has quick flashes of explosions, building collapses, train accidents, car crashes, fire scenes, stuck elevators, barricaded gunmen with hostages, large demonstrations. She imagines going through the pockets of a dead man, dealing with an emotionally disturbed person on the street, accompanying a city marshal who is evicting a poor tenant. In the same day she'll be both good guy and bad guy. Soon she'll be the S.O.B. cop she herself swore at in the past when she was on the receiving end of a parking ticket.

Police Science has given Stefanie a different view of the city. Instead of thinking of it as five boroughs, it's now seventy-five precincts, geographical areas ranging from ten square blocks to several miles. Manning the precincts are police officers and an assortment of superiors. Patrol officers, she has learned, are the backbone of the force, the defenders and watchdogs of the community, the front line of the department. Within the rank of police officer is the promotional designation of detective, whose job it is to investigate crimes. Ranking above patrol officers are sergeants, who, as patrol supervisors, oversee the work of officers on patrol, responding to all serious crimes and incidents, taking command and making sure proper procedures are followed and notifications made. Next come lieutenants, who may serve in a variety of positions: desk officers, in which they spend their tours in the precinct supervising operations in the command; Integrity Control Officers (ICOs), in which they check for "cooping"—napping or relaxing on duty—and pass by corruption-prone locations to see if any cops in the precinct are involved in activities such as gambling, prostitution, or extortion; or in other positions where they make inspections on scheduled tours, maintain disciplinary records, or command detective squads. The highest civil service rank is the captain, who commands or manages the precinct, being responsible for all personnel, crime statistics, and having ultimate power in deciding how the precinct is run. While Stefanie has heard disillusioning stories about ICOs who punish cops for the most minor infractions, or captains who run their precincts poorly, she has learned to respect the rank, for a superior officer can make or break her career.

The work covered in Police Science—making memo book entries; filling out complaint forms and aided cards; completing stop, question, and frisk reports and other paperwork; writing summonses; learning radio codes—becomes routine after a while. What worries Stefanie most is whether she will be overcome emotionally in the throes of an emergency. Will she remember common-sense tactics or will she panic, lose her professional demeanor, and set herself up for injury, even death?

Other, similar questions haunt her. Will training really prepare her to deal with the kinds of situations and people she'll be coming into contact with? Will wearing a blue uniform and carrying a gun and shield make her any different from the person she was a year ago? Will it make her the valorous purveyor of law and order a cop is supposed to be? Stefanie had gone through some rough times recently, uncertain about her future in every way. There were periods when she was broke, depressed about her relationships and what she'd do with her life. She felt helpless. Overnight, an inordinate amount of power has been thrust upon her, including, all too soon, the power of life and death. She wonders just how well she'll respond in a crisis.

In the first six months following graduation, the student officers are assigned to Field Training Units, details that are basically footpost work. This is still a learning period, with jobs, when they arise, ranging from individual drug busts to domestic disputes. Real emergencies are left to more experienced officers, unless they happen to be on the footpost cop's beat. Yet there are two radio calls every cop in New York City responds to in their vicinity: 10-85s and 10-13s. The 13 is the more serious of the two, usually used only when a cop has been shot or for some other dire emergency when he desperately needs backups. A notch or two under is the 85, literally "officer needs additional unit," which also brings in all available troops in the immediate area, especially when "forthwith" is tagged on. Just a few months into field training, Stefanie had a chance to test her mettle and put all her Police Science work to use when a 13 came over the radio.

It was a cold December day, and Stefanie, on footpost, was standing on the corner of 116th Street and Seventh Avenue in Harlem. She saw a driver disobey a sign for cars to turn right—the driver proceeded straight ahead—and she signaled for him to pull over. Stefanie's footpost partner, a woman walking a beat across the street, saw the stopped car and joined her.

Stefanie informed the driver of his traffic infraction and asked for his license, registration, and insurance card. Just as he handed everything over, they heard a crash. Stefanie and her partner looked up to see a minor automobile accident across the street. No one appeared to be hurt. They walked over and told the drivers that they were giving a summons, so the drivers would have to wait before the two cops could write up the necessary accident report.

Just then a 10-13 came over the radio. What grabbed Stefanie's attention was that the location was only a block away. She greeted the distress call coolly, casting a quick nod to her partner as if to say, "Okay. We know what that means. Now, let's get the hell out of here!" A cop—perhaps a friend—might have been shot or stabbed. The perps—perhaps armed with guns—could still be nearby. When a cop hears a 10-13, there's no time to mull over the possibilities, no time to consider the perils that may lie ahead. It is the worst radio call a cop can receive; after that it's pure instinctive reaction on the cop's part. But it's years of experience that translate that instinct into judicious behavior when the situation is fraught with danger.

With their hands over their holsters, Stefanie and her partner raced down 116th Street to Eighth Avenue. The 13 came from the subway. It didn't matter that a Transit officer made the call—all cops are brethren.

Some subway stations in the city have separate staircases for downtown and uptown trains. Without giving a thought to this, the two women plunged down the staircase at the subway entrance on the corner and ran to the platform. "Shit!" Stefanie said as they saw a streak of blue uniforms across the tracks. They would have to go back up, cross the street, and take another entrance. When they reached the street, there were already a number of radio and unmarked cars there. Down on the platform they found more than three dozen cops. It turned out that a cop had been struck and knocked down by a man as he tried to arrest him. The perp was in custody, and Stefanie and her partner were not needed.

Stefanie was relieved that the cop wasn't badly injured or killed, and that the attacker had been caught. If she had been the first officer to arrive on the scene and confront the perp alone, would she have been capable of it? She doesn't know, but the incident does reveal a few things to her. She didn't panic in the face of a distress call; she responded with zest and vigor; she made an attempt to help. She hopes she'll never have to go on a 13 again, or have to call one, but that's probably wishful thinking. In New York City these calls are part of the daily routine of the police force.

On the street around her, Stefanie saw many, many of New York's Finest. It's comforting to know, Stephanie thought, that if she was ever in trouble, real trouble, the troops would come to rescue her. After the experience, she has a better understanding of the camaraderie which exists among all cops. Your world is theirs, and theirs yours. You don't even have to know a cop to put your life on the line for him; he'd do the same for you.

Having exerted all her energy in the chase, Stefanie was

overheated and breathing hard in the bitter cold. This was just the kind of situation those grueling gym laps back at the academy prepared the recruits for, and now she really appreciated them. But not having run as much since she was in the academy, she had to get back into a regimen of exercise. And quit smoking, or cut down. She and her partner were offered a ride back to Seventh Avenue in a police van, and they gratefully accepted. Back on Seventh, Stefanie apologized to the driver she stopped for the 15-minute delay and wrote him up. The other drivers, those involved in the accident, apparently had exchanged the necessary information, because they were no longer there.

While Police Science and Law may be considered the recruits' technical education, Social Science teaches them how to deal with people. It's an easy subject academically, but a vital one, since effective interaction with people makes police work most manageable. If what began as a family dispute ended in an armed face-off because the police couldn't separate, calm, and talk to family members, then they failed to do their job. "Tactics and Law are academic," says Officer Michael Wilson of the Social Science Department. "I came on the job to help people. That's Social Science."

Cops are in the people business: aiding, protecting, rescuing, summonsing, arresting. Their tours are spent mostly serving people in need and safeguarding the public. Most of their contact is with basically law-abiding citizens. If people respect the police and respond to them positively, this in turn makes the cop's job easier. Knowing how to interact effectively with the public is vital; they must be able to defuse explosive confrontations rather than let them escalate.

Social Science opens a window on human behavior, teaching recruits to develop interactive skills in order to deal effectively with the broad spectrum of society they'll meet as cops on the street. With eighty-five percent of a cop's time on patrol spent serving people—from giving directions to making a death notification—good communication skills are essential.

A police officer parked near an intersection observes a young man driving a souped-up sports car roll through a stop sign when he sees no other vehicles. The officer pulls him over.

The man pulls up, cursing to himself, thinking he's going to get a summons. He'll have to pay a fine. He'll get points on his license, and his insurance costs will rise. He is seething as the officer approaches his car.

"Don't you know you're supposed to stop when you get to a stop sign?" the cop says impatiently. "You went right through it!"

"Hey, look, why are you wasting the taxpayers' money on me? Why the fuck aren't you going after the real criminals?"

"Look, buddy. Don't tell me how to do my job. And who the hell are you to talk to me this way? If you don't shut up, I'm going to give you another summons."

"This is bullshit, man. I slowed down at the intersection. And I did stop. It's just your word against mine, you know!"

Angry, the officer walks around the car and notices one of the back lights is broken. He completes his circle to the driver.

"You're getting another summons," he laughs.

"You fucking asshole cop!" The driver jerks open his door, gets out, and pushes the cop. The officer puts him against the car and handcuffs him. He calls his patrol supervisor to verify the arrest.

"What happened?" the sergeant asks.

"He pushed me."

"How did the job start?"

"It started as a summons. He ran a stop sign."

"It started as a summons and now you've got a collar? How the hell did that happen?"

Clearly, the officer handled this job poorly, letting the situation get out of hand. If this happened in real life, he might be walking a footpost next or working at an inside desk job. The academy devotes several lessons to teaching the recruits how to prevent situations from escalating in this way, through what is called Transactional Analysis.

Transactional Analysis, used as a model of communication by the NYPD, is a technique of evaluating a person's behavior in such a way as to evoke a desired response, or to prevent a situation from getting out of hand. It is also a psychological tool used by the police to remain neutral and professional, not to take a person's comments or behavior personally or get emotionally involved in a situation.

TA identifies three different ego states that people may fall into: the parent ego, adult ego, and child ego states. In the parent ego state, a person acts authoritatively; he scolds, moralizes, or gives instruction as to what is "right" or "wrong." He tells someone what to do. In the adult ego state, a person analyzes a situation and then reacts, using reason to decide how to improve the situation rather than losing his temper. Calmness and objectivity characterize the adult ego state. The child ego state is emotional; a person in this state is motivated primarily by feelings, reacting angrily or joyfully, for example. Officer Wilson compares the parent ego state with the Archie Bunker character from the TV show "All in the Family," the adult ego state with Mr. Spock from "Star Trek," and the child state with a clown.

With TA, the academy strives to prevent volatile situations from erupting, as when a person uses abusive language to a cop, who then fails to achieve what he set out to accomplish. The cop might lower himself to the person's child

55

ego state, and the situation could escalate. Using TA can prevent that.

The Social Science instructors don't guarantee that TA will always work. But they tell the recruits that it should be the first form of communication attempted in appropriate situations and not to give up on it, not to come down to a person's level and get hooked into his pattern of abusive behavior. Force against force, the instructors say, does not work. Police antagonism will make a person more frustrated and riled. To make someone understand, the cop has to explain himself rationally and not talk down to a person. An officer who keeps cool as abusive language is being hurled at him helps the angry person switch from the child ego state back to the adult ego state, in which the offender is able to recognize his guilt and accept the fact that the officer is only doing his job.

If a cop arrests someone for disorderly conduct at an anti-abortion demonstration, he cannot allow himself to get hooked by the person who protests, "You're a police officer. Your job is to uphold the Constitution. Babies are being killed, and you're arresting me?" A proper response would be, "Ma'am, I understand your position, but as a police officer I have to stay neutral. The people in that building have rights too."

In a case where a motorist rambles on, the recruits are taught to ignore any angry outbursts and to reply only "It's part of my job" if provoked. A traffic violation should not result in an arrest. It is also considered bad form for an officer who is annoyed by a driver's mouthing off to circle the vehicle looking for other violations. There is nothing in the NYPD *Patrol Guide* that says that a cop has to give a summons for a violation of the law. In practice, summonses are issued at an officer's discretion, and a cop may choose to warn and admonish instead. He or she should weigh the circumstances of a given situation. A man who breaks the speed limit driving his pregnant wife to the hospital could legally be issued a summons, but probably would not be.

The TA classes are essentially lessons in social psychology. Recruits are taught how to analyze different kinds of behavior, how to break down barriers of communication, how to listen effectively. They are taught techniques of feedback to elicit clarification of messages ("Do I understand you correctly? Are you saying that . . . ?") and proper words and phrases to use in addressing the public ("Ma'am," "I see your point," "Have you tried . . . ?").

The student officers voice mixed feelings about TA. Some say it's worth a try, but others brand it as ridiculous, unworkable, something that seems like a good idea in theory but is impractical for confrontational situations on the streets where a cop's authority depends on his perceived power. One recruit says he wouldn't address gang members, hoodlums, street rogues, or crack addicts, for example, with "sir," or say "Please do this or that," or bother to explain his actions, or approach a confrontational situation in a composed and courteous manner because that would weaken his position. And it wouldn't make a difference anyway, he says. Some people are just so uncivil, so lacking in respect for cops, that courtesy and reason wouldn't have any effect.

Indeed, soon after graduating, many recruits will talk about going on radio calls and finding a person who is yelling, acting violent, or who refuses to answer at all. So even with all they've learned at the academy, all the textbook responses, they often have to ask themselves, "What do I do now?" They improvise, they say, and ask advice of supervisors. They learn for the next time. One recruit in Company 20 said, "When I was at the academy, an idealistic student officer, I was gung-ho to learn TA and apply it once I got out. But you deal with so much scum on the street that you can't use it. They laugh at you; your authority is weakened. You've got to treat them the only way they understand." Officer Wilson says the New York Police Academy is sometimes called the ivory tower, a reference to training that is not always realistic for the streets of New

York City. But much of training is based on actual incidents in the city and the results of various studies. Furthermore, as representatives of the public and paradigms of law and order, cops should try to interact with the public, even its most denigrated citizens, in the most civil and reasonable way possible.

There are times when a cop will have to use a parent ego state. If a person is standing on a street with a gun, for example, the cop will sternly say, "Police, don't move! Drop the gun and turn around." But in non-life-threatening situations, the students are told they don't have to be authoritative. Talk to people. Give a reason. Explain.

As a former social worker, Lissette Sierra-Solis sees possibilities for TA. She believes she knows how to approach people and talk with them, but realizes that not all cops are able to. Some cops become emotionally involved. If they take something personally, she thinks, they're no longer functioning as professional police officers. Their individual personalities emerge and they feel under attack as individuals, not cops. Words are exchanged; the situation can turn into a physical confrontation. Cops often get hurt when this happens.

Many of Lissette's peers disregard TA. Lissette thinks they concentrate too much on the arrest, or power aspect, of the job, and that they neglect its social service aspect. When the student officers were told that as police officers they'll be serving in many roles, including social worker and psychologist, and that they could de-escalate situations through courteous behavior, some grimaced. Their concept of a cop was something else—if anyone gave them a hard time, cursed at them, or disobeyed them, they should take out their handcuffs and make an arrest.

It was just after ten in the morning, and Lissette Sierra-Solis, having graduated the academy, was at the Tremont Avenue

IND subway station in the Bronx, sitting on a bench on the platform. She was dressed casually, wearing jeans and a pullover shirt, her hair tied back in a bun. There had been a number of fare-beaters at this station lately, and Lissette was working plainclothes. Sitting next to her was her partner.

A young man, about twenty-four years old, quickly opened the exit gate and rushed through, looking left and right to see if there were any cops on the platform. He didn't see any uniformed officers, and was surprised a moment later when Lissette and her partner approached him.

"Sir," Lissette said, displaying her shield in her hand. "I'm a police officer. Do you have a pass?"

"No," said the man, who was thin and muscular.

"Sir, we saw you go through the exit gate, and I'm going to have to issue you a summons." Fare-beaters receive what is called a Transit Adjudication Bureau summons. "May I see some identification?"

Shaking his head angrily and grumbling, the man reluctantly handed over an employment identification card bearing his name, date of birth, weight, and a picture.

"Can't you give me a break, a damn break?" he pleaded as Lissette examined the card. "I didn't even know you were cops."

Lissette began to feel a little sorry for him, but remembered he blatantly broke the law. Other people have to pay fares, and it was beginning to irritate her that someone would try to pull a fast one because he thought no cops were around.

Lissette asked him his weight and he screamed, "It's on there! You wanted my identification, it's on there. Now don't ask me nothin'. I ain't saying nothin'." The man then complained that he was late for work.

From his angry protesting, it was obvious to Lissette that the man was in a child ego state. It bothered Lissette that the man broke the law, and now he was swearing at her. But she wouldn't let herself get hooked. She was rational and calm, she was using level eye contact, and she appeared confident; she was in the adult ego state.

She could have told him firmly to stop mouthing off and do exactly as she said, but that might have riled him even more. Instead, she chose to be polite and tried to get him to respond civilly. "I'm going to issue you a summons now. I understand you're late for work, but the quicker you cooperate with me, the sooner you'll be on your way. What is your height?"

"I told you, don't ask me nothin'. It's on there!"

"Sir, if you'd look at your identification, you'd see your height isn't on there."

"Five ten," he growled.

Other Transit cops have told Lissette she should be more aggressive, but that's not how she chooses to work. She often works alone, and getting into confrontations could be dangerous. In the subways, it may take a while for backups to arrive.

The ticket was written and handed to the man; Lissette told him that the instructions were on the back.

When fare-beaters get a summons in the subway, they often think they get a free ride. Not so. Lissette told the man he'd have to leave the station, and he protested that he should be allowed to ride a train now without paying a fare. Lissette informed him that he would have to buy a token.

For all her attempts to make the man understand that he committed a crime, and that she was just doing her job, he cursed under his breath as he walked toward the exit gate. As he approached it he slowed down and tore up the summons, turning his head to see if Lissette was watching. Though Lissette could have pursued him further through the courts, it just wasn't worth it, and she let it go.

Learning to deal effectively with people requires knowledge of the customs and cultures of ethnic groups and other communities whose life-styles and practices differ from those of the mainstream. As a long-time center of immigration, New

York City has absorbed peoples of all nationalities; as a major city, it has attracted individuals whose personal practices or beliefs might encounter fearsome opposition elsewhere. NYPD cops come in contact with all of these communities, and the academy tries to socialize recruits to understand and deal with whatever preconceptions they might bring to their training.

Each of the five boroughs—Manhattan, Brooklyn, Queens, the Bronx, and Staten Island—is dotted with large constituencies of people of common ethnic and religious backgrounds, each with its own distinctive personality. In Queens there are large populations of Greeks in Astoria, Poles in Greenpoint, and Indians in Flushing. In Brooklyn, Russian Jews dwell in Brighton Beach, Hasidim in Williamsburg and Borough Park, West Indians in Bedford-Stuyvesant and East Flatbush. In Manhattan are Little Italy, Chinatown, and Spanish Harlem.

If New York is a city of diversity, it is also one of extremes. Only a few blocks separate squalid urban ghettos from the most expensive real estate in the United States. New York is at once an impoverished realm of illiteracy and a center of higher learning. Individual streets have come to be known as centers of leading industry in the country—theater on Broadway, fashion on Seventh Avenue, advertising on Madison Avenue, finance on Wall Street. At the same time, certain neighborhoods have come to symbolize strife, danger, terror—the South Bronx, East New York, Harlem.

In Social Science, the student officers are required to prepare and deliver brief oral presentations on an ethnic group of their choice. Having lived in Puerto Rico for several years, Lissette Sierra-Solis feels capable of enlightening her fellow recruits about Hispanics. "As police officers, we will be coming into contact with a large number of Hispanics," she says. "In order to interact with them more adequately, it will be very helpful to know the differences in their cultures, which are often misunderstood." Lissette covers such areas as family, customs, food, and appearance, and addresses common misconceptions

61

about the people. She speaks with a slight Hispanic lilt, but she is clearly an acclimated New Yorker.

The recruits are mostly silent throughout her discourse, shuffling a little when she talks about voodoo and spiritualism, and emitting a few titters when she talks about words having different meanings in different Spanish countries. *Bicho*, for example, is a word which in some South American countries means an insect, but in Puerto Rico it refers to the male sex organ. She warns the students that Hispanics will become defensive or even hostile if they're stereotyped in an encounter, or the men made to feel embarrassed in front of their wives or girlfriends.

In each borough, New York City cops come in contact with people to whom they may not previously have been exposed. To serve effectively, police officers must understand the sociological backgrounds of the people in the communities they patrol, as the practices of these people may affect their work.

For example, the Orthodox Jewish community has restrictions during the Jewish Sabbath, which begins before sunset Friday and ends after sunset on Saturday, and on holy days. In certain sections of Williamsburg and Crown Heights and other Jewish communities, Orthodox members will not write, work, or operate mechanical or electrical devices; they may not even let vehicles pass through certain streets.

How does this affect the police officer who works in a precinct in these areas? The officer may be asked to come to the home of an Orthodox Jew to turn on a light or into a synagogue to turn on an air conditioner. A female police officer who wants to look for a man in an Orthodox temple might be asked by the rabbi to have a male officer do the search instead, because women may not enter certain sections of the synagogue. By complying with such requests, the officers are serving their communities.

Each ethnic group has its own holidays, sometimes marked by parades or other celebrations. St. Patrick's Day is in March, the Hispanic Day parade in October, African-American Day in September, the West Indian Carnival in September, the Italian Festival of San Gennaro on Mulberry Street in September, and the Festival of St. Anthony on Sullivan Street in June. The Muslim holy month of Ramadan is in August or September; Chinese New Year is at the end of January or the beginning of February. During parades, a cop's main objectives are to maintain peace and order and to take proper action in response to serious crimes committed. Street cops may be told by superior officers to overlook certain minor infractions such as Rastafarians smoking marijuana, which is considered by these people to have medicinal and spiritual value.

Many foreign words and expressions of various ethnic and religious groups are part of a New York City cop's vernacular. Students must learn to use these words. There might be a stickup in a *bodega* (grocery store) or *botanica* (religious shop and herbal store), an introduction to a *compadre* (close friend or relative), a request to turn on a light during *Shabbat* (Jewish Sabbath).

The academy stresses to its recruits that police officers who aren't sensitive to cultural and religious differences can have serious problems on patrol. They may lose the respect of the public they deal with every day, and their job will become more difficult. One young instructor with four years' experience on the street says, "Social Science gets a lot of knocks, but it's the best course. It teaches how to deal with people. How to talk to them. How to handle them."

A call comes over the radio for a 10-20; a person has been robbed. Two officers in the vicinity of the location respond. They knock on the door of the apartment, and a young man answers. He tells the officers he's not hurt, just upset about being robbed.

"Forty minutes ago," he says, "I was waiting at a bus stop when someone stuck a hard object in my back and

63

said, 'If you don't give me all your stuff, I'll blow your head off.' "

He says he handed over his red leather shoulder bag, which contained work from his job at a brokerage house, gym gear, an electric shaver, and a wallet with $500 cash and assorted credit cards.

The officers ask more questions and take down information on a complaint form.

"Was there anything else in the shoulder bag?" one of the cops asks.

"Yes. Two sets of leotards, an athletic supporter, and a vibrator."

A student officer in this role play, given in a Social Science class of Company 19, bursts out laughing. He thinks it is funny to hear the instructor talk like that. The part just doesn't go with him. There is also some laughter among the recruits.

Until now, Lissette was not aware that the victim is gay. There was no hint of his sexual orientation until he described some of the contents of his bag.

The role play continues. The victim adds that in his wallet was also a card given to him by a police officer who had befriended him when he moved to New York City two weeks earlier. Imprinted on the card was the name of an organization the officer said he belonged to, the Gay Officers Action League.

"Is there such an organization?" he asks.

"Yes."

"Then he really was on the level."

The instructor asks the students if there is anything unusual about this job.

"Yes," says a student. "The person is a homosexual."

"Does that make this job different?"

There are mostly puzzled looks.

"Well, he's a homosexual," comes a response.

"Yes, but does that change it at all?"

"No, it doesn't," another student says.

"Yes, it does!" the instructor responds. The whole class seems confused.

"The reason it's different is because a crime was committed against a person because of his sexual orientation, so it's a "biased" incident. You're right in saying you're not going to treat this victim differently than another victim, but we still have to be aware of the reason why it happened. You have to find out if the victim is a homosexual, and if he is, was the crime committed against him because he is a homosexual?"

The recruits weren't told ahead of time that the victim would be a homosexual. Their first impression was that this was just another role play to see how they would handle a victim of a crime, rather than the possibility of the crime stemming from a sensitive issue.

One purpose of the role play is for the instructors to see how the recruits would treat a homosexual, or their reactions to finding out a person they're helping is a homosexual. Does it mean they should stand away from the person, not put their hand on him or touch him as they would another crime victim? Not sit down in his home? No. The student officers are expected to treat gays just as they would anyone else, and to make sure they feel safe and secure with them as police officers.

After the scenario has ended, a sensitivity session on the gay and lesbian community follows. It's apparent that the majority of recruits don't know much about homosexuals, holding stereotypes as past classes have. Their ideas of homosexuals are basically dictionary definitions, with some perception that gays are effeminate males who sometimes dress and act flamboyantly.

A barrage of questions is put to the students: How can you tell if a person is gay? Is the homosexual a threat to society? Does a gay person have more of a tendency to molest children?

65

Whether the recruits are giving the answers they think the instructor wants to hear or are responding from their own true feelings is hard to tell, but no antigay machismo comes out during the session. At this point in the curriculum, the students know the department policy on prejudice: If they don't like or agree with a certain group of people, their prejudices have to be stowed away with their civilian clothes before they put on their uniforms. The recruits also know that adverse responses would have a grave effect on their standing and appear on their recruit evaluation forms. If a student responded in a classroom discussion to a homosexual's attempt to pick him up by saying, "I'd punch him in the mouth" or "I'd pull out my gun and point it in his face," it would be the instructor's responsibility to get the person counseling or weed him out altogether as soon as possible.

The recruits are savvy enough to not appear overtly prejudiced. After all, they passed an oral psychological exam to get into the academy. They generally express feelings that they know are acceptable to the department, and do not make any outlandish statements, even if they feel differently. But seasoned instructors claim they can tell when a student officer is hiding a bias, and when they do they will confront the student in the classroom and make a written record in their diary as well as inform their supervisor, who might refer the student for counseling.

It is not the purpose of Social Science to train recruits in the social psychology of why a person is a homosexual, but rather how to deal with sensitive issues. Biased incidents occur not only against blacks and whites and religious and ethnic groups, but against homosexuals as well. Crimes are committed against gay persons because they are gay, and the academy trains the student officers to pick up on these situations. Gay people don't necessarily come out and say they're gay, and for the police to process an incident as a biased one (in which a crime occurs against a homosexual simply because he or she *is* homosexual), the patrol cop has to be discerning and sensitive to the victim. The academy teaches recruits to use psychological first aid, crisis intervention, and victimology with all crime victims, including gays.

If gay people are reluctant to report crimes because they're treated rudely by the police, they'll become perfect targets for criminals because of this inhibition. If a recruit can't treat a gay person as fairly and compassionately as any other, he has no place, the students are told, on the police force. This is made abundantly clear, and the recruits seem to believe it.

After the sensitivity class, as Company 19 waits for their next instructor, Lissette Sierra-Solis overhears the recruits conversing with nervous laughter and using words like "faggot." She feels some recruits hid their true feelings in the discussion that followed the role play. She grimaced when the recruits were asked how they would react in such a situation and the responses came back, "I wouldn't discriminate, I would just take the report." She knows some answers weren't genuine, and that many of these officers may change after they are out on the street. She's heard from her husband how cops react to gay people, how they joke about them to their faces. Her husband would mimic a typical cop response in a gay voice: "Oh, your leotards? Did you have your tutu with you too?" Among her classmates, Lissette doesn't hear any cruel statements about homosexuals, just jokes. Some recruits seem to be tolerant of homosexuals, but do not accept their life-style because of religious beliefs.

In his three years at the academy, Officer Wilson says he has never seen a recruit in a homosexuality role play come off macho. Sometimes they become quiet, he's noticed, but thinks that's not necessarily bad. A few recruits may do most of the talking, and the others will keep quiet. Never, however, has he witnessed taunts or scoldings for a person's sexual preference. He realizes that after class or in the car ride home, jokes are made. But the instructors aren't out to change the views of the student officers. They're not saying that the recruits have to love gay people, blacks, Greeks, Italians, Jews, or Catholics, Officer Wilson says. But with the knowledge they're given at the academy, and their commitment to the job, the instructors hope the recruits will treat these people as they would want other cops to treat their brother or sister, father or mother, if they were the victims of a crime.

The student officers have learned to show sensitivity to a gay crime victim, and to try to restore his or her power, dignity, and security as for the victim of any crime. From the looks on some of the men's faces, it is obvious they're concerned that this might spark interest in them by the gay victim.

This concern is later addressed in a Social Science review session by an instructor, a large black man who has had years of patrol experience. He suggests that some officers might discriminate against homosexuals. Why? Because they feel threatened. If the officer is approached or propositioned by a gay person, the officer should simply turn the person down politely. "I've been approached a few times," the instructor says, "and I always compliment them on their taste. But I say no thanks."

5
PT—PHYSICAL TRAINING

New York's Finest? Hah. New York's Funniest is more like it. I never saw such a sorry bunch of people!" Welcome to PT—physical training. If the academic subjects show the instructors at their sedate, intellectual best, gym class is the place where they really bust chops. Instructors stand over the recruits, haranguing them to snap to attention quickly, not to slack off during exercises, to squeeze out that last ounce of energy in the thirty-sixth lap. Actually, draconian faculty are in the minority, but they set a tone that permeates the gym classes and keeps the recruits on guard.

Stefanie Hirschhorn can understand why it's important that recruits be whipped into shape. A finely tuned body is a cop's stock in trade. With all the tactical skills and knowledge that police officers bring to their work, the real foundation for carrying out the job successfully is excellent physical health. A police officer must not only be alert and vigorous, but be able to respond readily to the everyday calls of duty where physical stamina and prowess are crucial—chasing a perp on foot, running up a staircase to help an accident victim, controlling a hostile crowd, pulling a frantic nonswimmer to safety, frisking and cuffing two powerful brawlers. There may be a time when Stefanie's life depends on her strength, endurance, swiftness, or self-defense skills. Still, she thinks some of the gym instructors are overbearing and relentless. "There are certain instructors who do their routine through motivating you," she says, "and others who do it through abusing you."

The recruits are introduced to basic military commands early on. The purpose of these military drills is to build discipline and teamwork. Except for those with military experience, most fall out of step at one time or another or move clumsily. The instructors make sure they know it.

The experience brings Andy Varga back to the days of boot camp. "What did I get myself into?" he thinks. "Am I going to last the five months here?"

Within a couple of weeks the recruits are facile in executing the basic commands—attention, parade rest, at ease, present arms (a salute), right face, left face, about face, opening and closing ranks, dressing (aligning) right and left, close and normal—and are even able to march around the gym with impressive military precision. As an instructor calls out the drill, they march in normal step or half step, executing various types of column movements and flanks (turns).

Gym classes consist of a regimen of exercises, laps, and instruction for two hours every day. The recruits run out onto the gym floor, fall into company formation, come to attention, salute and pledge allegiance to the flag, open ranks for inspection, and do warm-up exercises. Then come the laps. Three days a week the recruits run one mile, two days a week two miles. Occasionally, these limits are stretched, and the run is pure agony. Sometimes the instructors take the laps at a merciless pace. After each lap, the recruits yell out the number. At the end they decelerate to a slow pace, then a march. The transition from one workout to another is smooth and quick, with little time to rest in between.

In the early classes some recruits are clearly out of shape.

During a run one day a winded young woman lags behind the pack and is ordered to the middle of the floor to "loosen up." The instructor yells at her, "Are you kidding me? You're twenty years old, and you can't keep up?" The instructors are stationed around the gym and single out recruits for talking or for maneuvering to an inside lane so they can run slower. The penalty is a round of push-ups. Toward the end of laps a number of faces register expressions of pain.

"We want everybody to graduate," an instructor says later. "To do your best, we don't want one hundred percent. We want one hundred fifty or two hundred percent. If you fall out of seven runs or get five Star Cards [because they cannot complete the exercises], you have to see your sergeant. Fourteen and you see Sergeant Gotay. More than that, Lieutenant Geysen. Then they'll send you to Health Services."

The recruits are told the gym warm-up builds "fire, spirit, and conviction." These are necessary "because if you're on the street and someone says he's going to fight, you'll have to as well. Stick it out. Do it here."

Then there are the exercises: push-ups, sit-ups, squat thrusts, windmills, jumping jacks, leg bends, leg raisers, hip raisers, toe raisers, toe touches, extended arm circles, backbends, overhead chin-ups. Throughout the exercises, instructors walk around the gym floor, criticizing and urging the recruits on: "I don't know where they found you. Are you on a bad batch of drugs, Officer?" One recruit, too slow in doing push-ups, is told, "Pretend you're with your girlfriend and her father comes home."

While out-of-shape or lazy recruits sometimes evade the vigilant eyes of the instructors, more often they do not, and the penalties for moving sluggishly may be harsh. Sometimes, after a couple of warnings, the entire gym class is punished for one recruit's infraction by having to start the exercise over. Clearly, no student wants to incur the wrath of his already exhausted classmates.

At the beginning and end of training the recruits are given a fitness exam consisting of a flexibility test, a one-minute sit-up test, a one-and-a-half-mile run, a bench press, and an agility test. Body fat is measured with a skinfold caliper. Those whose body fat exceeds a certain amount—it differs for men and women—must report to Health Services to get their weight down before their probation ends.

The fitness component is one part of a diverse gym program that comprises three broad areas: safety services, which includes courses in water safety, first aid, and cardiopulmonary resuscitation (CPR); overall physical fitness, achieved through daily aerobic and anaerobic exercises; and defensive tactics, in which the students are taught handcuffing and frisking, crowd control, self-defense, and how to use a baton.

There are several first-aid and CPR classes in which the students receive instruction in emergency treatment for drowning, shock, bleeding, wounds, choking, heat exhaustion, burns, and poisoning. Childbirth is taught by Officer Arthur Perry, a one-time Golden Gloves quarter-finalist who once assisted in a baby's delivery on the Long Island Expressway in Queens. This portion consists of a graphic film and a class discussion. At the end the students must pass written and practical exams.

Several lessons are devoted to handcuffing and speed-cuffing. In speed-cuffing, Sergeant Dennis Bootle, a Transit officer and expert on self-defense, tells the students, "Size doesn't make a difference," and one can believe him. Bootle is not a large fellow, but he looks tough and one need only watch him in action to see that that know-how can indeed enable a recruit to cuff and subdue a much larger opponent. The students practice on each other in pairs, taking turns: The cop comes from behind and grabs the perp's left hand. With the cuffs in the right hand, the cop quickly brings them up to the perp's arm and snaps one on. Then he brings the cuffed arm around the back, reaches for the other arm, and brings it

72

back to be cuffed. Students learn to appreciate the pain hand-cuffs can inflict. Once the hands are cuffed, a little twist can be torture.

The mechanics of frisking are covered in gym. A frisk differs from a search in that usually only the outermost garments are touched. The officer does not go inside the clothing unless he feels an object that could be a knife or other weapon.

Officer Dave Washington demonstrates the process for Company 20. Approaching the perp (played by a student officer) from behind at a distance of six to eight feet, the officer makes strong eye contact with the suspect, and in a loud, authoritative voice shouts, "Police! Don't move!" He orders the suspect to turn around or go up against the wall. Then, if the officer is right-handed, he takes two steps to his left, because if the suspect suddenly turns around with a gun, he will probably shoot where he heard the voice coming from. If the officer is left-handed, he takes two steps to the right. A right-handed officer will frisk the left side first. Then come the orders:

"Put your hands straight up.

"Wiggle your fingers." Dirt, razor blades, or any other object he may be concealing between his fingers fall free.

"Face your palms toward me.

"Turn your head to the right.

"Spread your legs wide.

"Bring your feet back toward me." The point is to keep the perp off balance if he is against a wall.

The officer comes up behind the suspect and begins the frisk, starting on the left side with his left foot on top of the suspect's left foot, in case he makes an offensive move. The gun is held in the right hand (if right-handed), and the touching is done with the left. The head is patted first. Razor blades and other sharp instruments can be hidden in hair or under a toupee. Then the officer goes to the neck, then to the left arm and down to the hand and up again into the armpit, across the chest, to the back, up and down, and around the waist. Then the left hand grabs and squeezes the groin, moves down the front of the leg, to the top of the shoe, to the back of the foot, and up the leg.

Having frisked the suspect's upper and lower left side, he steps back ("Distance is your greatest ally," reminds Officer Washington), switches the gun from the strong hand to the weak hand, and tells the suspect to turn his head to the left. The officer takes two steps to the right at a forty-five-degree angle and makes his approach as before, except that his right foot is in front. The procedure on this side of the suspect is the same as on the other. The frisk does not stop when a gun is found; many perps carry a gun and a knife or two guns.

Cops doing a frisk are under considerable stress. The person being frisked is suspected of criminal activity, may be facing a prison sentence, and may be violent by nature. If an officer is alone and believes a suspect is highly dangerous, he is to draw his gun and wait for assistance before making his initial approach. His finger should be off the trigger, however, as his nervousness could inadvertently make him squeeze it.

While cops are equipped with a nightstick, Mace, handcuffs, a radio, and a revolver, there's always the possibility that they may have to slug it out on the street. Their equipment may be knocked away or they may be overpowered, and their survival may depend on how well they fight hand-to-hand. This could be particularly daunting if an officer is alone and facing two or more vicious adversaries.

In gym there is a boxing exercise, but no face-to-face boxing. One student holds a punching bag while the other pummels it. Lissette Sierra-Solis tries to hold the bag steady as her partner, a burly male, drives her back. She is overpowered by his strength.

Many students lament that boxing is no longer a part of the gym curriculum; it was discontinued because there were too many injuries. Even some female recruits, who would probably have to spar with bigger, stronger males, regret it. "It's better to get punched the first time by someone who doesn't want to kill you," says Stefanie Hirschhorn, "than by someone who doesn't care if you die."

Self-defense training includes throwing techniques; methods to help break falls; leg sweeping (knocking down and getting control of an opponent who is pulling the cop); rear tackling; breaking chokes, headlocks, and bear hugs; removing a person clinging to a chair; resisting knife attacks; and preventing a perp from grabbing an officer's gun from its holster. Men and women are paired in these exercises, and usually the men feel awkward about being rough. Lissette Sierra-Solis implores her partners not to be gentle. She wants the simulated fights to be as close as possible to what she might experience one day on patrol.

There is an endurance exercise in which two recruits playing cops try to apprehend another playing a perp. To simulate a fatiguing chase before the struggle, the two recruit-cops first race up the eight flights of stairs, run down to the sub-basement, then up to the first floor and finally into the gym, where they have to jump a five-foot wall and then subdue and handcuff a fresh, waiting "perp."

Lissette Sierra-Solis is selected to play a cop. She is paired with a strong man, so she thinks this exercise won't present much difficulty. She and her partner plan their modus operandi: The man will grab the perp's hands and pull them behind his back; Lissette will do the cuffing. Up, down, and up the stairs they go, into the gym and over the wall. They confront a chubby man who falls to the ground, clenches his hands together under his chest, and curls up in a ball. After a couple of minutes of pulling, Lissette's partner gets one of the perp's hands behind his back. Lissette quickly cuffs it, and twists the ring to inflict pain and get the other hand cuffed. It doesn't work because the handcuff isn't on tight enough. She sighs.

Two swimming classes are held in the pool. The first class is two hours of water safety; the second, two hours of water rescue. The students learn how to rescue someone in the water without getting wet, using objects such as tires, ring buoys, and rope that are stored in a radio car. The classes begin with water push-ups along the edge of the pool, and five laps of any stroke desired. Though the vast majority of recruits do know how to swim, this is not something the NYPD requires of its cops.

In the first class, Officer Mary McCarthy, an attractive twenty-eight-year-old who is a competitive swimmer and former lifeguard with hundreds of rescues to her credit, gives the students some basic facts. Never dive into New York's water, she says. With all the debris floating around, you could hit something and be injured. She goes over basic rescues and has the students do some routine exercises. In the next class she shows the students how to pull someone to safety from land. Lying down on the tile by the pool, she demonstrates techniques used when the victim is not far from land, and when the victim is at various distances out.

There is a simulated ice rescue in which a large green mat is floated on top of the pool. Andy Varga is the first to try it. He slides himself across the mat and reaches out for a hypothetical victim. Later, the recruits form a chain across the mat to execute a rescue.

For most recruits, gym is a welcome relief from sitting behind a desk for hours using only their mental faculties. But it also creates stress: "Will I finish the run today?" "Will I get injured?" Most of the women, like Stefanie Hirschhorn and Lissette Sierra-Solis, try hard not to come across as delicate females. They want to be as good as, and treated like, the men.

There is no denying that gym is strenuous for all, and that an out-of-shape person would have extreme difficulty in making it through. The classes inspire the recruits to take care of their health; many recruits run after day tours and on weekends, and smokers realize they had better quit. Gym also confirms that this is a young person's job. Few forty-year-olds would be able to keep up with the daily regimen without suffering something close to a coronary. And although some people tend to think that cops spend almost all their time riding around in a patrol car (if they're not parked and munching doughnuts), the job, at least as far as big-city cops are concerned, is exhausting.

After the first gym classes have painfully demonstrated their limitations, most of the recruits are reconciled to the necessity of getting themselves in shape. They have learned to deal with the constant berating of their instructors by transforming it—at least in their minds, if not in their guts—into a personal challenge to become a superb physical specimen in order to be a formidable foe on the street.

Police officers may have guns and nightsticks at their disposal, plus an entire police force to assist them, but the first thing a bad guy intent on challenging a cop evaluates is the cop's size and physical condition. Street thugs are not intimidated by guns and shields. They have no qualms about taking on cops, especially one on one. Gym may not be able to duplicate the reality of the street, but it is a place for the recruits, knowing their survival is at stake, to test and hone their mettle.

6

THE PRACTICAL REVOLVER COURSE

All eyes are trained on the man before them, a menacing figure glaring at them and pointing his revolver at their hearts. He is their adversary—a thug intent on killing a cop. They crouch in combat position, two hands on their guns, waiting for a signal to set them into lethal motion.

A whistle sounds and forty-eight men and women spread across a line seven yards from their targets begin pumping bullets into the man. Shots ring out as if from a machine gun. The bullets land in a mound behind the targets, throwing up geysers of sand. As the spent shells fall to the ground, the recruits reach into their pockets for new rounds, loading quickly and looking up regularly to keep sight of the perps. With each round of firing, wisps of white-gray smoke whirl above, only to vanish a few seconds later, leaving behind the strong smell of lead and gunpowder. The action is swift. There's only fifteen seconds to get off two rounds, reload four manually into empty chambers, and then fire them with pinpoint accuracy.

For most of the recruits, this shootout is their first simulated life-and-death confrontation. It's a chilling welcome to their new job, a confirmation of both the power and risks they embrace as cops. For some, the exercise is entertainment, a real-life fantasy of their childhood cops-and-robbers games. For all, however, it's a grim awakening to the reality of being a police officer, an affirmation that at any moment they may have to take somebody's life, or that somebody may take theirs. There's a feeling of exhilaration among the recruits, a thrill like what they may have experienced driving their first car, when the power of something new and wonderful was in their hands. Everyone smiles and jokes, and it's obvious that they all love the experience. But there's also an inner sense of solemnity, a feeling that they've crossed a new bridge. The recruits are at the NYPD's outdoor firing range, and they are learning how to defend themselves with guns.

Starting in the third week of training, the academy begins sending companies on a rotating basis—eight companies, or about two hundred student officers at a time—to Rodman's Neck, a fifty-four-acre parcel of land at the southeastern end of Pelham Bay Park in the Bronx, for a week of firearms training. They learn safety, proficiency, marksmanship—it's called the Practical Revolver Course, or PRC. At the end of the week the recruits have to pass a shooting test to qualify to carry firearms as a police officer. Although many student officers have never fired a gun before, only two have failed to qualify since 1979, and both had neurological problems.

Firearms training reflects the kind of gun battles that take place on the streets of New York City. Every shooting exchange between a criminal and an officer is reported in detail, and those reports are then analyzed each year in a department document, the Standard Operating Procedure 9. The location, weather, time of day, rounds the cop fired, how many times he hit the perp, rounds the perp fired at him, the extent of injuries, and whether the cop was wearing a bulletproof vest—

all this is collected and considered. Accidental shootings also require the filing of a report. SOP 9s have provided much useful information—for example, that most gunfights in New York City last three to five seconds with both parties within seven feet of each other. In 1988 the NYPD hit potential in gunfights against perpetrators was eleven percent (of one hundred shots fired, eleven found their targets), while the perps hit NYPD cops ten percent of the time, this latter figure probably reflecting the perps' element of surprise.

At 6:55 A.M. on a Monday in mid-February, eight companies, including Tom Ramos's Company 32, line up in formation on the grounds outside Building 7. It is their fourth week at the academy. It is thirty-four degrees. Roll call is taken, and an instructor addresses the recruits.

"You will shoot twenty-five rounds today. Most of you have never fired a gun. The most important thing you have to remember is that everything on the firing range is designed around safety.

"No smoking, no horseplay. You will be armed here all day, every day, so you can't leave the base. If I catch you in the parking lot playing with your guns, you'll blow the best job in the world before you get there."

The recruits stand quietly, used to the rules of conduct student officers must follow while the instructor looks them over.

"How many people here were in the service?"

A number of hands go up, including Tom's.

"On our side?" he asks, deadpan. The recruits chuckle, and everyone relaxes a bit.

The recruits file into Building 7, a one-story prefab that houses one large classroom. It has a small stage in front and small offices at the corners. Police Officer Jim Martin begins with yet another set of rules. "Your attendance here must be perfect—five consecutive days. So plan to be healthy this week. If you miss one day, you don't come back." He spots a frown on one recruit's face. "And if you don't like any of the rules, you can go to Building 8 to complain about them." He pauses. "Of course, you'll also submit your resignation at the same time."

Officer Martin explains the procedures for the course. For training purposes, he tells the recruits, the instructors use guns whose barrels have been painted red to show they cannot fire. "On occasion," Officer Martin says, "I will have to point one of these guns at you. Don't dive or hide under your chair or give me karate kicks. But remember—all the other guns we deal with are real."

"The safe direction to point a gun is down range at the targets. You want to upset us, do something stupid. Break one of these easy rules, and we'll take a Star Card. You may carry the gun only at the range, under supervision. Nowhere else or you'll be terminated.

"We give you enough room to hang yourself," says Officer Martin. "The kid stuff is over. We teach you as adults. If you can't follow instructions with guns, which is serious business, get the hell out of here.

"I challenge any police department in the world to do what we do. We've never had an accident here that resulted in death—and we're not going to start now."

Officer Martin pulls out a handkerchief and wipes his face; it is warm in the classroom. Then he grins at the recruits. "I'm going to take my hat off. Yes, I'm bald. They say wearing a police cap loosens the hair follicles. But I don't believe that." He mops the sweat from his brow and continues.

"If you understand what we do, I think this will be one of the most enjoyable weeks you have of academy training. Be the best you can. Try the hardest you can. It can save your life. A gun is a defense weapon. You have to be proficient with this weapon. By the end of this week, you will be."

* * *

The NYPD uses .38-caliber revolvers made by two manu-
facturers—Smith and Wesson, and Ruger. The Smith and Wes-
sons come in three models: a four-inch barrel with a square
butt, a four-inch barrel with a round butt, and a three-inch
barrel with a round butt. There are two Rugers, a four-inch
square butt and a three-inch round butt. All the guns have six
cylinders and fire six rounds and have either checkered hard-
wood grips, or rubber grips around a steel shank.

Some students who know about firearms complain that the
.38 puts them at a disadvantage. Criminals on the street blaze
away with Uzis, MAC-10s, MAC-11s, and other automatic and
semiautomatic weapons. One of the most popular semiautomatic handguns among perps is the Intertech 9. But police
studies show that bullet placement—not size, shape, config-
uration, composition, caliber, or velocity—is the most important factor in winning a confrontation, and by far the majority
of weapons used against cops in New York City are still handguns. Nevertheless, the NYPD does have an arsenal of weapons
to meet every possible challenge, including submachine guns,
semiautomatic rifles and sniper rifles, as well as armored vehicles. Exactly how many guns does the "other side" have?
Experts estimate that there are about two million firearms in
the city of New York; in 1988 and 1989, cops took over 16,000
of them off the street.

At one of the shooting ranges, service revolvers are displayed
for the recruits to handle and select. Instructors guide them,
but the students remember the advice Officer Martin gave.
Each recruit, he said, would immediately recognize the most
suitable gun for him or her. "It will jump off the table and
smack you on the face: 'I know we don't know each other, but
we belong together.' It's a little like falling in love."

Having big hands, Tom Ramos is directed first to the four-
inch gun with the square butt. In successive turns he points
each revolver downrange, his elbow straight out, right hand
clutching the grip, left fingers curled around right; with his

right index finger he slowly pulls the trigger. Tom prefers the feel of the Smith and Wesson revolver with a round butt and a three-inch barrel.

The recruits march to the armory to get their guns, and then to another building, where they are issued holsters and two speed loaders each. Then, back in Building 7, Officer Martin addresses the group. "I'm a small guy, but that doesn't matter. It's what you have up here," he says, pointing to his head, "that makes the difference. There could be four perpetrators on the street and one of you. But you're better! The perps don't have any rules and regulations, but that's what makes us better. And we're getting better all the time."

While the student officers seem to take Officer Martin's comments seriously, once out of the classroom some will forget or ignore the warnings and basic precepts of safety they've been taught. Joseph Montalbano, a twenty-year-old in Company 32, listened attentively during this lecture like his classmates. Yet just over a year after graduating, his girlfriend, in a game of Russian roulette, fatally shot him in the head with his off-duty revolver in the bedroom of his parents' Long Island home. It was the third or fourth time they played the game. In a statement to homicide detectives, his girlfriend wrote: "He would leave one bullet in the cylinder, spin it, and we would hand it back and forth two or three times; after we pulled the trigger and the gun didn't go off, we would laugh." Unbeknownst to Elisa Beth Egger, in their last game each chamber of the gun held a bullet.

On the wall is a large painting of a gun. With a yardstick, Officer Martin points out the different parts, then the students receive instruction on how to put their paraphernalia on their gun belts. The gun belt is perhaps the most distinctive part of a cop's uniform, often a source of curiosity—what are all those things weighing him down and what do they do? The right-handed recruits follow Officer Martin as he holds up a gun belt with his right hand, with the buckle down and unfinished side facing him, and with his left hand slides on the pen and pencil holder, the whistle holder, baton holder, flashlight holder, handcuff case, holster, and two cases to hold speed loaders, devices that empty six rounds of ammunition into the chambers of a gun at the same time. Then they strap their belts on, the first time they have done so. This group sits down, and the left-handed people stand up and load their gun belts by doing the same procedure in reverse.

Officer Martin, always wanting to shape the recruits into model police officers, gazes at them. "You can be a hard-nosed son of a bitch or a compassionate guy," he says. "Did anyone here ever get stopped and think the police officer was a bastard?" There are lots of nods. "Why? Because he had the upper hand. Now you do. Don't take the guy who's intimidated by your gun to the cleaners.

"On the other hand," he continues, "the reputation I want the New York Police Department to have is, 'Don't get into a shootout with one of their cops, because he'll get you.' "

Officer Martin demonstrates how to "draw and present," a procedure for safely passing a gun to someone else. With the gun held at chest level and the muzzle pointed toward the ground, he pushes down on the release cylinder latch with his right thumb, pushes the cylinder (which holds the bullets, one in each of its chambers) through with his left index finger, wraps the rest of his left fingers around the barrel, and then turns the butt away from himself with his right hand, extending it to an imaginary taker. The students practice this, at the same time being warned never to hand over their guns to someone casually.

Next follows oral instruction on how to shoot a gun. The human eye can focus on only one thing at a time, which means one eye must be closed to focus a gun on a target. The rear sight is a U-shaped piece of metal located just before the hammer, on what's called the top strap. The front sight is a thin semicircular piece of metal at the front center of the barrel.

When aiming, a person aligns the front and rear sights so that the target is in the foreground of the front sight as seen through the opening of the rear sight. "We teach to fire center mass," says Officer Martin, meaning at the chest, where the vital organs are. "Don't shoot for the head, because if he's moving, you could miss. He'll fire back. There's less margin for error in the chest. We shoot to stop, not kill, but shoot center mass."

The reality of the street is that most of the time cops do not use sight alignment when shooting. When someone firing their gun wants to kill you, there's usually no time to aim properly. Cops want to react as swiftly as possible, so they usually respond by the instinctive or "point" method of shooting, where the gun is like a pointed finger and aimed where that finger points. However, as the distance between cop and perp becomes greater, aiming becomes more important; and so understanding sight alignment could be a lifesaving technique.

When the students first fire their guns, the motion of squeezing the trigger tends to cause the whole gun—and therefore the sight—to move around. Practicing trigger control, the smooth and steady motion of pulling the trigger without disturbing the sight, will minimize this.

In the afternoon of the first day of PRC the students are given their first opportunity to shoot on Charley Range, a large rectangular grass yard with concrete pavements stretching across the seven-, fifteen-, and twenty-five-yard lines. At the center of the firing line is a Plexiglas-enclosed booth, the tower, from which an instructor gives commands. Across the range from the tower are the stanchions, onto which the targets are stapled. Forty-eight stanchions embedded in concrete stretch across the range, with piles of sand behind them to catch the bullets. For added safety, there is a high hill in back of the range and small hills on either side.

The students receive targets, goggles, and headsets. The line instructors staple the target, a black outline of a body on yellow paper with a circle at the center, to each stanchion. Goggles protect the eyes from the "spitting" of lead shavings when the guns are fired, while headsets protect the ears from the loud gunshot noise.

Safety is paramount on the range. Talking is forbidden. If a recruit on the firing line has a question, he must raise his hand. There is no turning around or moving out of position. The goggles are never adjusted with a hand holding a gun. If anything drops on the ground, it stays there. In the summer, the students are warned never to wave away mosquitoes with a loaded gun in their hand.

Shooting follows only after a sequence of commands. First the recruits stand with their feet together and their hands behind their backs. "Draw the service gun and come to the standing ready position." Their nonshooting hand grabs the bottom of their holster and their other, shooting, hand withdraws the gun. In the standing-ready position, the shooting arm is bent, and the elbow and the gun point downrange. "Point the gun at the target." The revolver is brought up to eye level, arm extended, the nonshooting hand supporting the shooting hand. Unsupported shooting is with just one hand on the gun. The students are told to bend their knees and not to drop their chins—this could cut off circulation to the brain and make the shooter lightheaded. Right-handed people close their left eye, left-handed people their right eye. "Load the revolver with six rounds." They look at the target (their adversary) each time they put a bullet in. "On the whistle, fire two rounds." There is a short blast of the whistle, followed by a steady succession of shots. Another short whistle brings the action to a halt. The recruits are told to "combat-unload" and reload with six rounds.

Combat loading simulates loading the gun on the street while under fire. The body is twisted so that the opposite shoulder to the shooting arm faces front and the cop keeps looking up at his adversary, the whole action done as quickly as possible. Each of the students has twenty-five bullets in his or her right pocket. With the revolver in the left palm, the right thumb releases the cylinder, the left thumb pops it open. The right hand gets ammo from the pocket and puts one round into each chamber. The cylinder is turned counterclockwise. It should take only a few seconds.

A number of exercises are called out by the tower officer. His voice is loud, and there is no problem hearing him through the headsets. In back of the forty-eight recruits are five line instructors who provide individual instruction. At the end of the session, the recruits pick up their spent shells—"brass"—and place them into tin cans. Then they retrieve their targets and count their hits. The group instructors take their scores and critique the shots.

Police Officer Salvatore Manna looks at each target in his group and analyzes the shots. On one student's target, he sees scattered shots. "That's not good," he says. "It shows poor trigger control. You want the shots grouped. If the shots are too high, bring the front sight down a little.

"You're not going to be an expert in five days," he reassures them. "It takes years."

For Tom Ramos, this is not the first time he has shot a gun. His first experience shooting was with an M 16 in 1976 during air force basic training. "The experience was exciting," he says, "because I was nineteen at the time, and I looked at it as sort of a rite of passage. Holding that weapon and firing it gave me a feeling of power, that I was old enough now, that I was a man. But it was also frightening for me because this was serious business."

Tom enjoyed shooting. When he was transferred to Eglin Air Force Base, he joined the Rod and Gun Club, a chartered group sanctioned by the base for military personnel interested in learning about different firearms. The members, often collectors of weapons, shot at a firing range in the woods. But unlike most of the others, Tom didn't share their enthusiasm about firearms. He believed a military person should be knowledgeable about guns, but his fellow members seemed to have a morbid fascination with them. He didn't think that was healthy, so he dropped out of the club.

Several years later Tom had to qualify with a .38-caliber handgun while stationed at Langley Air Force Base in Virginia. When he first shot with a .38, he felt no emotion. "The kick was nothing compared with an M 16," he says. "With the M 16 you have to hold it against your shoulder, and you can feel it when it kicks back." He found the .38 jumped only a little after shooting and that the alignment is different. It was a matter of a mental adjustment. "Compared to the M 16," he says, "the .38 was a piece of cake."

Indeed, Tom appears relaxed on the range, but then again, his normal demeanor is one of calm confidence. Other students make nervous comments to their company mates, but Tom always is quiet and serious. If he's having a terrible time inside, he keeps a guard up, and some of his classmates have come to resent him as a company sergeant who's detached, unemotional, and icy.

Back in the classroom after their first day, Officer Martin asks the students to comment on their shooting.

"It was great!" shouts one recruit.

"That's an insightful description," Officer Martin says as the class laughs.

"I saw what point of alignment is," says another student.

The class breaks up into more laughter and applause.

"Point of alignment?" asks Officer Martin, raising his eyebrows. "You mean sight alignment."

At the end of the day the class stands and draws and presents, checking to see that their guns are empty. Then they put their guns back in the boxes, and give them to the company sergeants, who put them into plastic crates that are returned to the armory. Not until just before they graduate will they take their guns home.

Each day the students will shoot more rounds: 100 on Tuesday, 150 on Wednesday, 200 on Thursday, and finally, 500 for the PRC test on Friday. They must qualify on two weapons—their service revolver and their off-duty weapon. The off-duty revolver is different from the service revolver, with a smaller barrel (two inches versus three or four inches), five chambers (versus six), a smaller ejector rod, butt, and sights. It is easier to conceal because it is smaller but has more recoil and consequently less accuracy.

With each session at the range, the recruits are given various drills to improve their shooting skills and are taught new techniques. They do a three-round "ball-and-dummy" exercise, in which two rounds are loaded, a chamber skipped, then another round loaded in order to learn how to react to an empty chamber. They concentrate on trigger control, not forcing the shot, and sight alignment. Anticipating when the round is going to go off is the biggest distraction. Officer Manna tells his group that if they have trouble pulling the trigger, they should use hand grips to build their muscles up. The students try to develop good shooting habits by remembering the classroom slides showing the wrong way to shoot: one hand grabbing the wrist of the other, back arched too much, elbows bent, knees rigid, body leaning forward too much, two fingers on the trigger.

The recruits also learn to use their speed loaders. In a shootout, speed loaders, which fit over the cylinder to drop in all the bullets at once, are an efficient way to reload, especially since trying to fit bullets one by one by hand into the small chambers of a gun while under fire is difficult. Although skill with a speed loader is vital and important, the device itself is usually not used in combat. In armed confrontations, NYPD officers usually fire less than three rounds though most carry at least eighteen rounds of ammunition, six in the revolver and six in each of the two speed loaders. Many carry more in ammo pouches. Rapid reloading is usually necessary only in "cases of pursuit, barricaded persons, and other incidents where the action is prolonged and the distance exceeds the twenty-five-foot death zone," according to an NYPD Analysis of Police Combat Situations.

On the third day, Wednesday, the students begin practicing for the PRC test, which measures shooting skill and speed— shooting, unloading and reloading, both manually and with a speed loader, within certain time intervals. There are separate tests for service and for off-duty revolvers. A majority of rounds, sixty percent, will be shot from the seven-yard line, as most gunfights in New York City take place within that distance. A quarter of the rounds are shot from fifteen yards, fifteen percent from twenty-five yards.

The target now changes. The PRC target is a gold two-by-three-foot poster of an unshaven, bull-necked thug pointing a gun at the shooter with his right hand, his left fist clenched underneath his right. A large portion of his front area, as well as his face, is shaded and worth two points, while one point is given for hits between the shaded area and the outline of the body. Two points are deducted for hitting outside the man's body. A hit on the line between the areas is counted as two points.

For two days the student officers practice shooting from different distances while the clock runs. They shoot supported (with two hands) and unsupported. They shoot, unload, and reload, both manually and with a speed loader. On the fourth day of firearms training, the recruits shoot two practice sessions with their off-duty revolvers in the morning, and two with their service revolvers in the afternoon. By now many have open sores on their thumbs from prying their revolvers out of holsters designed to prevent anyone from snatching a cop's gun.

There is also classroom instruction covering regulations about off-duty revolvers. New York City cops are required to carry their shield, ID, and gun in their area of geographic employment, whether or not they are working. Exceptions apply in certain situations, such as if an off-duty officer is going drinking or playing sports or engaging in certain kinds of off-duty employment. If an officer is off duty and not carrying his gun, he will have to report the reason for this if he becomes involved in an incident.

When a New York City police officer may use deadly physical force—taught in regular classes as well as in the Practical Revolver Course—is the subject of an exam on justification given at the academy, an exam on which student officers must earn a perfect score to graduate. For NYPD cops, the gun is solely a defense weapon. It may be used only when the officers' lives are threatened or when the life of someone else is in serious danger. When a gun is used, the officer must be able to show through a legal defense called justification that he was allowed to use this deadly force.

Applying the rules of justification to real situations is not always cut-and-dried, but it's absolutely vital that police officers know when they can use deadly force. To this end, the police department has established its own guidelines which are even more stringent than the law. If officers fail to adhere to department regulations, they may be fired from the force, and if their actions are so flagrantly inappropriate that they violate the laws of justification, they may also be criminally and civilly liable.

A driver gets a speeding ticket, and the officer directs him back into traffic. The driver goes up the block, then suddenly makes a U-turn, racing back toward the officer in an obvious attempt to run him over. May the cop shoot the driver? No. Department regulations state that an officer may not fire at a moving vehicle unless deadly physical force other than the vehicle is being used against him—if, for example, someone in the car is also shooting at him.

Three men wearing masks run out of a bank and leap into a waiting car. Just then, a police officer turns the corner to see a person rush out the door of the bank screaming frantically,

"Help, help, we've been robbed!" The officer sees the bandits take off in the car. Can he fire at them? No. If they were firing at him, he could. If they were just escaping, however, the officer could not shoot at them to stop them.

A person in a large crowd on the street is pointing a gun at a cop. Could the officer shoot him? Yes, according to department procedure; the person is threatening the cop's life. There is, however, a moral dilemma. The officer's shot could injure or kill innocent bystanders. Must the cop shoot? No. The department doesn't say when a cop *must* shoot, but rather when he *can* shoot.

A small policewoman is confronting a large, muscular man when suddenly he punches her. Taken by surprise, she falls to the ground; the man jumps on top of her and begins to pummel her with his fists. Her nightstick has rolled away, and she can't get to her Mace. May the officer shoot the man?

There is no absolute answer for this scenario. For the officer to justify shooting the man, she would have to be able to convince the court that she was in extreme danger and had no other recourse but to shoot him.

A man cooking at home accidentally chops an artery in his wrist and calls 911. When a police officer arrives at the home, a vicious German shepherd, snarling and growling, blocks the path to the kitchen. The man is bleeding to death. May the cop shoot the dog? Yes. He has no other recourse, no other way to bring the animal under control. It's a life-or-death situation, and (contrary to popular opinion) the Mace the officers carry will not immobilize dogs.

A Housing police officer falls down an elevator shaft. Her legs are broken, her radio doesn't work, and no one can hear her cries. May she fire her gun? Yes. It's her last resort. Interestingly, although the officer may fire shots to summon assistance because of her precarious situation, department policy does not allow cops to fire warning shots at perpetrators.

All in all, the theory of justification is one thing, being in a deadly situation and reacting correctly is another. Cops are expected to make proper and legally valid life-and-death decisions instantly. Individual response, the recruits know with some anxiety, is a variable that is best honed through the least desirable method: perilous, real-life experience.

Friday, the 19th of February, is the PRC test. It is cold but sunny, and the sky is steel blue. At nine A.M., the recruits, with their service revolvers in their holsters, line up at the twenty-five-yard line on Charley Range. Officer Eugene Gibbs is in the tower calling out the commands.

Tom Ramos, feeling nervous, looks downrange at the target. He's concentrating, blocking out all distractions to create the mindset of a potentially lethal situation. To go one on one against his perp. Looking at the gun-wielding figure ahead, he's thinking, "He's out to take my life. No one can help me but myself."

Shooting as a cop provides a different psychological setting for Tom than when he was in the military. "There was always the possibility of war," he remembers, "times when we'd hear about a development and would say, 'Wow, this could really stir up into something major.' " But Tom was never shaken. Combat always seemed remote to him. He never felt that his life was in danger.

It's different being a cop. You don't patrol in a group, carrying sophisticated weapons. You don't engage in combat with an enemy so far away you can't see their eyes. You're on top of the enemy. You are the whole regiment until the backups arrive. The figure of a perp several yards away pointing a barrel at his face underscores the real possibility that as a cop, Tom could be shot and killed.

And Tom will be a cop not just anywhere, but in New York City—turf of savage drug dealers, home to America's most powerful organized crime family, host to more homicides (and hence, murderers) than any other city in the world. What fate awaits Tom in this crazed landscape? One day in the future he could be casually going about his job when he unwittingly crosses the path of some punk who just held up a store or a gang who just pulled off a heist. Despite the more routine aspects of the job, he must fight complacency, for his survival may depend on his proficiency.

"Combat-load two rounds."

Ramos bends his knees, turns to the left, and puts two bullets in the chamber. He hears a line instructor yell out, "Trigger control, concentration. Take it easy on the trigger squeeze."

For a moment it occurs to Tom that this is not the way a shootout would really happen. His weapon would be loaded, but he might not be as mentally prepared to fire. These thoughts flash through his mind but are quickly overtaken by his excitement. He's also trying to remember all the rules he's been taught over the previous week.

Tom waits, then hears a hard and short whistle blast signaling the start of this round of firing. The test begins. A barrage of gunfire erupts all around.

"This is the guy that wants to kill you. This is the guy that wants to kill you!" The instructors are yelling behind their students, scrambling from one end to the other.

The whistle sounds for a cease-fire, and a last pop is heard. Tom stands with his gun drawn, his shooting arm bent at the elbow and held closely against his hip. It is quiet as everyone waits for the tower call. Tom is looking straight ahead and can't see anyone else, but he feels some fidgeting going on. Line instructor Sal Manna tells one jumpy student to "settle down."

"On the whistle, four rounds supported, twenty-five seconds. Unload and reload with the speed loader, and fire two more rounds."

Tom flexes his neck slightly, raising his eyebrows. "What the hell'd he say?" That's a lot of instructions, and encumbered by the earphones and goggles and shivering from the cold, he hopes he heard correctly.

The whistle blows, and the students carry out the command. Bullets spew out until the whistle blows again. The students stand at attention.

"Four rounds supported, fifteen seconds. Combat unload and holster." The whistle blows.

Tom realizes that fifteen seconds is not much time to get off four rounds when you're trying to concentrate, align the sights, and squeeze the trigger without jerking it.

The students pick up their speed loaders and the empty cartridges, which they drop into the cans, and move up to the fifteen-yard line.

"Combat-load six rounds using the speed loader. Four rounds supported, ten seconds. Two hands on the gun."

Tom's nervousness builds; he has difficulty with the speed loader. When it is put over the gun's chambers, you have to twist the knob and sometimes shake the device before the bullets fall into the chambers. Under pressure, Tom sometimes twists the knob and pulls up the speed loader simultaneously, rather than waiting until the bullets are in place. Occasionally, one or two rounds fall to the ground instead of going into the gun.

All the loud gunfire doesn't disturb Tom. He's in a gunfight, facing off with a killer, and only one person will emerge the victor. His instinct of preservation has overtaken him. The only sound he hears, faintly now, is the voice of the referee, the tower caller.

The whistle sounds and Tom, deep in concentration, carries on. Shots. Gun smoke. The smell of lead. More orders come in a flurry. It is slightly unreal. Tom is shooting, looking the perp in the eye. He looks vicious. He hates. He means to kill. The whistles seem to bleed into each other as the recruits follow the commands like automatons. Move to the twenty-five yard line, back to the seven. Four rounds supported, fifteen seconds. Unload, reload with the speed loader, two seconds. Four rounds supported in ten seconds. Three rounds unsupported, five seconds. How does it feel to be hit by a bullet? Pain. Excruciating pain. No. I'm gonna get him. Two rounds supported, three seconds, three times. Combat-unload and reload with the speed loader. Six rounds supported, ten seconds. Squeeze the trigger. Bend down. Reload. Squeeze. Brrrrrrrrrr!

Tom is panting now, his mouth is dry. He awakens from his concentration to find the test over.

Tom's usual cool seems a bit ruffled. He is eager, not so much to pass, which he is certain to do, but to do well. Tom sets high standards for himself and feels that he has to do better than everyone else. He'd feel this way even if he weren't company sergeant. But he also thinks that his performance is a barometer of how he'd fare in a real gunfight.

The recruits are told to retrieve their targets and score them. The line instructors go over the scores of each student in their group.

Tom's score is a 93. With 75 as the passing grade, it's good; but Tom's not happy. He shot expert in the air force while this score is only average in his group. A number of students shot in the high 90s. For a moment he rationalizes why he didn't do better, but dismisses this line of thought immediately. He just didn't achieve his limit, he knows, but he can live with that. There is one failure in the company; the person will have to practice at the range at One Police Plaza and then come back to try to qualify at a later date.

The test is repeated with the off-duty revolver. The off-duty PRC is the same as the service, except that it is carried out in reverse, beginning on the seven-yard line. Tom scores a 91, finding the shooting a little more difficult with the adjustment to the smaller gun.

On Friday afternoon the student officers finish the day with a written quiz, five multiple-choice and five fill-in questions (which the entire group of two hundred passes), and a gun-cleaning class. Tom has heard that cops are notoriously lazy when it comes to maintaining their weapons. He takes the class seriously. A gun is a mechanical object with moving parts that must be properly taken care of. If he's going to rely on it, he'll have to inspect it regularly and keep it in optimum condition.

The first phase of firearms training is over. While it has bound the students together—the less formal atmosphere at the range and the shared experience encourage camaraderie—it has also opened the recruits' eyes to cop reality. They're now saying, "Hey, maybe I can get injured, maybe I *can* get killed on this job." Officer Manna says this revelation happens with every class. The recruits come enthusiastically to the range and end up asking themselves, "Should I have taken this job?" They don't actually admit this aloud, he says, but the anxiety and disconsolation can be seen on their faces.

In a month or so, near the end of March, the student officers will return to the range for instruction in tactics. They'll be put through chilling scenarios in which Central will dispatch them on gun runs, jobs in which they'll confront people with guns in apartments and alleyways and in which they will all "die."

—7—
STRESS

Four weeks into training, in the doldrums of February, Lissette Sierra-Solis's initial enthusiasm is wearing thin. The four and a half months ahead to graduation loom longer and longer, and, for the first time, she seriously questions whether being a cop is what she really wants. Between her difficulty in adjusting to the weekly shift changes, the demands of her courses, and the physical and mental exhaustion of being under intense pressure to measure up even off duty, things have gotten to be too much. The breaking point came during the PRC test at the firing range, when it was snowing and raining, the wind was blowing furiously, and it was unbearably cold. She was surprised when she passed, but asked herself, "Do I really need this?" Indeed, being a student officer at the academy is arduous, and for most, necessitates a drastic change in life-style.

Every day five days a week for eight hours, the student officers attend academic and physical education classes (with the exception of the eight days of firearms training, four days of driver training, and the one-day car-stop workshop). The academic training is college level but more intense: forty credit hours per week, more than twice the normal college student's course load. But there are other factors to be considered when distinguishing academy training from conventional college training.

Every week the recruits change tours, from a 7:30 A.M. to 3:30 P.M. shift one week, to a four P.M. to midnight shift the next week. It is not only difficult to make the schedule adjustment after an entire week of settling into the last one—most recruits, as well as instructors (who change tours similarly), complain that for the first night or two they can't fall asleep—but the demand not to be late is, for some, overwhelming. (Since this class, all precinct patrol officers are being phased into steady eight-and-a-half hour shifts, a major change enacted by new Police Commissioner Lee Brown.)

Dan Jackson, a strapping blond twenty-five-year-old recruit, has worried about being late since the first day of orientation. He commutes from Massapequa Park, Long Island, to the academy by railroad and subway. The early morning and afternoon traffic jams on the highways leading into New York City make driving too ridiculous even to consider. At the academy, if a recruit reports late for a tour, a Star Card is pulled; lateness of more than an hour is punished with a Command Discipline. Very few excuses are tolerated.

Dan's greatest fear is that he'll sleep through his wake-up alarm. Many recruits use two alarm clocks, one a backup in case the other should fail. Dan uses three clocks, two of which run on batteries in case of a power shortage. Yet even with this security, Dan's anxiety about being on time overpowers his rational self.

One night Dan dreamed that his alarm clock went off. He leapt out of bed and rushed to shower, shave, and dress, his usual routine, and headed for the train station. There was no one on the platform. "Where the hell is everybody?" Dan wondered. He asked the only other person there, a drunk, if the train had come in yet, and gathered that it hadn't. He looked at his watch. It said 12:15. It must have stopped, he thought.

Then he looked at the station clock, and it said the same thing. Dan ran to check the clock in his Jeep. Sure enough, it was just after midnight. There were four precious hours of sleep he could still get, so he raced back home and dove into bed. On hearing the story, Dan's fellow officers in Company 10 dubbed him "Boob of the Week."

Student officers come from as far as eighty miles away, and for the day tour have to rise as early as 3:30 A.M. On weeks with late tours, they are dismissed at midnight and may not arrive home for another couple of hours. They all have to do their assigned reading and written work, which may be not only substantial but difficult. Unlike college, where professors aim to accomplish a predetermined syllabus of work but are not required to do so, every academy instructor *must* complete the specific material in his course.

Lissette Sierra-Solis finds it most difficult to do homework after a late tour, so she often goes to sleep first and does it when she rises. She doesn't find the course work hard, but it is time consuming. Still, she does it scrupulously because not being prepared may mean getting a Star Card pulled. Lissette has seen how nasty the instructors can be in taking one. She wants to avoid the black mark on her record, and just as important, doesn't want to be embarrassed in front of her peers.

There are many other small pressures. Lissette would be on the way to the academy only to remember she forgot her uniform pin. She'd rush home to get it and hope there'd be no other delays. Uniforms must be worn on every tour at the academy, as well as while traveling to it. Conspicuous to the public, the male and female recruits are frequently stared at. Lissette Sierra-Solis takes the subway each day, and there are sometimes situations that require police action. People look at her as if to say, "So what are you going to do?" and she feels awkward. At the academy the recruits are urged not to get involved off duty but to dial 911 and avoid any kind of confrontation.

But there are times when she feels a confrontation is inevitable. Teenage boys and young men on the trains often give her funny looks and snicker among themselves. Some people blow kisses to her or make condescending remarks. Sometimes they even seem to want to challenge her. Once three men sitting on the D train kept looking up at Lissette and laughing. They huddled in conversation, then one stood next to Lissette as if to challenge her. She returned his mean stare but said nothing. Eventually, he sat down. But then he continued looking at her and laughing.

There are also tremendous family and social pressures. If a student officer lives at home or with a spouse and children, family members also find themselves making adjustments. The recruit may have to make new friends and be selective about which of his old pals to see. If they smoke pot or are rowdy in any way, they could endanger his future.

One B Squad recruit knew his mother-in-law was a drug dealer. Just after he was appointed to the NYPD, he urged his wife not to take their children to her mother's nearby home, but the woman continually made a fuss to see her grandchildren. Finally, he was so worried that his job might be in jeopardy that he moved his family out of the neighborhood.

If a family member is breaking the law in any way, a recruit cannot even mention it casually to an instructor, or the officer will be obligated to take official action. The student officers aren't encouraged to report lawbreakers—the academy doesn't want them to rat out everybody they know who is involved in illegal activities—but rather to avoid them. Some of the recruits live in areas where there is much drug activity, for instance, and obviously know some people who are sellers or buyers. It's not that they're supposed to report these people, just not to associate with them.

The recruits are also encouraged to avoid bars while on probation. Getting drunk and doing something stupid could cost them their jobs. If a recruit does go to a tavern, he must leave by four A.M., the mandated closing time of licensed premises in New York City.

As well as the stress created by the academic rigors of the academy and the restrictions associated with being on probation for two years of your life, there are also the everyday pressures inherent in being a recruit at the academy, whose training is by its very design stressful. In the middle of one of Lissette Sierra-Solis's Social Science classes, a gravely visaged sergeant enters the classroom. The student officers jump to attention, the proper protocol for any visiting superior officer. The students are told to sit down, and a forbidding silence permeates the room in anticipation of the announcement of the purpose of the sergeant's call. Then alarm sets in as the students see an envelope prominently marked "Resignations" held by the sergeant. Even the instructor looks up in surprise.

The sergeant says that there have been some problems with background investigations. He opens the envelope and glances at the list within. "The following people are to come with me," he announces as the recruits exchange puzzled glances. What could be wrong? Of course, they know that background investigations weren't considered complete when they entered the academy, and a problem found later might result in their termination. But the initial investigations seemed thorough enough, and the department must have been searching hard to uncover any skeletons at this point.

The sergeant reads off four names and tells the students he has called to bring their gear with them. Now there is considerable tension in the classroom. After they leave, the Social Science instructor continues as if nothing happened, but the subject on everybody's mind is the episode just past.

In the hallway the sergeant explains to the rattled students that they have just been victims of a role play on stress. Nervous smiles fight through the fear on their faces, and their hearts begin to slow to normal. All return to the classroom, and their classmates are similarly informed.

The instructor, who was of course privy to the skit, assures the recruits that this role play will not be repeated, and asks the recruits how they felt. Racing hearts, sweaty palms, inability to swallow are some of the responses, both from those whose names were called and those who remained in the classroom. A student officer who shares the surname of one of the recruits who was called admits he felt quite relieved when the first name was given.

The purpose of the role play was to demonstrate what the body experiences in stressful situations. One day a cop might get a radio call, "Man with a gun," and he may actually have to shoot or come under fire. The adrenaline will be flowing, and the recruits need to recognize the feeling and know how to deal with it.

Officer Michael Wilson of the Social Science unit tells of a cop he knew who went to his locker several times a day for a swig of Mylanta to fight severe heartburn. "The department itself can be stressful enough," he says, "but we don't have to make things worse. Be in control of yourself." Officer Wilson says the police academy tries to give the recruits all they need to handle the pressures of the job. Indeed, the academy simulates station house discipline, preparing the student officer to meet the demands of the department.

Stress produces a variety of reactions on the human body, ranging from an increased breathing rate to, very rarely, death. Stress is not always necessarily bad; some amount can trigger body responses that may help a person face a tense situation with great strength or drive. But in general, stress is like the elements of nature wearing away at a surface. The less resistant the surface, the faster it erodes.

A cop's world is one of stress. Stress from the street—seeing good people's misfortunes, dealing with the dregs of society, constantly having to meet the public's high expectations—is well known. Conforming to the standards of the department, some cops say, creates equal or even greater stress. Inundated with rules and regulations, they feel that they're trained in a negative way. Worst of all, they say the department doesn't back them up when there is a problem like a complaint allegation by a civilian. Perhaps that's because the department bends over backward to please the public.

The stress of the job is so substantial that it can have serious consequences—alcoholism, mental breakdown, even suicide. Aware that stress is likely to become one of the great maladies in the neophyte cop's future, the academy covers various aspects of this phenomenon, from what it is physiologically and how to recognize its causes to reducing and preventing it.

Despite all the pressures, Lissette now approaches getting through the academy as a personal challenge, one that she feels compelled to meet. And she enjoys the spirit that has developed in Company 19, where everybody roots for each other. Lissette is happily surprised to see the men in her company push along a female recruit with a newborn baby and two other children. Lissette thought the guys would say her friend couldn't handle the responsibilities of being the mother of an infant and being a student officer at the same time.

The Police Academy is a quasi-military institution with rules for conduct in and out of the classroom, for mustering, for appearance, and for uniforms. When a recruit breaks a rule, an instructor may pull one of the recruit's two Star Cards, or issue a reprimand, a reminder which ends up in the student's records.

A Star Card can be taken for any infraction at all. Each day before class, for example, the company sergeants are supposed to check their mailboxes in Room 610 for memos. Andy Varga had gym for his first class one day, and didn't feel like climbing six flights of stairs. During the class Lieutenant Geysen came in and pulled aside Andy and three other company sergeants. He yelled at them all for not going to their mailboxes, and pulled a Star Card from each.

When five Star Cards have been pulled (company sergeants

have a supply and replenish extracted cards), the student is placed on disciplinary probation. Having seven cards pulled results in a Command Discipline—a hearing before a high-ranking officer of the academy that may result in some kind of disciplinary action. The student officer will have a Patrolmen's Benevolent Association delegate present with him at such a meeting to make sure that the department follows union rules. Certain violations, such as parking in a restricted area, automatically result in a CD. Penalties include loss of vacation time, suspension, or worse. Since little reason need be given to terminate an officer on probation, a CD can be a harrowing experience for a recruit. Many students end up in tears during these tense confrontations. Disciplinary action isn't meted out frequently, but the anxiety about having a card pulled or having a CD can ultimately be worse than the punishment. All infractions are reported to Room 610 and the academy's Integrity and Discipline Unit.

The Integrity and Discipline Unit (IDU) is the academy's police. Working under the aegis of the commanding officer of the academy, the unit handles all investigations that are reported to it, and maintains computerized records of all recruits and of the academy's personnel, who are not immune to disciplinary action either. IDU's commanding officer and five sergeants, who are always in plainclothes, may pop up anywhere around the building or in the geographic area of the 13th precinct, enforcing the rules of the NYPD and of the academy.

Integrity and Discipline is headed by Lieutenant Pasquale Petrino, a twenty-five-year veteran who served in the marine corps and was a military policeman in Pearl Harbor. He doesn't look like the typical hard-ass cop. Rather, he looks dapper, sporting a short, trimmed mustache and close-cropped hair. He wears a gun around his left ankle. A fitness freak, every morning he drinks cod liver oil and works out in the academy's gym. Before his assignment at the academy, he had the unsavory task of catching precinct cops doing things they shouldn't: shopping on duty, working off duty in the precinct, driving cars with out-of-state license plates, frequenting local bars.

"We police the police, but I can live with that," says Lieutenant Petrino, who considers himself the "shoo fly" of the building. Lieutenant Petrino has unannounced tours. He has even been known to show up at four o'clock on a Sunday morning to observe security personnel.

Each day, entering and leaving the academy premises, the recruits are observed by the plainclothes officers of IDU, who stand in front of the building looking for violations: gum chewing, eating on the street, a toothpick in the mouth, long hair, a crooked cap, no name tag, or carrying a paper bag or newspaper—these may result only in an admonishment. But a CD may be imposed if a student officer is caught receiving food or merchandise free or at a discount, or while on duty leaves the precinct, enters a bar, or consumes an alcoholic beverage anytime or anywhere. IDU also monitors drug-selling locations in the academy area. Any recruit or staff member found buying, selling, or using a controlled substance is immediately suspended from the force. "Some people should not become cops," notes Lieutenant Petrino. "Our aim is to find out who they are before they bring discredit to the department."

Lissette Sierra-Solis says that all the recruits fear the officers from IDU, that these officers carry themselves in a way that makes them intimidating. "They never smile at anybody," she says, "and if they say anything to you at all, it's negative: 'Straighten your tie' or 'Take your hands out of your pockets.' I had my hands in my pockets one day because it was cold, and Lieutenant Petrino told me to take them out." When Lieutenant Petrino isn't by the booth on 20th Street, he may be peering out of his fourth-floor window through a pair of binoculars.

One morning Lieutenant Petrino spotted a female recruit

outside the academy kissing a man good-bye. Petrino told her such behavior doesn't look good for a professional police officer.

"But he's my husband," the recruit responded in dismay.

"The people across the street don't know that. We try to keep the department from getting a black eye. We try to uphold the reputation of the department."

Socializing between the recruits and the instructors—both in and outside the academy—is forbidden. In fact, all the student officers signed a document acknowledging that they knew and accepted that all fraternalization with instructors was forbidden and could result in termination. If a student officer even so much as sees an instructor at a restaurant, for instance, he should either avoid talking to the instructor or leave the restaurant. An instructor who develops a relationship with a recruit could get transferred. It's difficult not to become paranoid under the ever-watchful eye of IDU. IDU might even take heed of a male physical education instructor conversing with a female recruit for longer than it takes to issue instructions or deliver a reprimand.

The instructors encourage the students to make complaints about their peers if they see blatant violations. The department, they say, believes everyone is responsible for everyone else.

What's permissible and what's not at the academy and on the force was conveyed to the recruits during their first week of classes. Alicia Parker, a sergeant in IDU who has served on the NYPD for more than fifteen years, addressed the women recruits separately. A former model and a semifinalist in a Miss Teenage America contest, Sergeant Parker is six feet tall with expressive eyes. She discussed rules of special interest to the female recruits and the obstacles they would encounter at the academy. Except for watches (which are required) and wedding bands, no jewelry is allowed. No garish makeup or lipstick may be worn. Wear pale nail polish only and keep your fingernails short. Keep long hair in a bun. Among the recruits, Sergeant Parker soon became known as the Dragon Lady.

The adjustment for women is sometimes more difficult than for men, Sergeant Parker explained. Fewer women have been in the military and so have had less experience with discipline. Fewer have been involved in athletics, and some are not in their best physical shape. A menstrual period, Sergeant Parker noted, is not an excuse to miss gym class.

After hearing all the IDU lectures, Stefanie Hirschhorn thought she pegged the student officer experience. "The idea is to get out of the academy without anybody knowing your name," she said. "Unless it's for a good reason."

Similar to IDU are three agencies in the department that serve as watchdogs for police misconduct—Internal Affairs Division (IAD), Field Internal Affairs Unit (FIAU), and the Civilian Complaint Review Board (CCRB). Most cops loathe them or fear them, or both. These units do create stress, because even small matters of corruption may go severely punished. Can a cop talk freely with a stranger on the street, or is that person from IAD looking to hang him?

The most-feared unit is Internal Affairs. IAD will investigate physical abuses—when a suspect is seriously injured while in custody, for example—or allegations of serious wrongdoing such as when a cop is suspected of being on the take. IAD responds not only to allegations, it identifies internal hazards and acts to prevent corruption. The department, in theory, tolerates no corruption and, in fact, goes after rogues with a vengeance.

IAD dispatches representatives to the academy to familiarize the student officers with the unit and to explain how minor infractions could lead to transgressions of a more serious nature. Some recruits have preconceived notions about IAD based on the infamous stories they've heard from other city cops. IAD stories do become exaggerated over time, but they are usually rooted in fact. At the very least, such stories demonstrate both the nature of the activities of the unit and the paranoia that cops have about it.

An incident at a nearby precinct three months into their training opened the recruits' eyes to the reach of IAD. There was an allegation that a certain midnight tour at a precinct was committing burglaries. So IAD began surveillance on all radio runs of the unit. A break-in was reported at a super-market, and when the unit arrived to investigate, the officers saw no one inside. They helped themselves to two cases of beer, which they put into the trunk of their radio car—right under the watchful eye of an undercover IAD team. The officers drove back to the precinct and were observed putting the beer into their own cars. IAD approached them and called a patrol supervisor. The two officers were requested to open their car trunks. They lost their jobs.

It is common for an NYPD cop to respond to a DOA (dead on arrival), and then sit around for hours waiting for the med-ical examiner and others to arrive at the house or apartment. Staring him in the face may be jewelry and other valuables. But a potentially corrupt cop can never be sure the DOA is not a setup by the IAD; the expensive necklace on the bureau or the wad of cash in the desk drawer may be a plant.

Officers from IAD give a series of lectures at the academy over four days, explaining the role of their unit and the nature of corruption to each of the companies. The students are con-stantly told what the department expects of them, and what it will not accept. They are shown a film of how one graduate, due to financial and social pressures, took a wayward path, first by accepting a free meal, then eventually getting into extortion. After the lectures, the recruits are down in the dumps. "The job tells us that we have to get this person or report that person," one student officer says. "That's not the type of job I thought it would be."

The Field Internal Affairs Unit operates like IAD, filtering out corrupt officers, but on a boroughwide level. The unit often investigates cases referred by IAD, which usually handles only the most sensitive or complex cases. FIAU investigates minor improprieties—for instance, officers not being on their posts when they should be. On completion of a "job," a radio call assignment, NYPD cops have to report back to Central. If it appears that an officer is taking too long to "give the job back," then he or she may be investigated. If they notice a pattern of long completions of jobs, FIAU may monitor later radio calls to follow and observe suspected officers undercover. The department wants its patrol officers to finish jobs as efficiently and quickly as possible, otherwise calls for police assistance will pile up. If a cop is sitting in his patrol car munching sandwiches, the public is endangered. FIAU will also check out other alleged improprieties, such as cops "cooping"—napping in a radio car under a bridge, at a junkyard, an airport, or in a parking lot.

The Civilian Complaint Review Board investigates only allegations of wrongdoing made by civilians against police officers: rudeness, excessive force, abusive language, racial slurs, or threats of harm. If the claim is substantiated, action will be taken that could result in a Command Discipline, a transfer, or even termination. Civilian complaints are taken seriously by the department; even if unsubstantiated, they may hinder a cop's career because every complaint, proven or not, ends up in his permanent record. One officer reports that the possibility of getting a civilian complaint on the job bothers some cops more than the possibility of getting shot.

During training, CCRB, which is composed of both police and private citizens, also dispatches staff members to the academy to address each of the companies. Detective Hugo Parilla, an eighteen-year veteran, addresses Company 20 in Room 436. "I'm here to try to prevent our paths from ever crossing," he begins.

Detective Parilla says the CCRB code is the acronym FADE: force, abuse, discourtesy, ethnic slur. If an allegation falls under FADE, it's a civilian complaint; otherwise it falls under the jurisdiction of another police investigating unit.

"You're on the street issuing a summons to a guy for making an illegal U-turn," Detective Parilla says. "He's cursing you, calling you a fascist pig. What should you do about it? Nothing. Sometimes it's tough to stay polite. But you don't have to do it for the guy who's cursing you. Do it for yourself. You'll come out the winner in the end." There should be no basis for a civilian to make a complaint, even if the civilian provoked the confrontation, he notes.

Anyone can make a civilian complaint. No matter how distorted or grossly exaggerated it may seem, each complaint that comes to CCRB will be investigated. Case in point: An individual wrote a letter to the police commissioner saying that a police officer beat him up, cursed at him, shouted racial epithets, and broke his finger. He said he was front-handcuffed so he would be tempted to run away in order for the police to pursue and kill him. He did run away, and the police caught up with him and, he claimed, beat him mercilessly.

In actual fact, CCRB discovered the following: The complainant was standing on a loading platform when two plainclothes officers from an anticrime unit approached him. The van he was loading matched the description of a van stolen that day. The officers began asking the man questions when he suddenly turned on them and began fighting. He was finally subdued but had to be front-cuffed rather than rear-cuffed because he was so violent that the officers couldn't get his hands behind his back. By the time other cops arrived, he had been put in the back of a radio car. Shortly after, however, he broke free and climbed into the rear of the van, which was still idling. He put the van in gear as one of the officers jumped on its hood, and the officer went flying. A call went out over the radio, and the man was soon caught and brought to a station house.

In his letter the man made complaints against a sergeant and one of the police officers. He didn't think it made a difference that he had just committed a burglary and was driving a van he had stolen from Kennedy Airport, or that he had slammed the van door on the sergeant's hand or that the officer he sent into orbit was injured so badly that he was forced to leave his job for six months. The officers who stopped him were only asking general questions while the sergeant was waiting to receive confirmation that the van was stolen.

"Can we see the two sides of the story here?" asks Detective Parilla. "Were the officers justified?"

Of course the officers were justified, the students say. That's the only side to the story there is. The man should never have even been allowed to make a civilian complaint.

The fact that the man had committed crimes, notes Detective Parilla, doesn't take away his right to make a civilian complaint. The system provides for anyone who believes he was subject to police abuse to file, and for CCRB to investigate.

It is NYPD policy that cops use only the necessary force to subdue an individual. "Use as much force as it takes to get the individual under control," says Parilla, "and don't be afraid to use your nightstick. It's part of your equipment and was given to you for a reason. If you can prove that what you did was right, then by all means use as much force as is necessary to get the individual under control, and don't worry about getting a civilian complaint."

Sometimes individuals file a complaint because they think it will help their case in criminal court. It won't. "They think their defense lawyer will be able to plea-bargain with the district attorney by offering to drop the complaint charge against the officer," says Detective Parilla. "We explain to the complainant that one thing has nothing to do with the other. CCRB investigates only the alleged misconduct by the officer. Filing a complaint has no effect on the case. The complainant's crime is separate and apart from the alleged police misconduct."

"Any time you use force," the detective reminds the recruits, "document it. Don't deny using it." Civilians sometimes see police using force out of the context of a situation, and this can lead to complaints also.

Cops are constantly observed by the public, adds Parilla, and may not even be aware of this. When they realize someone saw them doing something that could lead to trouble for them, they shouldn't try to abuse their power to cover up their mistakes or get back at the citizen.

The NYPD discourages off-duty action: a civilian in an encounter with a person in street clothes may doubt the person is really a cop. This could lead to trouble—or to corruption. If an off-duty officer threatened to issue a summons for a traffic violation, the civilian might be inclined to offer a tempting bribe. The cop might be inclined to accept it; he's out of uniform and thus can't be identified.

Detective Parilla warns the students about making threats of arrest. If they respond to a job and threaten an individual with arrest, there had better be a justifiable reason for it. Otherwise, they may get a civilian complaint.

"Try to avoid getting civilian complaints," he says. "Years later, when you're applying for a detail, you're going to find they'll take the individual with the fewest complaints."

Every complaint, whether substantiated, unsubstantiated, or based on an incident that did not occur, goes on an officer's record. Even if the officer is exonerated because his actions were deemed proper, the allegation goes into the folder.

CCRB makes every attempt to conduct a full investigation of every allegation. It contacts and interviews the complainant as well as any witnesses, and reviews relevant police records. It presents a report to a review board, which submits its determinations to the commissioner for action.

If a complainant can't be found for one reason or another for a follow-up interview, CCRB staff will send certified letters, question neighbors, and do anything they can to reach the complainant in order to record the details of his or her allegation. If the complainant doesn't wish to follow up on the charge, he is given a withdrawal letter and asked to sign it.

Like many street cops, the student officers look upon the whole system of civilian complaints with contempt. They've heard stories that enrage them—of pimps who tell their prostitutes to make civilian complaints whenever they're arrested, of cops whose careers have been screwed up because of absurd and vindictive civilian complaints. The potential of getting complaints, they say, will make them afraid to do their job.

Detective Parilla points out that the unit doesn't create the complaints, it only investigates them. "A complaint is made by an individual we have no control over," he says. "One thing a police officer has to realize is that he can't do whatever he feels like doing just because he's an officer. If you follow the rules, there's no reason to be scared. No one's telling you not to do the job—just do it correctly."

—8—
ROLE PLAYS

Y ou're a cop. You're walking your beat one day when someone runs up to you breathlessly and says that a store around
the corner is being robbed. When you get to the store you see
the man behind the counter pointing a gun at the person in
front of him. You quickly consider the possibilities. Did the
perp go behind the counter to take money out of the cash
register? What if the store owner pulled a gun and forced the
perp to drop his? Certainly, if things flare up, you don't want
to shoot the wrong man.

So you shout, "Police! Don't move!" You order the man to
put the gun down, you pick up the weapon, and then search
for any others. The man in front of the counter, visibly upset
and shaken, cries out that he's the store owner, then pulls out
a wallet and shows identification. But you're not aware that
when he first pulled a gun on the real store owner behind the
counter, he demanded his wallet. In the aftermath of the event,
when you're trying to sort out the situation, the perp slips
away. Then it turns out that the real store owner doesn't have
a license for his gun, so you have to arrest *him*.

Indeed, the recruits soon come to know that appearances

115

can be deceiving, and that on the street truly anything is possible. But the academy prepares them for the unexpected in the closest way possible outside of throwing them onto the streets and into real life-and-death dramas—through role plays.

In the role plays, which take place throughout training, sometimes in class and sometimes before the entire assembled squad, the student officers face the kinds of distressed people and enigmatic or volatile situations they're likely to encounter as police officers. The scenarios, most based on actual cases, address the urgency, rawness, and spontaneity of the street. Of course, the academy can't prepare its students for everything they're likely to encounter, for every situation is as different as the people involved. Still, role plays provide a superb opportunity for recruits to develop their skills as cops interacting with the public, closely approximating what they will soon be called on to deal with every day.

In the role plays, the students are patrol officers, and the instructors play victims, complainants, and suspects. There are basic preplanned plots, but the instructors improvise according to the recruits' responses, trying to confuse them, to draw their sympathies, or to glibly evade charges when arrest is possible. The instructors' intent is to force the students to ask more questions, to use their common sense, to look beyond the manifest, and to sniff out hints.

The major role plays at the academy are interdisciplinary, where students try to utilize the principles they've been taught in each of their subjects while instructors from the three academic areas analyze the skits from the perspective of each of their disciplines. Interdisciplinary role plays are held in the auditorium, and the student actors are understandably nervous performing in challenging situations before their peers.

The role plays rivet the students' attention and sometimes make them giggle nervously or break up with laughter at their performing peers' maladroit responses. But more often, the instructors are so convincing in their roles that the students forget for a moment that the scenarios are fabricated. A palpable tension descends on the auditorium, and the students are moved to disquietude, to sympathy, and occasionally to tears.

Officer Michael Wilson of the Social Science Department moderates the B Squad role plays. He implores the students to take them seriously. "We'd like you to get the maximum benefit from these role plays," he says. "Those who participate, place yourself on the street. Those who don't, observe and learn from the active participants. This is the best possible place to make mistakes."

The stage is dressed with amateur props to simulate different milieus. The student participants are given radios and receive calls from "Central." They are told to call for backups if they feel it is necessary. They are constantly reminded to use the tactics they've learned, and that there's always the possibility that the situation might be something other than what was described in the call from Central.

The victimology role plays attempt to teach student officers that the most important aspect of a crime scene is the victim. In years past, the cop would take care of the crime first, then address crime prevention, and finally deal with the victim. Now the NYPD wants its cops to address the victim first, then crime prevention, and lastly, the crime.

> A woman wearing a bathrobe over jeans walks from her bedroom into the kitchen. She is clearly in distress. She is standing in the kitchen holding her robe together at the collar when suddenly there is a knock at the door. She doesn't respond. Another knock. She goes to the door and opens it a little.
>
> "Police, ma'am."
>
> "Do you have identification?"
>
> The woman inspects the proffered IDs and lets the of-

ficers in, a white woman and a black man. "I was robbed," she says. "A man came into my house and robbed me. He took my pocketbook. I came into my house, he pushed me, and then went out the window in that room." She points to the bedroom. "He said if I told anyone . . ." Her voice trails off.

"Ma'am," one of the officers says, "would you like us to call an ambulance?"

"No! No! I don't want any of my neighbors to know. I don't want anyone to know!"

The officers question her. The woman says she is married.

"It's my fault," she exclaims. "My husband told me not to work late, and I worked late."

Her mind shifts again to the perpetrator.

"He said he's going to come back. He's got my keys. The keys to my house." The woman, in a frail voice, keeps repeating that it's her fault. Finally, she breaks down weeping. The officers try to calm her, telling her everything will be okay.

"He took me into the room," she confesses now, nearly hysterical, her voice breaking. "He tore off my clothes. He hit me." She stops a moment to contain herself. In a barely audible voice, she reveals the secret she's been hiding from the officers and for which she feels shame: "He raped me."

The officers look at each other but manage to contain their shock. "My husband will kill me," she sobs softly. One of the cops reassures her: It's not her fault, and her husband won't kill her. She excuses herself to take a shower when her husband walks in. He is a solid, husky man, wearing a bright red jacket.

"What happened?" he asks, seeing the two officers. "What's going on here?" He looks at his wife and sees she has a black eye. "Tell me what happened!" he demands.

The wife, weeping, stammers that a man hit her. Her

husband is incredulous. The male officer pulls him aside and tells him his wife was raped.

The husband explodes with anger, bellowing at his wife: "I told you not to work! I told you not to work!" In fury, he knocks a glass off the kitchen table. "It's your fault, bitch! Why do you wear those tight clothes?"

The husband is enraged. In his anger, he continues hurling objects to the floor. An officer asks the woman again if she wants an ambulance.

"How many times did I tell you?" the husband interjects. "It serves you right." He turns to the police officers and snaps, "So what are you going to do?" Before they can answer, the man turns to his wife and screams, "I've told you a hundred times, stay home, take care of the kids!"

"It's not her fault, sir," the female officer says.

The husband is oblivious to the cops now. He turns to his wife, who is sitting with her head buried in her arms. "I'm sorry," he says, trying to control himself. He begins awkwardly to comfort her, when the action is abruptly cut.

The Social Science critique begins with a personal comment by the woman who played the rape victim, Officer Aida Perez, a thirty-one-year-old Social Science instructor. "I could certainly sense the fidgeting in the audience," she begins. "I could feel the discomfort, particularly when I was crying."

Officer Perez says that in the role play she was the ultimate victim. "When someone violates your body and you survive, you live with it for the rest of your life. The perp goes away, and you live with it. When you're killed, you're dead."

The effectiveness of Officer Perez's performance wasn't just due to natural dramatic ability. Early one morning eleven years ago a man attacked her in her building. She resisted but was beaten badly, with serious internal injuries. She kept screaming, and eventually the assailant dropped his knife and fled. But the terror of the attack remains.

She says the two "police officers" in the skit weren't sure what was really going on. Officer Perez asks the audience what might clue them in that something more than a burglary or robbery had occurred. There are several responses: She was holding her robe together very tightly; there were marks on her face; she didn't seem to want the police officers to go in the bedroom; she didn't spend much time discussing the property that was stolen; she said someone did terrible things to her.

Officer Perez cuts in. "Who do rape victims blame?" she asks. "Themselves. I blamed myself. That was a clue." Then she adds a commendation for the young female recruit performing the role play. She says that it was the first time she had ever witnessed honest compassion from a role-playing officer. "She looked me directly in the eyes, was not afraid to touch me, and she listened patiently when I spoke, showing real concern."

"How many victims were there?" asks Officer Perez. No one responds. "The answer is two: the wife and the husband," she says. In the original case on which the role play was based, Officer Perez points out, the husband went into a crisis and became emotionally disturbed. She asks what an officer can tell a husband who reacts turbulently in a similar situation: "Think of your wife. She needs you."

Officer Gary Lombardo begins the law critique. The issues involved in determining exactly what crimes have been committed in a given case are complex. A good portion of the recruits' time at the academy has been taken up with mastering the labyrinthine structures of the penal code and the criminal procedure law. But for an arrest to stand up throughout the trial process, the crimes with which the accused is charged must be precise and appropriate.

The call that came over the air was for a burglary, says Officer

Lombardo. While most people think of burglary as the breaking into of a building and the stealing of property there, it is a crime committed any time a person enters or remains unlawfully on a premises with the intent to commit any crime in that place. So if a man breaks into a house and rapes a woman, he has committed both a rape and a burglary. In the skit, the perpetrator unlawfully entered the victim's apartment intending to commit a crime there, thus committing a burglary.

Robbery is the taking of property by the use of force or by the threat of force. It is committed when, in the commission of a larceny (the taking of property), force is used or threatened to overcome a victim's resistance to the larceny. Force was used by the man in this case to take the woman's pocketbook.

The perp punched the woman in the face. If in the commission of a felony a perp causes any physical injury to anyone other than an accomplice, the crime is felonious assault. Assault, the unlawful causing of physical injury to a person, may be a misdemeanor or a felony. The extent of the physical injury, the perp's state of mind, and whether the injury was caused by a deadly weapon or a dangerous instrument determines the charge.

In the role play, the perp forcibly compelled the woman to engage in sexual intercourse and is guilty of rape in the first degree. The legal determinant of rape is the lack of consent. A rape occurs either when force is used, or if the victim has a mental disorder or is physically helpless, or mentally incapacitated (drugged or rendered intoxicated). If any of these conditions exist, consent cannot legally be given, and the male is guilty of rape.

If normal sexual intercourse occurs in an alleged rape situation and the victim is not mentally deficient (retarded), physically helpless, or mentally incapacitated, the ages of the parties are then considered in determining the charges. The academy instructors use a table to determine whether a charge is rape, a felony; or sexual misconduct, a misdemeanor.

121

Male	Female
21 or over	16, 15, 14
20, 19, 18	13, 12, 11
17, 16	10 or younger

The ages of the parties are located on the chart. If a line drawn between the age of the male and the age of the female runs across or down, the charge is rape. If it runs up, it's sexual misconduct. For example, if sexual intercourse occurred between a sixteen-year-old male and ten-year-old female, the charge would be rape; between a sixteen-year-old male and thirteen-year-old female, sexual misconduct. The age of consent varies from state to state; in New York it is seventeen.

The woman in the role play said she had been raped, but Officer Lombardo raises the possibility that an additional sexual crime, sodomy, may have been committed. Sodomy, under New York State law, is deviant sexual intercourse between two people without consent (either party may be male or female) "consisting of contact between the penis and the anus, the mouth and the penis, or the mouth and the vulva." The same table may be used to determine whether a charge of sodomy exists in a given case, the only difference being that the aggressor's age is in the left column and the victim's in the right, regardless of the sex of either perp or victim. If a twenty-one-year-old man has deviant sex with a thirteen-year-old boy, that is sodomy. If a twenty-year-old woman has deviant sex with a ten-year-old girl, that, too, is sodomy. If a seventeen-year-old male has deviant sex with a sixteen-year-old male, that's sexual misconduct.

Summarizing the role play from a legal perspective, Officer Lombardo says the crimes committed were burglary, robbery, felonious assault, and rape.

From the Police Science perspective, the instructor emphasizes certain points to the recruits. First, when police officers approach a scene, they have to use sound tactics. They should observe anyone leaving the premises—they might be a suspect. If an officer believes there may be danger, he may unholster his weapon. Officers shouldn't stand in front of a door when knocking.

An officer has much on his mind at this time: the crime scene, and whether the perp is still there or nearby; getting the victim aid if needed; guarding the scene for the detectives; the paperwork. There are two basic reports the officer must fill out: an aided card, required whenever a person is injured; and a complaint report, a form used to record the victim's description of the crime.

"Don't upset the lady any more than she is," says the Police Science instructor. "You can get the information later, at the hospital, if the woman elects to go. Worry about your victim's condition." Where is the case referred to? The Sex Crimes Unit, because it involved forcible, or first-degree rape. If the officers don't know how to make that referral, they can ask the desk officer. As a sex offense, the officers may not reveal information about the case to the victim's neighbors, or the give the victim's name to the news media. It is confidential.

When the woman said she wanted to shower, the officers should have persuaded her to wait and allow a doctor to examine her at a hospital. If she persisted, they would ask for the clothes she had on, because washing or showering can destroy evidence like semen or body hair, which would be vital to the prosecution of her attacker.

Many hospitals use Vitullo Evidence Kits, which contain swabs, slides, and other equipment to do pubic combings and other procedures for the collection and analysis of evidence. All evidence goes to the police lab.

The Police Science instructor also points out that the two recruits should have separated the husband and wife initially. The husband should have been informed when alone and less abruptly and his reaction gauged. The officers should each have been in a different room, although they wouldn't want to lose eye contact with each other for a long period of time. "Remember tactics," says the instructor. "Under certain circumstances family members become hostile and will even turn on the police."

Rape is a serious crime; the scars that remain with the victim are not fully realized or understood by many. To educate everyone about what this rape victim is going through, Michael Wilson paints a scenario, which he addresses particularly to the men.

"Imagine leaving here tonight. You're walking home, proud that you're in the police academy. All of a sudden a van pulls up next to you. Some men rush out and grab you and your books. There's three of them, one of you. They decide they're going to sodomize you in the back of the van. They do this, they throw you out on a street corner. You're bleeding. Your books are missing. Then you go home. How are you going to feel? How are you going to explain it? The next day will you feel like coming to the academy? Do you see now how a rape victim feels?" The audience is still. The message seems to be sinking in. "Just because you're a recruit in the police academy, don't think it can't happen to you. Think of that when you go on a job."

A few additional comments close the critique. One recruit

thinks the officer should not have told the husband so directly that his wife had been raped; the husband should have been told more gently. Officer Perez points out that perhaps the wife didn't know the definition of rape and that beating around the bush might have ultimately increased the husband's anger and suspicion. Each rape situation is different, she says, and police officers should temper discretion with patience, understanding, and gentleness. Their main role is to help the victim overcome the trauma she has experienced.

The static of a police radio is heard, pierced shortly by a call from Central. Ten-twenty-one, past burglary. Two thirty-five East 20th Street, Apartment 1M. Two officers in the vicinity respond to the call and find a woman in her late twenties; she's very upset. Her apartment is a modest studio, a kitchen and a bedroom; there is a National Rifle Association sticker on the front door. She complains it's been forty-five minutes since she called the police. She is quite agitated.

"They stole everything!" she says shrilly. "My fuckin' Sony Trinitron, my CD player . . . They even pulled the extension out of the fuckin' wall." Pointing to the refrigerator she says, "They helped themselves. They ate all my fuckin' food!"

"Would you like a seat?" an officer asks.

"No."

"Do you mind if I take a seat?"

"No. I don't give a shit."

The woman continues bellowing. "I could have walked in here. Then what would have happened?"

"But you didn't," answers the officer, a woman. "You're safe now. What's your name?"

"Grace."

"Your last name?"

"Telesco."

Grace mumbles that her father will kill her and worries out loud that the burglars will return. The other officer says the chances are ninety-nine percent they won't.

"A one percent chance!" Grace yells. "They'll be back, I know it!"

"What time did you arrive home?"

"Nine o'clock."

"Is there anyone you'd like us to call? Friends? Relatives?"

"I have no friends. Now what am I going to tell my father? They took my lampshade. Who the fuck takes a lampshade? They fuckin' took my CD player, my scuba equipment, my shotgun. . . ." Her voice trails off and she picks up the phone. "Forty-five minutes ago the phone was working. It's dead now. Why?"

"Do you have any neighbors who would have been home during that time?" an officer asks.

"Maybe my next-door neighbor. She's very nosy."

"It's not urgent now, but do you have a serial number for the stereo equipment?"

"I might have that. Do you think I could get my stuff back?"

"We'll make every attempt. I can't guarantee anything, but the more information we have, the better. I want you to come with me to a locksmith. Officer Mascia will stay here."

The role play is cut and Officer Gary Lombardo begins the law critique. He asks the students what offenses were committed and then defines each. First there was burglary, then larceny, the stealing of property. But was it petit larceny—a misdemeanor, or grand larceny—a felony? If the value of property stolen is $1,000 or less, it is petit larceny; over $1,000, it is grand larceny. Even if the perpetrator stole just the shotgun, a grand larceny would have been committed because in New

York it is a felony if the value of stolen property exceeds $1,000, or if among the property stolen is a credit card, secret scientific material, firearms, or a motor vehicle whose value is over $100.

To gain access to the apartment, burglar's tools were needed. These could be anything from a screwdriver to hairpins. A person who possesses an article intending to use it to illegally enter a premises is guilty of possession of burglar's tools. "Is someone who throws a rock through a window to force entry guilty of possession of burglar's tools?" asks Officer Lombardo. Yes, he answers himself: it matters less what the article is than how the article is used.

Then there is criminal mischief, the intentional damage of property, a misdemeanor if the value is under $250, a felony over that amount. There is also criminal possession of stolen property, and Officer Lombardo tells the recruits to be sure to request that the latent print unit come to take fingerprints if the job is big, if a lot of goods were taken. The unit will dust whatever it thinks is necessary—the refrigerator, cups, coffee cans, and glasses (plastic foam cups are no good for getting fingerprints). If burglar's tools are found, they should be vouchered and sent to the lab. He asks Stefanie Hirschhorn, who played the female cop in this role play, what she should have told the woman. "To avoid touching anything," she answers.

Officer Michael Wilson covers the Police Science perspective. He discusses the paperwork and adds that the police must search the home for the perp. A complaint report worksheet should be kept in the memo book as a guide in asking questions: Get serial numbers of the stolen items if possible. If a firearm is stolen in a burglary, the precinct detectives and the Stolen Property Inquiry Section should be notified.

None of the student officers noticed the National Rifle Association sticker on the apartment door. That should have warned them that the occupant might have a gun.

The Social Science critique points out that the officers

should check around for the perp before entering an apartment and listen to what's going on inside before entering rather than rely on what Central broadcasts.

Once inside, checking the apartment also makes the victim feel more secure, helping to restore her sense of security, power, and dignity.

"The victim said her father is going to kill her. How do you deal with that? You can say, 'Ma'am, these things happen. The most important thing is that you weren't hurt. Your father will understand.' "

When property of only nominal value, such as a car radio, is stolen, the police are usually not going to be able to find it. But they can make a victim feel better. By calling the latent print unit to dust for fingerprints, there might be a chance of recovering stolen property. But most of the time that effort is to just show the public that the police are doing all they can, unless it is in response to a wave of robberies in the same area over a week, for instance. How would a victim feel if a cop just said, "Come on, lady. This is only a little thing. Just your TV. You're never going to get your set back, so I'm not calling the print unit out"? Not only would she feel violated by the burglary, she'd wonder where her tax dollars go and what the police are good for anyway.

Grace Telesco, the officer who played the victim, adds some important points. First, a victim doesn't want to hear percentages. She wants the door fixed or secured—a superintendent or janitor could do this right away. Next, the police should show some compassion despite the unpleasantness of the victim's attitude. As a rule, victims tend to maximize the value of their stolen belongings; the police tend to minimize it. This may be the ninety-ninth burglary for the officers on the case, but perhaps it's the victim's first. "Let the victim 'ventilate,' " urges Officer Telesco. "Let her rage and get out her emotions." For the police, silence is golden. A final subtlety: if the victim doesn't want to sit down, the officers shouldn't either since eye contact will be lost. But if the victim sits down, the officer should also sit.

At three o'clock in the morning, two New York City Transit police officers arrive at the 59th Street, Columbus Circle subway station. They approach the token booth clerk, who called for the police. He tells them that a young girl has been sitting on the platform for hours. He can't leave the booth to find out if there's a problem.

The officers go up to the girl, who is visibly upset and shy. She is wearing a white cap, a white T-shirt, and blue jeans, and is bouncing a ball in a desultory manner. One of the officers begins asking questions.

"Hi, how are you doing?"

"Am I in trouble? I'm just not sure which train to take."

"Where are you going?"

"To my grandmother's house."

"Where does she live?"

"Up in Nyack."

"How old are you?"

"I just turned thirteen."

"Where do you live?"

"Bayside."

"Do you want to go home?"

Looking down, the girl does not answer.

The officer asks whether she'd like them to take her home. The girl shakes her head no, then starts crying.

"Is there a problem? You don't want to go home?"

She shakes her head no.

"What's your name?"

"Linda. I want to go to my grandmother's house."

"I'll ask the token clerk which train you should take."

The cop goes to the token booth. After a brief conversation with the clerk, he returns. He says, "The train you want has stopped running for the night. Would you like

to come with us? Maybe we can call somebody for you."
The girl looks doubtful but finally nods. The officers take
her to a substation of Transit District Number One. The
girl sits, and the cop asks if she wants to call her mother.

"My mother's dead."

"Your father?"

She shakes her head no.

"Your grandmother?"

The girl sits silent. The officer again asks the girl about
her father, and she insists she doesn't want to call him.
"He's the reason I left. He does things to me. Ever since
my mother died when I was six."

"Your grandmother's not home?"

"She is. She just can't hear. She's fifty."

She pauses and then says, "You can't help me. You can't
do anything!"

The action is cut and Michael Wilson, the moderator, asks
what type of job this is. A recruit answers, "A runaway child,"
and Officer Wilson queries, "Just that?" It could also be child
abuse, says the recruit after a moment's thought. Zeroing in
on the recruit's hesitancy, Officer Wilson says the role play
didn't continue precisely because the questioning wasn't leading anywhere.

"No one's going to hold cue cards up for you on the job,"
Officer Wilson admonishes them. "A police officer has to make
decisions." When a cop gets to a job, it may not turn out to
be what Central said it was. By asking questions, you find out
the nature of the circumstances and can make effective
decisions.

The legal perspective of the role play is addressed. The girl,
Officer Lombardo says, as much as said her father was a child
abuser. She should be asked if her father touched her and, if
so, how. The unlawful touching of a person is sexual abuse,
a misdemeanor or a felony depending on such factors as the

ages of the parties, whether the abused person is incapable of consent by reason of being physically helpless, or whether there was forcible compulsion.

A child-abuse victim should be asked if she has siblings and, if so, whether they are being abused. If a child is having difficulty responding, be sympathetic. Talk to her about getting her out of the home.

For legal purposes, officers need to determine then or later how the child was touched. Aggravated sexual abuse, a felony, is when a foreign object is inserted into the vagina or rectum. Was the victim raped? Sodomized? The officer also has to notify his desk officer, the precinct Youth Services Officer, the Society for the Prevention of Cruelty to Children, the Sex Crimes Unit, and the New York State Child Abuse and Maltreated Registry in Albany. In fact, failing to call the State Central Registry is itself a crime, a misdemeanor, for which a police officer could lose his gun and shield.

The Social Science critique dissects interviewing technique. To communicate with the young girl, the officer should speak on her level, and not scare her during questioning, which only victimizes her again. If the questioning is intimidating the child, then someone else, perhaps a female officer, should be called in.

A cop shouldn't be so intent on finding a suspect that he forgets the victim's feelings. However, if the cop makes mistakes because of his emotions, then maybe, the Social Science officer says harshly, the cop is in the wrong job. If the officer is too cynical, he's not going to display any outward emotions and come across as cold and unsympathetic. He's got to have a little feeling for what's going on and empathize with the probably frightened child because if he doesn't, it's just going to be mechanical. Joe "Just-the-facts-ma'am" Friday wasn't concerned about the victim's feelings; he just wanted the cold facts. That's wrong.

After the recruits leave the academy to go out on the street, says Officer Wilson, they'll see many pitiful situations. They may become hardened. This doesn't mean they can treat victims callously, however. How they handle a job can affect a victim for the rest of his or her life.

Adult victims as well as the young are affected by how the police treat them. Officer Perez remembers fondly a "big Irish cop" who carried her down four flights of stairs to a radio car when she was assaulted; his concern made a remarkable difference to her at the time. The real-life police officers who once helped a frightened young girl sitting by a subway track one morning felt their own reward in the satisfaction of helping someone.

The three role plays have a profound effect on the student officers, not just academically but emotionally. After the session ends, there is a brief silence. Then the recruits spring back to life, discussing among themselves what their feelings were, what *their* reactions would have been. What emerges from these conversations is the awareness that the instructors who performed in the role plays were effective because they had compassion for victims and empathy, too, for what the student officers would soon be experiencing. "They're young," says Officer Perez. "They're your babies. You pray that they'll stay alive."

——9——
STUDENT LIFE

To get by at the academy academically—an overall average of seventy percent is needed to graduate—a student has to keep up with his studies. He cannot slack off. Some of the work is common sense, some is challenging; but anyone who is accepted can pass—provided he applies himself throughout the term. That means doing homework every night and having little time left for a social life, even on weekends.

With the considerable investment the city has in each recruit, the academy does all it can to help the students succeed, offering regular tutoring classes and counseling.

In the week prior to a trimester exam, the recruits find themselves fully immersed in reviewing their subjects in preparation for the big test. The academy helps out too. For the three days prior to the trimester exams, review sessions are held in the auditorium for each of the academic subjects and separate sessions are held for each squad. The auditorium is usually filled to capacity, particularly for the law review. For each session, an instructor from the department sits on the stage and goes over the important material from each lesson included in the test.

Many students also form their own study groups. Andy Varga ran into some of his company peers at a diner before a day tour in the fourth week of training, and they decided to start a study group. All young and idealistic, and sharing a common goal—"to get through the academy and become the finest of the Finest, with the help of each other"—they became close friends. They call themselves the "Breakfast Club," since they usually meet at breakfast before class.

The club is composed of three men and one woman. Besides Andy, there is Frank D'Elia, a twenty-five-year-old former construction worker from Queens who hates crime, particularly drug dealing, with a passion; and Henry Ramirez, a stocky twenty-two-year-old army veteran. The lone woman is Carolyn Chew, a reticent twenty-four-year-old graduate of the State University of New York at Buffalo. She is the first female Asian officer ever to join the Transit Police Department.

The Breakfast Club meets formally once a week on a Saturday or Sunday at Andy's studio apartment in a high-rise on East 93rd Street. One subject is reviewed at a time, with one person asking questions, the others answering in rotation. If a person is weak in an area, the others drill the victim cold until he or she grasps the material. The sessions are productive and long—they may start at noon and run fourteen hours straight.

Relieving the intensity, they break into good-natured banter, impersonating their instructors and reaming out the victim before demanding a Star Card.

At unpredictable moments, one will suddenly jump another, like Kato attacking Inspector Clouseau, to practice cuffing uncooperative suspects. While avoiding the real violence of the street, they do play rough. Frank, much smaller than Andy, might leap on top of him. They fall to the bed and end up grappling on the floor, where Frank manages to cuff one wrist, maneuvering Andy to get the cuffed hand behind his back. He pulls up harshly, the pain forcing Andy to put his other hand behind him to be locked to the first. Henry will later play perp to Frank and Andy's cops, then steal the cuffs from Frank and end up cuffing *him*.

The Breakfast Club conducts these mock manaclings because in the two hours of gym on every tour, when cuffing is practiced, partners don't put up much resistance. These recruits want to experience what an actual street confrontation might be like. They know that a perp knows an arrest means jail, and he's not going to put his hands behind his back and stand politely to be cuffed. "When you cuff someone on the street," Frank says simply, "you're probably going to have to use force."

On weekends Andy occasionally relaxes by listening to music at a local bar, or watching a movie or video. But usually, if he's not visiting family, he's studying. He tries not to run around too much, particularly when a week of day tours is coming up, lest he exhaust himself before the week begins.

For day tours Andy goes to sleep anywhere between ten and eleven P.M., depending on how much homework he has. He rises early; his father, a church custodian, phones him at 4:30 A.M. to make sure he hasn't fallen back to sleep. It takes Andy an hour to get ready, half of which is spent standing in the shower, energizing.

At 5:30 A.M., Andy meets Henry Ramirez, who lives down the block, to take the Second Avenue bus downtown to 23rd Street, where they usually go to the Cosmos diner for breakfast. By 6:05 A.M., Frank and Carolyn have arrived at Cosmos also. About 6:45 A.M., they'll all start heading to the academy. They walk into the building and salute the flag behind the desk.

Each day before a tour begins, every company in a squad musters, lining up in formation twenty-three minutes before a tour on either the Campus Deck in front of the academy or on the Muster Deck off the third floor. The company sergeant stands in front of his group, which is divided into three ranks, and waits to greet the first class instructor and present the attendance. If anyone is absent, the instructor will want to

135

know why. Mustering is a formal procedure, and the instructor and company sergeant acknowledge each other by exchanging salutes.

Inspecting the three rows of recruits in a company with the company sergeant in tow, the instructor walks deliberately before each row, making square turns to face each of the student officers. With a sharp eye he slowly looks each student up and down to see that his appearance complies with department standards. The recruits stand stiffly at attention, eyes fixed ahead. A Star Card may be pulled for deficiencies: long hair, beard stubble, untrimmed mustache, stained uniform, dirty shoes, or a forgotten logbook.

After several weeks the recruits master the military formalities of this procedure and appear sharp and confident. This is in stark contrast to the very early musters before instruction was given. The first muster was a disaster since, without previous military experience, many had no idea what to do. Beginning about the third week, everybody seems to have gotten the hang of it.

After a muster, each of the companies files into the building and proceeds to the classrooms or the gym to begin their daily tour.

On each eight-hour tour at the academy, one hour is designated for a meal, and most recruits go out to eat. One popular spot is the Riss East Coffee Shop, across the street from the academy. It is clean and reasonable, but most importantly, the help is kind to recruits. One waitress, Kathy Hand, a forty-three-year-old, pleasant-looking mother of five (one son an NYPD cop) is known by all as "Police Academy Mom." Her warm and genuine concern for the recruits, not to mention her motherly instincts, come out when they walk through the door. Kathy lends them money if they are short of cash or forget their wallets, consoles them if they have problems, and handles uniform emergencies from a rack where she stores recruit shirts, ties, caps, tie clasps, and name holders. She is usually able to help one way or another, although ingenuity and quick thinking are sometimes necessary.

She saved one burly male recruit who lost his name tag; luckily none of his instructors noticed that the name on his replacement tag read "Kathy." Then there was the time, four months after classes started, when a student officer on a late tour came into the diner, panicking because his uniform jacket had been stolen the night before from his car. Fearing that he would receive a Command Discipline, he begged Kathy for help. There were no jackets on her rack, and she was momentarily perplexed. But then she went outside and snared a rather large recruit getting off an early tour. She slipped the student officer $20 for the use of his jacket, plus fare for a cab, so that he himself wouldn't be caught out of uniform. Like a scene out of an espionage thriller, the off-duty student officer was hidden until a taxi could be found to take him to his car. The much smaller recruit on the late tour was relieved to be reporting for duty in an official academy jacket, even if it was several sizes too large.

The only times a recruit may miss a tour at the academy are for a death in the family, an injury, or an illness. It would be virtually impossible for a recruit to feign either of the latter two. At the least, it would be more trouble than it's worth just to have a couple days' respite. Consider the rigors Stefanie Hirschhorn had to endure when she had a fever.

At six A.M. on a Tuesday morning in March, Stefanie awoke with a 102-degree temperature. To report sick, a recruit has to call the NYPD Sick Desk at least two hours before a tour, and since her tour would start in an hour, Stefanie dragged herself out of bed and made her way downtown to the academy. She arrived freezing, yet dripping with sweat. When, before her first class, the people she spoke with started "going in and out of focus," she decided to "go sick." She went to the administrative office and was instructed to call the police surgeon. She was given a log number, then returned home, and called

137

the police surgeon for an appointment. She was told to go to Lefrak City in Queens to see the surgeon the next day at 10:30 A.M.

After a night of fever, she awoke with her temperature still at 102 degrees. The trip to the police surgeon seemed formidable, but she thought she had no choice but to go. Instead of taking a subway, Stefanie opted for the more expensive—$35— car service. She waited three hours for the police surgeon, who saw her for five minutes. He asked questions but didn't examine her. He told her she was on sick leave until four P.M. Friday.

That appointment was the only time Stefanie was out of her apartment during her four-day reprieve from the academy. The recruits are not generally allowed to leave home during sick leave, except for a visit to a physician. If Stefanie needed to go to the bank, the drugstore, or the supermarket to get food, she would have to get permission from the Sick Desk or risk disciplinary action. The academy may call or even visit student officers to make sure they are home.

Eleven weeks into the training, the first trimester exam is held. By this point the recruits have learned to shoot, muster, had Star Cards pulled, and have applied themselves diligently to their work. The process of absorption, assimilation into the cop's world, is already taking place in the quasi-military environment of the police academy. In fact, the pressures of being student officers make them feel cut off from the rest of the world. As the winter cold disappears, spring seems to taunt them from the windows outside, though training is far from complete. Not until summer comes will they be cops, real cops.

On test days the academy takes on a different personality. Gone is the reined-in energy that usually permeates the tours, of students marching through the corridors and bantering with peers and instructors during breaks. The academy becomes somber, the atmosphere glum. The hallways and rooms are guarded with the utmost strictness.

On the fifth of April, test day, the B Squad comes pouring into assigned classrooms to muster, instead of on either of the usual two decks. The recruits' faces are serious, their manner nervous. Many are like Andy Varga, who hasn't slept for two nights and whose stomach is in a knot. It is the first major test at the academy, and Andy doesn't know what to expect. The single dominant thought in his mind is the instructors' warning that the test will start weeding out unprepared students.

After Andy takes roll call for his company, an instructor answers questions about course material for the next hour and a quarter. At nine A.M., the company is given a meal break, and an hour later the recruits report to Room 415. Minutes later Officer Frank Dwyer comes in and gives each student a room assignment.

To eliminate or reduce the chances for cheating, students do not know ahead of time in which room they'll be placed, and the test rooms are mixed with student officers from different companies. Andy is assigned to Room 516 and finds twenty-five recruits there, mostly strangers. He sees one familiar face from his company across the room.

Each trimester test consists of one hundred multiple choice questions divided equally among the three academic subjects. During any particular trimester, two separate tests are administered. They are called by the color of the pages they are printed on—white or green.

During the test Andy begins to relax. It is not as complicated as he had feared. He has prepared thoroughly, and he is confident that he'll not only pass but do well. At 2:45 P.M. the exam is over, but the recruits must sit silently in the classrooms for another hour. Then they line up in the hallways, waiting until a sergeant receives word over his radio to release them. One by one the student officers file down the stairs as the instructors check that the classrooms are empty.

As the B Squad files out the door facing 20th Street, they see the 16 A Squad companies waiting quietly and anxiously. Hordes of instructors are there, preventing any talk between student officers of the different squads. Even though any recruit found cheating would probably be terminated from the department, the system is so iron-clad that Lieutenant John Madigan, head of testing, jokes that if a student *could* succeed, he or she should be made an inspector.

Two days after the trimester exam, the scores are handed out. A list of recruits with failing scores goes automatically to the academy's Counseling Unit, which follows up with interviews. The counselors try to determine why the students performed poorly—whether it was due to personal or academic problems, or inadequate study practices—and give guidance to help them improve. Andy Varga is satisfied: He got an 81.2 in Police Science, an 82.35 in Social Science, and an 81.82 in Law, for an overall score of 82. He can sleep soundly now, or at least until the next trimester. Lissette Sierra-Solis, who earned an overall score of 97.3, is jubilant, as are Tomas Ramos, with a 93; and Stefanie Hirschhorn, with a 95 overall.

10
DEALING WITH DEATH

Few weeks go by at the academy without some type of special class. Fingerprinting, AIDS, drug awareness, fire scenes, radio communications, and summons writing are the subjects of special workshops; officers from CCRB, IAD, and many other police units come to talk about functions carried out by their divisions. These classes acquaint recruits with various realities of police work not covered in detail in the regular curriculum.

Perhaps the most unnerving class of the entire training is that given by Crime Scene. The Crime Scene Unit, a division of the Detective Bureau, responds to homicides and major felony cases like rape, robbery, and burglary, and from the physical evidence collected attempts to identify suspects and link them to crime scenes. With an average of six homicides a day in New York City, the unit (one lieutenant, six sergeants, and sixty investigators) works around the clock and will inevitably be working with these officers-in-training once they are out on patrol.

The first officer on the scene of a homicide does not take fingerprints, search for evidence, draw outlines around the body, take photographs, or conduct any other type of investigation. All of that is the Crime Scene Unit's job. Often tied up on other important cases, however, it is sometimes several hours before Crime Scene investigators arrive. "Don't get annoyed with us," says Detective Jerry Donohue in his talk to the recruits about what they should expect out in the field.

The scene of a homicide is likely to be a macabre spectacle that will stay with the cop for some time. Some will outwardly make light of it, while others accept it stolidly as a common part of police work. But all are affected in one way or another by witnessing the depravity of the human mind and the often gruesome sight of a human life so cruelly ended. Investigators in the Crime Scene Unit, inured to the horror of murder by daily contact, accept the brutality in a casual, though not perfunctory, way.

The first cop at the scene of a homicide has the unfortunate disadvantage of not knowing exactly what he will encounter, what to expect. But he must maintain his comportment and handle himself professionally. First the officer determines whether the perpetrator is hiding anywhere on the premises, or if anyone present needs an ambulance. Then he must guard the scene.

That means permitting only authorized personnel to enter, and following the three cardinal rules: don't touch anything, don't add anything to the crime scene, and don't remove anything from it. The officer must not use anything at the location—not the phone, not the toilet, not an ashtray. This may be a considerable inconvenience, as it sometimes takes Crime Scene several hours to arrive. Investigators will search, collect, record, photograph, and sketch the scene. Ballistics evidence (spent shells, powder burns, trajectories), hair, fibers, semen, and blood will be collected.

"Curiosity is our enemy," says Detective Barney. It is March 15 and several Police Science classes have gathered in the auditorium for this special class. "Keep unauthorized people away."

It is important, he continues, for the first officer to keep careful records—who is at the scene when he arrives, names and addresses of witnesses verified by identification, and initial observations. Was a television on? Tuned to what channel? Were the lights on or off, any windows open? This information may be important in a trial that may take place years after the crime.

The recruits watch two slide presentations. The first one is "Crime Scene Procedures," a series of cartoons that illustrates the techniques of preserving, searching out, and collecting evidence at a crime scene. It also amplifies previous information. For example, if a gun is found at the crime scene, it should be picked up with two fingers around the checkerboard grip or with a string that has been tied around the trigger guard. The next group of slides shows the recruits what they may see at a crime scene. The slides are disconcertingly real.

There is a screen-sized photograph of a naked woman lying in front of her apartment door with her legs stretched apart and her hands by her side. The woman's husband was in the navy, and she left her kids with their grandmother when she decided she wanted to go out for some entertainment. She met a man with whom she had a sexual encounter, but unfortunately for her, the only way he could achieve satisfaction was by killing her and inserting an object into her body, an act known as pequism. The man strangled her on the bed and then, to humiliate her in death, positioned her in front of the door. With one thrust, he drove a butcher knife into her chest so forcefully that it passed through her body and embedded itself an inch and a half in the floor.

Two women with their heads and hands cut off are seen lying on a bed. Their bodies were burned when the room was set afire to destroy evidence.

The slide that follows shows a woman with her breasts cut off. These mutilations were the work of Richard Cottingham, a programmer for Blue Cross/Blue Shield, who lived in a nice home in New Jersey with his wife and three kids. An investigation led to him, and police found belongings from dozens of different individuals hidden in his house. The killer fit the psychological profile of a "trophy hunter," a criminal who collects clothing, identification, or jewelry from his victims. He was tried and convicted in New York and New Jersey, and during the investigation inquiries were made from California, Nevada, Florida, and other states.

Organized crime is a fact of everyday life in New York. The daily newspapers frequently have accounts of the latest mob rub-out, to which, of course, the NYPD responds as to any other crime. A slide shows the corpse of a mobster, eyes open and bulging. It also shows normal decomposition of the body. The victim had incriminating information in a case coming up against "Big Paulie" Castellano, who himself was later gunned down in December 1985 in front of a midtown restaurant. Detective Donohue notes that the police frequently find mob victims in the trunks of cars in airport parking lots—led there by the stench.

Much can be learned from the way glass is shattered by a bullet. A photograph of a window hit by a bullet appears on the screen. Detective Donohue tells how investigation of the shattering led to discovery of the truth in a controversial trial. A police officer on patrol looked through a window of a restaurant and saw a man holding a gun. The man looked up and saw the cop, aimed the gun, and shot at him. The officer returned the fire and hit a bystander. It turned out that the man was showing off an illegal gun to some friends. When he saw the cop, he panicked and shot. The man's friends testified in court that the cop shot first. Glass ballistics revealed, however, that the officer responded only in self-defense.

There is a picture of someone's legs and buttocks, found in a barrel. One sneaker was found next to the barrel; this sneaker led to the killer. Emergency Service conducted a search and found a matching sneaker in a trash can. In the same can was junk mail that led to a suspect. Some weeks later an unfortunate passerby, who probably bore the grisly picture in his mind for the rest of his life, found the top half of the victim's body in a steamer trunk.

A woman committed suicide by jumping from the fortieth floor of a building. She hit a railing in her plunge and her body split in two. A picture shows the woman's intestines, stretched out like a long string, extending from the top half of her body over the railing down to the bottom half of her body, some thirty feet below.

Detective Donohue tells of two men who picked up a stranger and invited him back to their apartment so they could all have sex together. The stranger killed both men by stabbing them in the chest, then removed their heads as well as one victim's ring finger. He filled the bathtub, intending to bathe with the two heads, but changed his mind. Before he fled the apartment, he put the two heads on the lap of one victim and disemboweled the other. He intentionally went through a series of red lights so he would be pulled over by a cop and could confess his slaughter, but he wasn't caught. ("There's never a cop around when you need one," quips Detective Donohue with macabre humor.) Finally, in frustration, the murderer rammed another car, giving himself up to the cops who arrived. When asked why he put the heads on the lap of one body, the killer said he thought the cops would get a kick out of it.

There was the case of the woman who kept asking her husband what happened to his first wife. She persisted until, finally, he showed her. On the screen appears the second wife, chopped up and drenched in her own blood. Detective Donohue adds dryly that the man made his second wife's fourteen-year-old daughter watch the dismemberment.

Detective Donohue, a veteran of more than 4,500 investigations, relieves the tension of his shocking presentation with some levity, referring, for example, to the discovery of a single buttock as a "half-assed case," the investigation of the slain mobster with the bulging eyes as the "I Only Have Eyes For You" case, and the woman whose intestines stretched like a long string from the railing as *Fiddler on the Roof.* "After seeing these things year in and year out, you have to have a sense of humor," he says in defense. He adds that he can completely obliterate cases from his mind when he's off the job: "Unless I refer to my notes, I have trouble sometimes remembering what the case was the next day."

Another informative lecture and (almost as grisly) slide presentation comes from officers who work out of the office of the medical examiner, at 520 First Avenue at 30th Street. The building is a high-rise graveyard, a temporary depot for unidentified bodies found on city streets, waterways, abandoned buildings, and empty lots. The vertical mortuary contains 126 stainless-steel refrigerated compartments; the floor is of a nonporous tile that helps prevent the spread of disease. Of the approximately 75,000 deaths each year in New York City, 34,000 come to the attention of the M.E. More than 12,000 receive post-mortem examinations, 8,000 are autopsied, and about 22,000 cases are actively investigated.

Detectives at the M.E. get twenty-five inquiries a week from families looking for lost relatives; they have to come down to the M.E.'s office to make identification.

In the past, a staff member rolled the body in on a cart and lifted the sheet covering the corpse. But when an ID was made, the family members often became emotional, jumping on the bodies, and so the practice was discontinued. Bodies are now identified through a glass partition; there is no physical contact, and distraught family members can more easily be comforted separated from the body of their loved one.

Sergeant Jack Hackett of the Missing Persons Morgue Unit explains that visual identification is not always possible. When a body is decomposed or badly burned or is otherwise unidentifiable, forensic investigators must use other methods. Clothing is examined for clues, the corpse inspected for anomalies, tattoos, and dentures. X rays and fingerprinting are also used. The students see slides demonstrating the difference between a "wet floater" (who decomposes in the water) and a "dry floater" (found in a dry place). Sergeant Hackett tells the recruits they will have to deal with each type of corpse at some point in their careers.

The slide presentation shows examples of advanced decomposition; mummification—a woman who died in bed and was kept there by her family to collect her social security checks; an arm chewed up by dogs and rodents; senile people who died alone and were eaten by rodents; chopped-off fingers, heads, and feet (organized crime groups dismember their victims to hamper identification); a body with 137 stab wounds; the remains of the face of a person blown up in an explosion; the guts of a person who fell into a meat grinder; a person who committed suicide by jumping from the 82nd floor of the World Trade Center; the keys, curlers, and hair barrettes found in the stomach of an institutionalized individual who would swallow anything he found; the tattooed genitals of a man whose arms and legs had been chopped off—the victim's girlfriend identified him by the markings.

A police officer who comes to a scene where a human corpse lies must follow certain procedures: He must request an ambulance and patrol supervisor; obtain the names of any witnesses if the death is suspicious; cover the body if open to public view; and permit only authorized persons to come in contact with the body—a physician or Emergency Medical Service attendant to formally pronounce the person dead. Then the M.E., D.A., precinct detectives, and the Crime Scene Unit begin their own routines. The patrol officer places an ID tag on the body and notifies the family of the deceased.

Death is one of the more unpleasant aspects of the job, but it is a natural part of police work. In their daily grind, police come in contact with bodies of people who have died in both natural and unnatural ways. Except for deaths in hospitals, almost every type of DOA involves the police, either in notification or investigation of cause.

Once the student officers leave the academy, they'll be seeing dead bodies and dealing with bereaved families. The academy prepares them for this experience. Maintaining control is the message.

In a crisis situation, people want to be able to lean on the police. They expect police officers to be cool but compassionate, removed but helpful. Like other Social Science instructors, Officer Michael Wilson covers the three main things police officers should provide in making a death notification. An officer should allow people to borrow from his *strength*, which he gives by showing he's in control. He should provide *support*, or compassion. He should give the bereaved family or friends *structure*. They'll be asking, "Who do I call? What's going to happen with the body?" The cop gives direction.

Soon after he graduated from the academy, Officer Wilson had his first DOA. The body, covered with a sheet, lay in the bedroom, the family huddled around it, weeping. Wilson was struck by their grief, and after expressing his sorrow, asked the family to move into the living room, away from the body. He also asked them if they wanted anything to drink or eat, if there was a friend he could call to help comfort them. They had many questions about what they were expected to do. He answered them to the best of his ability. He explained that their next step was to pick out a funeral parlor. The family chose one, but none of the members was calm enough to actually make the call. So Wilson made the call himself and arranged for the funeral director to pick up the body.

Police officers aren't required to make phone calls for families of the deceased, Officer Wilson tells the students, but they should show compassion for the survivors. They should recognize crisis behavior and try to ease the pain.

News of death should be given gradually. An officer

shouldn't ring a doorbell and say to the woman who answers, "Ma'am, your husband is dead," and walk away. The officer should sit down with her and break the news gently, in steps.

"Ma'am, I'm afraid I have some bad news."

"What do you mean? What's wrong?"

"There's been an accident."

"What happened?"

"I'm very sorry to have to tell you this, but your husband was crossing the street and was struck by a car and killed."

It sounds cliché but it is actually compassionate. The officer then helps the wife to understand and accept the fact, for she may deny it, saying she just spoke with her husband. The officer explains that he was at the scene or received a communication, and tells her where the body is, and what she needs to do.

Several instructors describe their experiences of DOAs. These personal anecdotes, and the gruesome photographs the students have been shown, are intended to give them some idea of what to expect so their own first such experience won't be quite as much of a shock.

"Somebody will report a stink coming out of an apartment," says an instructor, "and you'll go and investigate. You'll find this decomposed old lady who reminds you of your grandmother. But maggots are coming out of her nose. Then you have to stay with the corpse for ten hours till the coroner gets there." He tells them cops often vent their frustration through humor. "One time a woman had been dead for a few days, and there was no one to feed her dogs. So when we got there, the two of them were chewing the skin off her head. When I went out with my cop buddies that night, did I act freaked out? No. We joked about it."

If a corpse has been lying around for any length of time, there will be a distinct odor. "It's hard to explain," says Officer Wilson, "but it'll hit you from fifty feet away. You'll know it's a DOA." The body may be a sickening sight. Officer Wilson

explains how bodies swell up when the process of decomposition produces gas in the tissues. He tells them they might
find skeletons. "There have been times," says Officer Wilson,
"when we've pulled bodies out of the water and found that
fish have eaten the eyes out of the face." Some students squirm
in their seats; others look down.

If the deceased person lived alone, the officer might have to
knock down the door or have Emergency Service take it down
to get into the home. A cop will have to "sit" on the body until
the medical examiner arrives, safeguarding the premises. The
officer will call a patrol supervisor before conducting a body
search. For many cops, going through the pockets of a dead
person is revolting. Jewelry has to be taken off, and this may
also be a difficult experience. Officer Wilson tells of one fellow
officer who was trying to remove a ring and succeeded, but got
a little more than he wanted. The finger came off with the ring.

Henry Ramirez, Andy Varga's Breakfast Club buddy, had his
first experience of violent death while doing field training a
few months out of the academy. He was driving his sergeant
around when a call came over the air: "Shots fired in the four-
six on Mount Hope Place and the Grand Concourse." Units in
the area rushed to the scene. By the time Henry and his sergeant
arrived, there was confirmation of a double killing. The sergeant turned to Henry. "Did you ever see a dead body?"

"No, Sergeant, let's go!" Henry replied. He felt "like an excited little kid going to Disney World."

The two entered the building and saw an EMS technician
in the elevator.

"Are you going up to take a look?" the technician asked.

"Yeah."

"The guy's naked, and it's ugly."

"I want to take a look anyway," Henry answered defensively.
His sergeant had seen so many that he was pretty nonchalant.

When Henry got to the apartment, he saw the door slightly

ajar. He put his hands in his pockets so he wouldn't get fingerprints on anything. With his elbow he shoved the door, but
it didn't open very far. Henry's eyes immediately were drawn
to the floor. A man lay naked, his head leaning on an ottoman.
Crimson-red blood was splattered on it; Henry noticed more
blood dripping from the dead man's earlobe. He moved back
to catch his breath for a moment. A further glimpse into the
next room revealed another pair of legs. He stuck his head into
the doorway and saw a woman's head with a piece of the back
missing. There was blood everywhere. "Holy shit! Holy shit!"
he repeated to himself, only to be interrupted by a cop inside
yelling not to come in. When Henry went outside and the cold
November air struck his face, he realized how profusely he
had been sweating.

A short time later Henry had to "sit" on a DOA.

A man had died sitting up in a chair in his kitchen. When
Henry and his partner arrived at the apartment, they noticed
a strange smell in the entryway. When they entered the apartment, they found the DOA in the kitchen. They exchanged
uneasy glances.

They knew they would have to sit with the body, although
the two rookies naturally expected to be relieved by the midnight tour. They both called home. There was nothing to do
in the apartment but wait. Unfortunately for the rookies, there
was no TV or even a radio. The DOA must have drunk a lot
of beer, Henry told his partner, because the apartment was
filled with empty beer cans. A few times they entered the
kitchen, where the corpse was slumped over in a chair, one
arm dangling on the floor.

Finally, the medical examiner arrived. He put on rubber
gloves, lifted the corpse's head, and slapped it vigorously
across the face.

Henry's mouth fell open; he couldn't believe how the M.E.
was manhandling the dead body. "What the fuck are you
doing?" Henry said. "Testing for effect? The guy's dead!"

Rigor mortis had set in by that time, and the M.E. propped the DOA up in the chair.

Close to midnight, Henry told his partner he'd better call the desk sergeant to verify that someone would be coming to relieve them. His partner was jittery, and Henry kept teasing him that the DOA was moving.

The desk sergeant had some bad news. A lot of cops weren't coming in for midnights. They were low on sector teams, he said, and they didn't want to break up a unit just for a cop to sit on a DOA. "So one of you will have to collect overtime."

Hanging up the phone, Henry said to his partner, "One of us has to stay. Do you want to?"

"No, I don't want to fuckin' stay!"

"I'll tell you what. I'll flip you for it."

Henry flipped a coin. His partner called heads. The coin landed tails.

"Sorry, pal," Henry said with a smile.

But his partner looked as if he was about to cry, so Henry said, "I'll tell you what. I don't know why I'm doing this, but I'll flip you one more time." Another toss of the coin, and Henry's partner lost again.

"I'm out of here!" Henry announced.

The next day Henry asked his partner how sitting on the DOA went.

"Henry, it was fucked up. I was waiting for the morgue to come. I sat on his bed. I was thinking about something and fell asleep. Only I didn't know it. The next thing I know, the doorbell rang. I forgot where I was for a minute. I jumped up and ran to the door. As I passed the kitchen, I looked to the right and saw the dead body. When I got to the door it was the morgue. They saw the expression on my face. They looked at me like, 'What the hell's wrong with you?' "

* * *

152

"You'll hear some cops say that after the first few DOAs you'll become immune to them," Officer Wilson tells the recruits. "But I don't think anyone can ever become completely callous or hardened in dealing with the dead. It affects us all. But we can't show our distress to the family, friends, bystanders, or witnesses. They'll be looking to the cop for strength and support."

—— 11 ——
TACTICS TRAINING:
GUNS

On a hot evening in June 1984, firearms instructor Salvatore Manna was on routine patrol in the 32nd Precinct in Harlem. At around 11:40 P.M., ten minutes before he and his partner were to go off duty, the radio crackled, summoning them to a nearby 10-52, a dispute.

"Nuts. Another couple of jerks fighting over a dame, most likely. Let the midnight shift take it. I just want to get out of here and go home," Manna's partner muttered.

"Well, look, it's just around the corner from the precinct," responded Manna. "We can take care of it on the way in."

"What the hell," his partner said, leaning forward to acknowledge the call. "But if we get stuck in some mess, you owe me dinner."

As their radio car turned onto West 133rd Street, they saw a small crowd ahead. Officer Manna put on the turret lights and hit the siren a few times. The crowd scattered, revealing the tangled bodies of two young men writhing in the street.

As the car drew up next to the fight, the cops could see one of the men had gained advantage: He was on top of the other, pummeling him viciously. The face of the man underneath was covered with blood, and he wasn't putting up much resistance.

The first man, about to administer another blow, stopped midswing as he caught sight of the cop car. As the two officers were getting out, he pulled himself off his bloodied victim and took off in the direction of the nearest building.

Just then another police car pulled up. Officer Manna leaned down to the window.

"You take care of this guy; call an ambulance, he's hurt. We'll get the other one." The cops inside nodded, and Officer Manna and his partner followed the assailant through the crumbling doorway of Number 125.

The man was already halfway up the staircase. The cops managed to close the distance to a few feet as they chased him up to the third floor. Officer Manna couldn't figure out why the man kept running. "Doesn't he know he's cornered? That he'll have to jump out a window to get away from us? He must be desperate," he thought. "Watch it," he gasped to his partner. "This guy's already in some kind of trouble."

At the third floor landing, the man turned left and ran down the corridor. The cops could hardly see. The ceiling light was out, but the perp clearly knew where he was going. Officer Manna drew his gun, motioning to his partner to do the same.

The door to Apartment 325 was ajar, and the man pushed it open and disappeared through it. He tried to close it, but Officer Manna's partner threw his shoulder against it. "Forget it, buddy, we've got you," Officer Manna shouted.

In the light from inside the apartment the officers could see the perp's silhouette as he struggled to close the door. Suddenly his right hand moved to his waistband.

"Look out!" Officer Manna yelled, darting back against the

wall. But his partner was off balance and couldn't move quickly enough. There were three quick shots from inside the apartment.

"Oh, God, I'm hit, I'm hit!" Manna's partner crumpled to the floor as Manna squeezed off a shot through the doorway. He was at a bad angle and didn't think he'd hit the man, who moved back into the apartment. There were no more shots.

Officer Manna grabbed his partner, who had taken a .38 slug in the forearm, dragging him back to the staircase, where they huddled while Manna radioed a 10-13 to Central.

Seconds later the two cops from the street pounded up the staircase in response to the shots. Their first priority the wounded cop, they hustled Manna's partner downstairs and into the patrol car for the drive to the hospital. It took only a few minutes more for police cars to arrive from all directions after hearing Manna's 10-13. The area was soon flooded with cops: on the surrounding roofs, on the ground, on every floor of the building, in the air in a helicopter.

A woman appeared at the door of the apartment. She was the suspect's mother, she said; another child, a baby, was inside. She pleaded that there be no trouble and let the police in. The perp was climbing out the window when the officers grabbed him and placed him under arrest.

In the station house under questioning, the man filled in the details. Nineteen years old, he had been fighting with his brother. He had intended to shoot his brother after beating him up because his brother had been seeing his girlfriend behind his back. The gun was later found by detectives in the alleyway below the apartment window.

For his part in the incident, Salvatore Manna was awarded the NYPD's Police Combat Cross, as was his wounded partner.

In gunfights, the element of surprise is usually with the perps. The cop has no way of knowing when he's about to be fired on, but he has to respond swiftly, taking whatever cover he can find. There's little time to establish sight alignment and maintain trigger control as he was so carefully taught as a recruit. As Sal Manna did, a cop usually returns fire instinctively—by pointing and shooting.

In their first trip to Rodman's Neck, the recruits learned to shoot, developing their skills on stationary targets. But perps don't stand still in gunfights. They move. And gun battles may erupt after long chases and violent physical struggles. To train the students for these sudden life-and-death street situations— which they'll be facing in less than four months—each recruit company returns to the range for a three-day tactics course.

At seven o'clock in the morning of March 22, the temperature is seventeen degrees. Company 32 is in Building 4 at Rodman's Neck, a small prefab that houses a classroom. Jim Martin is discussing cops in danger, tactics, Mace, and reviewing radio codes. The recruits have memorized the codes up to 39. "Codes are important," Officer Martin says, "but when you're calling in, tell where you are, give your location."

He asks the student officers which units respond in the case of an emergency—a 10-13, for example—and the names come flying back at him: sector cars, footpost cops, patrol supervisors, outer precincts, Task Force, Housing and Transit police, plainclothes Anticrime officers, Emergency Service, Aviation, Street Crime (who operate out of Randall's Island in taxicabs and unmarked cars), and on and on.

In talking about the Street Crime Unit, Officer Martin says, "I'm going to tell you what kind of taxicabs they work out of. It's one of the few secrets we have left, and God help you if you tell anybody."

A student raises his hand and says he already knows the secret. He's wrong.

Officer Martin goes to the blackboard and writes a mythical medallion identification consisting of numbers and letters. He then reveals the magical ingredient.

What would happen if an undercover taxi were responding to an emergency and a neophyte cop, not knowing the driver's real identity, took off after him? "Three things will happen if you pursue the cab. You'll chase him, he'll smack his shield against the window, and he'll come looking for you at the precinct," says Officer Martin.

"There are two joys to this job," he continues. "Reviving a blue baby, one that can't breathe, and getting into a 10-13 and having other cops come to aid you." With respect to the former, he says, "On Thanksgiving you'll have dinner with the family, and every year you'll get a Christmas card."

Officer Martin discusses how cops should enter and sit in restaurants. "Look in first," he says. "If you don't see a robber, look at the people's faces." He advises sitting not at the counter, but in a booth. One cop should watch the front door, the other the back door. It may be uncomfortable to sit with the gun belt on, but it should never be taken off. He suggests putting the holster between the legs. The radio should be turned down low, but not off. If people come over because of some problem, either handle it or say you have ten minutes left to eat, and you'll handle it when you're finished. But don't be rude.

Officer Martin displays a can of Mace and discusses how effective it is as a defensive weapon for a cop, another thing he can use before he has to resort to deadly physical force. It instantaneously makes the eyes and nose run and burns the skin painfully. With three one-second bursts, a person will usually fall down and roll on the ground. Yet despite its potency, it is not used much by NYPD cops: 22 times in 1987, 118 times in 1988, and 180 times in 1989.

Civilians can purchase and carry Mace but can't legally use it in New York City. Department regulations even prohibit NYPD cops from carrying it off duty. It would be too tempting to use in minor altercations like fender benders. Officer Martin points out that normal Mace will not work on everyone—for example, persons extremely intoxicated or high on drugs.

Officer Martin tells the recruits that their radio is one of the best defensive pieces of equipment they will have: "You can really hurt a perp if you hit him over the head with it."

Martin then plays a videotape, "Off-Duty Weapons Control," which presents different scenarios the student officers could face one day. In the first, an off-duty cop is eating in a restaurant with his girlfriend and leaves the table for a moment. A former boyfriend comes over to the table and sits down. When the officer returns, the former boyfriend asks the woman, "Why don't you tell your friend about some of the good times we had?" The cop, angered by the lascivious reference to his girlfriend and by the challenge to his manhood, pulls his jacket back to display a gun in a holster. Instead of becoming unnerved, the man responds by telling him to "stick it up!" The bartender interferes, and everyone starts shouting and screaming.

Officer Martin stops the tape and asks the student officers what they would do in a situation like that. "Get the hell out of there" is the response. Martin adds that even if the girl doesn't want to go, they should leave anyway.

Another scenario shows a man at a bar with a gun. One student says he would approach the man with his gun drawn. Officer Martin says that would be the wrong response. There could be others present with a weapon. Another student says he would drop a quarter and make a phone call. Martin interjects that it doesn't cost anything to dial 911; it's free. "Why is it so difficult to be a police officer in this city?" Officer Martin asks. He answers himself: "Because there are so many millisecond decisions to be made."

In a final scenario a man and woman are arguing loudly in public. The man slaps the woman. One student says he would rush over and identify himself as a police officer. "But," says Officer Martin, taking the scenario one step further, "you get there and identify yourself, and the guy says, 'Don't tell me what the hell to do!' and smacks you. So you open him up because he assaulted you, and then you arrest him." Originally, the cop was the savior, the girl was the victim, and the man the aggressor. But in the station house, the man is bleeding, and the girl is crying. "You, the cop, are now the aggressor," says Officer Martin. "The girl, consoling her boyfriend, is the savior, and the man is the victim." If off duty, Martin advises, students should call 911 to relay what has happened at the location instead of trying to handle it themselves.

Another videotape, "Off-Duty Law Enforcement," shows a couple out shopping who watch two men break into a store across the street. The husband, an off-duty cop, rushes to a phone and dials 911.

"Did the officer act correctly? What action would you have taken?" Officer Martin asks the students. Martin says what the cop did was correct, but some students say the cop should have sent his wife to make the call, and he should have watched the store.

The tape continues—the off-duty officer sends his wife to their car, and he runs to the store and looks through the window. The third burglar, waiting in a van, sees him and comes up behind him. At gunpoint, the cop is forced to go into the store, into the clutches of the burglars.

"That move was stupid," Officer Martin says. "He had no backups, no one knew where he was." Again, he advises the students that if they encounter such a situation, they should go to the nearest telephone and dial 911: "Don't be a hero!"

During the course of a police officer's career, it is indeed possible that he might happen upon a situation where someone in street clothes has a gun drawn. The question: Is that person a police officer?

Martin paints a scenario. A man in civilian clothes holding a gun has two men against a wall. A police car comes by. One cop informs Central there is a "man with a gun," and alights with his partner. What should the cops do? Take cover, says Officer Martin, and say, "Police, don't move!" He adds, "If you happen to be the cop in plainclothes, *do not move!*"

How do the partners decide who does the talking? The students all answer at once: the cop with seniority, whichever cop got there first, the one with the loudest voice, the one with the best cover. No, no, no, Martin says, shaking his head. The officer with the radio does the talking. Why? The perp can hear the position of that cop, but won't know where the other cop is. Each pair of partners has only one radio, which should be turned on.

Returning to the scenario, Martin asks, "What if the man with the gun who claims he's a cop throws his shield on the ground to prove it?

"You ask questions," Officer Martin says. "They sell shields on Forty-second Street that look better than the real thing. Ask where he works. If he says something like the one-three, you have reason to be suspicious." While certain precincts are referred to by digits, others, such as the 13th, are not. "If you ask him who commands that particular precinct and he gives a name you don't think is correct, you can't jump to conclusions. There could have been a very recent change. You can ask him a radio code or his six-digit police tax registry number. But if he stumbles," warns Officer Martin, "don't jump on him. He could really be a cop, and maybe he's nervous." Other possibilities include asking what the color of the day is, or what some acronym of police lingo (like "RDO"—regular day off) means. Even if he doesn't know the answer to any of these, conclusive proof still cannot be drawn since he could work for the FBI, Secret Service, or some other organization. Some of these groups' shields actually look fake, says Officer Martin, smiling sardonically. The best thing to do is keep everyone there until backup or a patrol supervisor gets to the scene.

In the afternoon a videotape on bulletproof vests is shown, followed by a taped interview with Willie Washington, a retired NYPD cop whose life was saved by a vest. He shows his scar. Rodney Dangerfield pops up, exclaiming, "Put on that vest. Show your life some respect." (Since this class, the wearing of protective vests by patrol officers has become mandatory.)

The final videotape is on "accidental discharge." An off-duty cop is shown at home with his wife and baby. He is cleaning his gun when it accidentally goes off. In another scenario two officers in an RMP are racing to a crime scene when they are forced to stop suddenly. The cop on the passenger side has his gun drawn; it hits the dashboard and blows out the windshield. There are proper safety precautions to take in such situations.

At eight A.M. on Wednesday, March 23, the second day of tactics training, a police van takes half of Company 32 from Building 8 to Building 9, the Tactics House, sometimes referred to as the "Fun House" or the "Horror House." It is dark and dank inside. Here the students will go through variations on a frightening theme: "There's a man inside with a gun. Go get him."

The twelve student officers file into the building and line up against a wall. Several firearms instructors are present. Officer James Rafferty explains to the students the purpose of the exercises.

"This class is designed to show you how to handle certain types of jobs without getting hurt.

"You will work in teams of two. Your job is to look for a man with a gun. Central has called. But just because you get a call for a gun run, it doesn't mean that there really is a gun. It could be a family fight, a rape, a burglary, sexual abuse.

"Never lose sight of your partner. Don't split up. Call for a backup team. There is safety in numbers. If the perps split up, give a description on the air. If you split up, you may get hurt.

"Always think one more. If you see one individual, think two. They use bulletproof vests too. They have better weapons than we do, more bullets.

"If you find weapons, continue the search. Don't stop there.

"Never stand directly in front of a door when responding to

a call, regardless of the type of call it is. Bullets can pass through doors."

The students are tense. The possibility of confronting a perp with a gun has instantly become a grim reality. What lies ahead? There are so many deranged people on the streets. Is the job worth it?

Officer Rafferty shows the students a yellow-barreled revolver used in the exercise. It fires an empty shell casing with a live primer attached to it. When it goes off, there's a loud bang. Officer Rafferty cautions, "When you shoot at someone, you have to know why. Suspicion is not enough. And remember, the bulletproof vest does not work in this building."

He describes some of the physical effects of going through the Tactics House: rising blood pressure, racing heart, paralysis—being unable to pull the trigger for fear of killing an innocent person, becoming speechless or stammering. "One student panicked," Officer Rafferty says, "and yelled out, 'Fots are shired!' " The student officers of Company 32 laugh. He doesn't tell them that in the past some students have broken down and dashed outside crying. Or that a female recruit who recently stepped into an imbroglio there and was fired upon had a bowel movement in front of everybody. Cop legend has it that no person has ever gone through the House without getting "killed" at least once, except an FBI agent armed with a heat sensor device that detected the presence and location of human bodies.

"If someone jumps out and points a gun at you, that's dangerous. If it's a knife, perhaps you could use Mace.

"We hope that you retain some of the things you see in here in the back of your mind. They could save your life."

Officer Rafferty tells the students to pick a partner. He looks first at the company sergeant. Tomas Ramos looks around and asks, "Who wants to die with me?"

A number of the firearms instructors quietly drop out of sight. Ramos and his partner are told to stay there while the other students are led to a flight of wooden stairs. They climb up and find themselves on a platform where they can look down at the first floor, which has hallways, doors, and rooms, but no ceilings. It is dark, but they can see down.

Directly below is a hallway. At the beginning of the hallway is a closet. A few feet down is a faint light near the top of one of the walls. On the other side of the hallway are two doors. Both are closed. There is a lot of old furniture inside the first apartment—a chest, a couch, a chair, a table—and several guns.

The student officers gaze anxiously down from the platform, waiting for the action to begin. Suddenly Tomas Ramos and his partner are seen peering out from the end of the hallway below. They are tense, not knowing what to expect. The hallway is dim. Their beaming flashlights are held in one hand, drawn guns in the other. They advance cautiously down the hall, one step at a time. They work their way to the apartment. There are two doors. Ramos stands in front of one, the other officer a few feet away. They stand there for a few seconds waiting, thinking. In a flash the door bursts open and a hand reaches out. Bang! There is a loud cracking sound, and a flashlight drops. Ramos has been shot dead.

A call comes in from Central; a man with a gun has been reported to be in Apartment 1B at 9 Range Road. As two officers approach the apartment, a burly, disheveled man is leaving. The officers order him against the wall, and the woman officer begins a pat-down.

"What's the matter, honey?" the suspect drawls. "Not getting enough from your boyfriend?"

She ignores him, continuing her search.

"Oh, that feels good, baby," he says with an unpleasant smirk. "You're getting closer. Feel anything interesting yet?"

Around his waistband she touches a hard object. She reaches in and pulls out a revolver.

"You're under arrest!" she says.

"Oh, shit, that isn't what I wanted you to find. You got me. Just take it easy, I'll go quietly."

The officers step back, relieved to have found the weapon. Quick as lightning, the man reaches down to his ankle, pulls out another gun from his sock, and fires two shots at the officers point-blank.

Two officers walk down a corridor and knock on the apartment door at the end. As they face the door and wait for an answer, a gunman slinks out of a closet at the front of the hallway and takes aim. The cops are shot dead.

One male and one female officer stand in front of the apartment door, guns drawn. They are quiet, assessing the situation; they've already seen enough to know there are surprises in store. Another door opens and someone darts out toward them, his hands raised. One officer is startled and reacts too quickly. Her hasty shot kills an innocent person carrying a basketball.

A male and female officer stand at the end of the hall-way, flashlights in hand. The male officer opens the closet door. It is empty. Suddenly the hallway light goes off; it is pitch black except for the flashlight beams. Two men come out the far door. They see the officers' guns and rush back into the apartment.

"You two, get out here quickly!" shouts the female officer.

"Nothing doing. I'm calling the police!" comes a voice from inside.

As the two officers concentrate their attention on the apartment, two men appear at the entrance of the hallway.

They have plenty of time to aim; the cops are not aware of their presence.

Bang! Bang! The officers are dead.

Two cops are creeping slowly down the hallway when three men storm out of the apartment.

"It's about time you got here!" one shouts to the officers. "A guy with a gun just came in here and got away with a thousand bucks!"

The officers order the men against the wall and start to frisk them. Furtively, one puts his hand under his chin and whips out a tiny .25 automatic. He whirls around and pulls the trigger. Another cop down.

The call is for an emotionally disturbed person, or EDP, who may need to be taken away in an ambulance; it's not supposed to be a gun run. The two cops are making their way down the hallway when a man comes out of the apartment. He is very agitated. "There's a crazy man in the bedroom," he tells them. Inside there's a crash, as if a trash can has been thrown against the wall. Then a large man with a cloth draped over his head emerges. He weaves erratically, screaming, "You're going to die! We're all going to die!"

Another man follows him out of the apartment. "He's got a gun!" he shouts. The EDP lunges wildly and tosses a live grenade at the officers' feet. It explodes, killing them both.

Two officers respond to a report of a deranged person. A man comes to the door of the apartment, relief showing on his face at the officers' arrival. "My brother's gone nuts," he exclaims.

"What's he wearing?" one of the officers asks.

"A red shirt and jeans," the man answers. "He's in the apartment, but I'm not sure where."

There is a noise, and the officers' attention is drawn to a closet door several feet in front of them.

"He said he was going to kill me," the man continues. The officers draw their guns.

The noise in the closet grows louder. Suddenly the door bursts open and a young man in a red shirt comes toward the cops, screaming incoherently. An object is partially concealed in his hand. One officer quickly extends his hand and fires at him. As the man staggers, his hand opens, and a radio clatters to the floor.

Two cops approach the apartment; the door is unlocked, and they enter to find two men sitting on a couch; another stands nearby. One of the men on the couch points to the person standing. "Look out! He's got a gun!"

The two officers turn to the man, and the one sitting on the couch reaches under his leg. He draws forth a gun and shoots both officers.

The call is a burglary in progress, with a gun possible. Two officers enter the apartment. A man is holding a revolver on another up against the wall.

"Police! Don't move!" one of the officers says, pointing his gun at the man with the revolver.

"Wait, I'm a special guard, plainclothes," he responds. "I'm on the job."

"No, he's not!" the man against the wall yells out. "He's a drug dealer. I'm the guard. Help me!"

The officers don't know whom to believe. "Let me see your ID," one says to the man with the gun.

"Man, he's running a line on you," says the self-professed guard, holstering his gun. "Can't you see through this shit?"

167

"Watch him, he's tricky," the other warns.

As the man with the gun turns toward the cops, the other swiftly grabs him around the neck and plucks the gun from its holster. "Back off, or I'll shoot him," he orders the officers. Using the prisoner as a shield, he makes his way toward the apartment door. When he is almost there, he takes a quick shot at the female cop, killing her.

A few more gun runs follow. The final body count: fourteen student officers and two innocent people "dead." The recruits are stunned, but the point has been made; the simple act of walking down a hallway will never be the same. To enter a building and navigate its corridors can no longer be a routine stroll but a cautious, step-by-step journey through a maze of danger. Behind every apartment door may lie a homey living room, but it may also be a potential battlefield.

"I was sure I was going to get shot any second," Lissette Sierra-Solis says later. "When I went into the apartment, my heart was pounding as if it were for real."

"I was pissed because it was over before we even had a chance," says Andy Varga with a frown. "But that's the way these things go, I guess. My partner and I were both in the service, so we had some training to start with. We tried to figure out what tactics to use, but it all happened too fast. My heart was in my throat the whole time. I was glad when it was over."

Stefanie Hirschhorn has a slightly different reaction. "I had no idea what to expect, and I was worried about what my partner was going to do. I was nervous, but I wasn't feeling real fear because I've been in the middle of crime scenes before. I think we should have spent more time with it."

The underlying message of tactics training is that the recruits should avoid getting into confrontations in which rather than being in control, they are forced to react. They should not have to make what the firearms instructors call a "reflexive response." But sometimes such confrontations can't be avoided, and the recruits have to be able to handle them. Tactics training is designed to show them how.

Each of the scenarios has portrayed vividly at least one potentially disastrous mistake in tactics, and the instructors now examine them one by one. The recruits, all too aware that their lives may one day depend upon their ability to absorb and internalize this information, are intensely focused on their instructors' words.

"On a gun run," the first instructor begins, "before you take a single step into the building, stop and put together a strategy with your partner. Set up hand signals so you don't have to talk when you're inside. Know exactly what each one of you is going to do. You're going to get plenty of surprises from the perp; you don't want to have to worry about your partner doing something unexpected as well. Once you're inside, you should move like a team. Go down the hallway facing in opposite directions, or back to back, so you can see what's going on behind you. Keep your eye on all the entrances and exits.

"If you have to go down a dark hallway alone, move from side to side and swing your flashlight back and forth. It'll make it look like there's more than one of you, and it will keep the steady beam from being used as a target. If you need to take cover all of a sudden, you can toss the flashlight away from you; that'll buy you a few seconds.

"When you get to the apartment door, check the hinges so you know which way the door's going to open. If you're with a partner, don't talk; signal him you're going to open the door with a nod. Never stand directly in front of the door. If there's a guy inside with a gun, he can shoot through it and hit— maybe kill—you.

"Once you're inside the apartment and you've checked the closets, keep the doors open. You can use a closet for cover quickly if you need to."

The second instructor takes over. "If you're actually faced

with a man with a gun, forget about his eyes. Never lose sight of the palms of his hands. If someone has a hat or a wig on, knock it off. There could be a gun underneath.

"Often you shouldn't even go into an apartment to begin with if you know there's a perp with a gun inside. You don't have to play Superman; your job is to 'isolate and contain.' Call for backups, especially if you've got an irrational EDP. If somebody comes at you with a grenade, get the hell out of there; never assume it's a dud."

"When you're frisking a perp," the first instructor continues, "just because you find a gun doesn't mean there isn't another one, or two, or three, or a knife, or a razor blade. Keep looking. If you find another gun, don't stop. Don't take your hands off him until you've covered every inch of the guy's body."

"Never put a perp against a wall with a hole in it," the second instructor adds. "He could have stashed a gun there. And don't put a perp up against glass. Can any of you guess why?" One recruit responds swiftly: "He'll be able to see reflections, and you don't want him to know what you're doing, exactly where you are."

The instructor nods. "Good," he says. "That's the way you have to think. You've got to keep the perp off balance. You need every bit of advantage you can get."

"What was the big mistake the cops made in the scenario with the fake guard?" the first instructor asks the recruits. There is a silence as the students run through the scene in their minds. One remembers the sequence of events. "They let him holster his gun so he could get out his ID, and the other guy was able to grab it," he suggests.

"You got it. If they weren't sure he was a cop, they should have made him put the gun down on the floor and put his foot on it. Never let a gun out of your sight."

The second instructor says, "If things get out of hand and a hostage situation develops, as it did here, keep your radio on.

Central will be listening, and you can keep them informed without being obvious about it. Say things like, 'Don't shoot that cop! We'll get out of 1B. We'll leave 9 Range Road.' And then do it. Call in the Emergency Service Unit. They have dogs, grenades, helicopters, electronic stun devices, lights, sound—everything that's needed. You aren't equipped to handle it. Besides, ESU looks to the perp like a S.W.A.T. team, so they have a psychological edge."

The standard "Police, don't move!" challenge, the instructor explains, was developed in response to an incident in the 1960s in which two police officers responded to a burglary at an off-duty cop's house. The officers saw a man at the top of the stairs with a gun in his hand. "Freeze!" they shouted. The man turned toward the voice, pointing the gun at the cops, and they shot him. As he fell down the stairs, his shield fell out of his hand. "Since that challenge was incorporated into the training program in 1975," the instructor says, emphasizing each word to the recruits, "there has not been one deadly confrontation between officers."

Every so often a cop shoots someone who turns out to be unarmed. In January 1990, for example, a twenty-five-year-old NYPD cop responded to a call of a dispute involving men with guns in front of a building. She took a teenager into custody, but he made a sudden unexpected motion, and she shot him in the chest. Days later another unarmed youth in Brooklyn was shot and killed by a cop when the boy reached into his jacket as the officer was arresting him. As a result of these incidents, a commission was convened to determine if department tactics could be improved or deadly force guidelines modified to decrease the chance of further occurrences.

Sometimes, too, a radio report can be misleading. "Some idiot civilians call in and say that a cop has been hurt, or that shots have been fired, or that they saw a man with a gun, because they want the cops to respond faster," the instructor

171

says with disgust. "So you'll get all pumped up for what you think is going to be a dangerous gun run and then have to suck adrenaline when it turns out to have been a false alarm.

"Think before you act. If things become confusing, if you don't know what's happening, get the hell out of there. Rethink the situation and regroup."

And most important of all: "Never, never let yourself get complacent. There are no routine jobs. If you start to get cocky, you're going to forget the tactics, and the first time you forget is the time you'll get hurt. I guarantee it."

At this point the students' actual shooting experience has been limited to stationary targets. It is now time to practice in shootouts with moving adversaries. In the afternoon of the second day of tactics, Company 32 goes to Eddy Range for this training.

Nicholas Giacobbe, a firearms instructor, addresses the students sitting on the bleachers.

"I'm going to start off with a scenario. It's August. You've graduated and are assigned to a Field Training Unit out of the Bronx, the Four-four Precinct. You're on a day tour, eight A.M. to four P.M. You have a partner and you're patrolling a particular area of the precinct. On the radio you get a 10-50, a large disorderly group, in Claremont Park. Central gives you the cross streets. You ask if they have any descriptions, and Central says negative. You go to the park and see a large group of people clustered around. There is some kind of dispute over a drug deal. You hear a few bangs, and pandemonium sets in. What do you do?"

"Take cover," one student responds.

"What physical properties must cover have?"

"It must be solid. Have mass. It's something that'll deflect or absorb rounds. You use cover to protect yourself from injury or death," comes another response.

Officer Giacobbe warns against the "stand and fight" syndrome. That is the response of many new police officers. They

172

assume the combat position in the open instead of seeking cover, greatly lessening their chances of surviving an armed confrontation. "Cover also gives a police officer time to evaluate the situation, to map out a game plan." The added time also helps the cop get used to the rapid physiological changes of adrenaline released when he is in danger.

"Now, what's the most common example of cover on the street?"

"A car," says a student, and the discussion segues into where it's best to take cover (in the front behind the engine) and what to beware of (glass, gas tanks, and the space between tires; a traveling round can go underneath, hug the surface, and hit a person standing on the other side).

Previously, the students learned to distinguish between cover and concealment, which is anything that can hide one's physical presence but through which bullets can strike. Officer Giacobbe discusses what, in and around the home, may be used as cover or concealment. Cover may be taken behind a refrigerator, television, dishwasher, couch, or any other solid piece of furniture. Concealment is offered by drapes, tall grass, and hedges.

"A telephone pole is an excellent cover," says the instructor. "It will deflect almost any round you'd encounter."

Officer Giacobbe lists the calibers of guns that are commonly used by street-level criminals: .22, .25, .32, .38. Why? The guns are small, compact, and hence easily hidden in a pocket for, say, a grocery stickup. They can be carried anywhere, and ammunition is cheap and easy to get.

Eddy Range is the moving-target range. Here students have fifty-round "gunfights" with an adversary, a silhouette target that moves one and a half miles per hour. "Every time you see that target," says Officer Giacobbe, "you shoot." The targets are mounted on metal rods or hinges; each target moves between a pile of tires. Several feet in front of each target are items of cover: a car, a telephone pole, a mailbox, another

173

telephone pole, a fire hydrant, a third telephone pole, a trash can, and a brick wall.

Officer Giacobbe reviews the combat kneeling position:

"Take a step back with your right leg. Kneel down on your right knee, but don't sit on the heel of the right leg.

"Two-hand combat grip on the gun.

"Keep your back straight, your arms extended. Never lean the gun down or against the item of cover. The first round could hit the cover, deflect, and cause an injury to you.

"Protect the vital areas of your body—the T-zone—your brain and chest. And *always* know where your adversary is."

Officer Giacobbe then stresses the nature of the exercise the students will perform shortly; this *is* combat. Eddy Range was prepared for this, to help recruits build up their speed and accuracy. On the street, he says, it's up to the cop to decide how many rounds to fire. "Use only enough force to stop that person from using deadly physical force on you."

Officer Giacobbe warns the students not to drop their speed loaders in front of them in a combat situation. Otherwise, their adversary might be able to determine how many rounds they have left. "Keep your gun pointed down when speed-loading. Now, I want you to get your reloading speed down to three seconds, because the average gunfight is less than five seconds."

He gestures at the targets. "The second you see a target," he repeats, "shoot back. That's a man shooting at you."

"Here, you know you're just firing at a piece of paper," Officer Giacobbe continues. "We can't instill real fear into you. But we try to simulate the conditions and make it as realistic as possible to try to get you a little nervous, because that's going to happen in a gunfight, only more so. This will give you a taste of what it's like out there."

The students, eight at a time, line up behind their cover on the range. On the whistle, the targets begin moving—right to left, left to right, to and fro in jerky movements, out behind their cover, then retreating immediately back. There is a barrage of gunfire. At the end of the exercise the students collect their targets and add up their scores.

After the exercise, Officer William Stagnitta gives a demonstration of other types of guns they may encounter on the street and explains why the NYPD uses a .38 Special revolver as its weapon when it could use a weapon with more knockdown power.

A myth: A weapon of heavy-duty caliber has the capacity to knock someone back. "The entire concept of knockdown power is a fairy tale," he says, "but your mind's response to being shot, or even thinking you're being shot, can make you respond by moving back as if the bullet has pushed you." The students look dubious.

"Look, it's like if your head is under a car hood and someone blasts the horn, your head's going to jerk back and hit the raised hood, even though there's no physical force behind the horn. Remember when President Reagan was shot? He didn't even flinch, right? Well, it wasn't because he was brave, it was because he hadn't seen the sniper, hadn't heard the gunshot. His mind didn't have a chance to prepare his body to be hit."

The pros and cons of using automatics as opposed to revolvers are covered. Automatics, which have only one chamber, are only as good as the ammunition in them; if the bullet in the chamber does not fire, the chamber will jam and have to be cleared for the gun to fire again. Revolvers have six chambers, so if there is a bad round, the cylinder will spin to another chamber and a fresh round. Automatics have more moving parts, so there's more of a chance of breakdown. True, automatics have more firepower—the number of rounds that can be fired before reloading. The average 9mm gun carries sixteen rounds in its magazine, ten more than the six rounds of a revolver. But, says Officer Stagnitta, only two or three shots are fired in a typical gunfight by a New York City cop. For all the drawbacks of the 9mm gun, why do cops need sixteen rounds?

Another hurdle to accurate street shooting is fatigue. An officer may be involved in a gunfight after chasing the perp, and being winded may affect his accuracy. On the third and last day of tactics, the students go to Boy Range. They line up at their stations in front of their targets. The tower caller gives the signal, and the exertion course begins.

"Draw your service revolver and combat-load six rounds— like your life depends on it.

"Take your finger off the trigger and safely holster. Take off your safety equipment; hold your nightstick in your left hand.

"Now, jog forward to the three-foot line."

Company 32 then jogs around the perimeter of the range, with nightsticks in their left hands and their right hands on their holstered guns. They run two laps to the seven-yard line, and then continue jogging in place at their stations. This is followed by a ten-second sprint in place, then five push-ups. Next, they put their safety equipment on and draw their service revolvers.

"Six rounds, two hands supported, five seconds.

"Combat-unload, reload. Take off your safety equipment. Pick up your nightstick.

"Jog in place.

"Now jog to the three-foot line.

"One left-face.

"Do a one-lap sprint. Run as quickly as you can." The students race, again holding their nightsticks in the left hand with the other hand over their guns.

"Run like you mean it!"

The students return to their stations and jog in place.

On the next whistle the students jog heavily in place as if, they are told, they are running up a flight of stairs. They do a half about-face and five push-ups, yelling out the number each time.

They put on their safety equipment and, on the whistle, fire six rounds, unsupported, in eight seconds. Then they combat-unload and reload manually with rounds in the pocket, in fifteen seconds.

Over the next several minutes the recruits alternate jogging and sprinting around the range, and doing push-ups and stationary sprints at various firing stations before shooting. They run with their nightsticks and jog in place with their hands over their guns. The tower caller eggs them on, saying, "You're chasing the perp up the stairs," as they're sprinting, and, "We're wrestling with him at the top of the stairs," as they're doing push-ups. There is more shooting, with combat unloading and reloading, within set time intervals. The students are out of breath when a long whistle finally brings the test to conclusion.

While the exertion test is grueling, its purpose is to show the students they can shoot just as well when they are physically stressed. It is a qualifying test, and they need thirty-seven out of fifty points to pass. All do pass. When they finish, the tower caller says, "Shooters, give yourself a hand. You looked good."

The last shooting exercise of tactics training is the multiple-target exercise. A cop responding to an armed felony is likely to encounter two or more persons with weapons. Tactically, he should have called for backups, but often a cop will happen on a crime in commission and find himself in a life-and-death situation. Several feet away he is being fired upon by one man, then by a different perp from another direction; and perhaps by accomplices from still other directions—shots discharged by criminals who'd rather be killed than face a stiff prison sentence. The officer must take cover yet remain calm enough to pivot gracefully while shooting rapidly and accurately.

At 12:30 P.M., Company 32 assembles again in Boy Range. The scenario: Each student is having a gunfight with two perps, one seven yards in front, the other fifteen yards to the left. They are to shoot six rounds in a sequence of two, three, and one. It is their choice as to which target gets the first shot.

The students have fifty rounds in their pockets. They need to score at least thirty-seven out of fifty. The most they can score with any one target is twenty-five. Following the sequence is imperative, or they will fail.

The first group comes to the firing line. They draw their guns and come to stand-and-ready. Again they listen to the sequence: two rounds into the first target, pivot, fire three rounds into the other target, pivot back, and fire one round into the first target again. This is a six-round exercise in eight seconds, two hands supported.

This is repeated. Then they combat-unload, reload six from the pocket, and shoot six rounds unsupported in the same sequence in ten seconds. Then they combat-unload and reload six manually.

"Six rounds, two hands supported, eight seconds.

"Combat-unload, reload six.

"Six rounds, two hands supported, eight seconds.

"Combat-unload, reload six."

The orders come from the tower at a blistering pace, and, before they know it, the recruits have finished the test.

"Combat-unload and present," the students hear, and finally lock their guns in their holsters. They end the day, a mild winter afternoon, cleaning their guns at a group of outdoor tables by the mess hall. The students seem to have a love affair with the range, but they won't return again until they have graduated from the academy and have served as professional police officers out on patrol.

The recruits seem annoyed that they are at the firearms range for only a brief time. One student says, "We need this, we need more of this. We're at the academy for more than five months and we're here for only eight days. It's not enough. We want more—three weeks."

"We can always read up on Law, Police Science, and Social Science," says another recruit. "But this is life." Indeed, of the thirteen New York City police officers who died in the line of duty from 1986 through 1988, ten were shot to death.

Once again the experience at the firearms range has deepened the recruits' sense of what being a cop is about. Writing fake summonses and reports at the academy has served to continue the illusion for some that the job is basically harmless at the same time it bestows power upon them. But when the instructors in the Tactics House fired at the recruits and shouted "You're dead, pal, you're dead," the young men and women felt a strange and rude awakening.

This latest excursion to the range has also changed the recruits' perception of the environment. Do they still see fire hydrants, mailboxes, telephone poles, and cars as nothing more than objects? No. Hopefully they now see them as places of concealment or cover. Are doors just doors, or are they screens behind which perps can hide as they spray the unwary cop with bullets? Indeed, any object can be used as either a weapon or a cover, the recruits now know, and depending on how astute observers they are, this knowledge and awareness may one day save their lives.

——12——
DRIVER TRAINING

At 4:30 A.M. on the last day of May, Andy Varga awakes feeling a little more cheerful than usual. Today is the first day of driver training for Company 20, and he will have a brief respite from the academy. Just a few weeks earlier he passed the second trimester exam; sometimes, he thinks, his entire life seems to be monopolized by studying. Graduation is in six weeks, but it might just as well be an eternity away. He picks up Henry Ramirez down the block and stops to buy breakfast at a nearby restaurant; by 5:15 the two are on their way to Floyd Bennett Field in Brooklyn, the site of the NYPD driver training course.

The first impression Andy has of the field is its great expanse. Turning to the training facility, he sees a huge stretch of concrete, formerly one of the runways when the field served as an airport.

Andy and Henry park in a little field adjacent to the driver training building and parking lot. A few other recruits are there, waiting inside their cars. All have New York State driver's licenses; that was a requirement to enter the academy. Soon the area is filled with cars, and by 6:30 A.M. the company starts heading to the front of the building. They line up in three squads, with Andy in front. Minutes later, Officer Thomas Gambino, who will be the company's classroom instructor for the four-day driver training course, comes out to conduct muster.

At seven A.M., Company 20 is seated in a classroom in the one-story driver training facility. It is a large room with several rows of chairs and yellow walls. At the front is a lectern with the NYPD insignia, a television monitor, a blackboard, and two signs: CONTROL THE RESPONSE! DON'T LET THE RESPONSE PUT YOU OUT OF CONTROL and BE A PROFESSIONAL DRIVER.

Andy realizes the importance of the training. Like other civilian drivers, he's had his share of close calls and has flirted with danger more often than he would like to admit. But driving as a cop is something different. In responding to an accident or an explosion or a family dispute, it is vital that a cop get to the scene as quickly as possible. What about the worst scenario, a 10-13 call over the radio that says a cop is shot? Maybe it's his buddy. There's much to be aware of in responding: traffic, pedestrians, intersections, stop signs, red lights. Driving on emergencies is part of the daily routine of being a cop in New York City, where traffic is heavy from morning rush hour to late evening. And no response should ever be considered routine. It's always dangerous. Andy is grimly aware that his actions as a driver can not only save lives, but take them too.

A cop must develop the skills needed to drive a patrol car safely and efficiently to calls. Radio car accidents delay responses and create a poor public image of the police. And though when a cop is shot the media glamorize it, little is ever heard when a cop has a car accident. Shortly after Officer Steven McDonald was shot in Central Park in July 1986 and paralyzed from the neck down, Albert Cortez, another NYPD police officer, responded to an emergency distress call. His car struck a railroad support beam, and he, too, sustained injuries

181

that made him a quadriplegic. McDonald gained national attention, but the other officer received no publicity other than a blurb of newsprint the day after the accident. Cops have car accidents on patrol much more frequently than they use their guns or have guns used against them. There is an average of eight radio motor patrol car (or RMP) accidents a day in New York City; one of these is bad enough to total the vehicle.

Thomas Gambino, a young cop with curly brown hair and wire-rimmed glasses, addresses the class. He speaks with the cognizance and wit of a lawyer and does, in fact, attend law school. "As police officers," warns Officer Gambino, "you shouldn't think you have carte blanche on the roads off duty. New Jersey is notorious for summonsing our cops." More important, of course, is safety. A cop on duty wants to get to the scene of a call quickly. But what happens if he has an accident and doesn't get there at all? Speed depends on the weather and other conditions. The cop may have to travel more slowly than he wishes.

The consequences of a car accident while on patrol can be dire. Cops may be held criminally liable for an accident, even on an emergency response. Was the officer to blame? There may be departmental discipline, trial, termination, or even arrest. "You're not a civilian," says Officer Gambino. "You may lose vacation days, walk a footpost, never drive an RMP again. You may have to come back for retraining. The job will indemnify you for negligence but not recklessness; sometimes there's a fine line between the two."

In New York City there are traffic jams everywhere. When a cop has to rush to a job, he has to know where the bottlenecks are so he can avoid them. If he has to go through them, it's best to go right through the middle. "Ten miles per hour is better than nothing at all," says Officer Gambino.

After lunch, Company 20 is assembled for muster on the blacktop. The temperature has climbed to ninety degrees, but all the RMPs are air-conditioned. Now the driving begins.

Everyone must wear a seat belt, including passengers in the back. Gambino also recommends wearing seat belts on regular patrol.

The company is split in two. One group drives a basic proficiency course while the instructor critiques their overall coordination, acceleration, braking, steering ability, control, fender judgment, and reverse maneuvering at low speeds. The other half goes on the street for off-site training. With an instructor in the car, the recruits take turns driving through the community at routine patrol speed. They are told what to look out for to be a good defensive driver and the pitfalls of driving an RMP in New York City. The instructors observe and comment on their driving skills.

Andy Varga and one other recruit drive through the local neighborhood of Mill Basin, where their driving skills are evaluated. In three days they'll be given a road test exercise similar to a New York State licensing road test to determine whether they can operate a vehicle to the standards of the NYPD.

On the second day of classroom instruction Officer Gambino covers definitions of various terms—friction, acceleration, velocity, centrifugal force, inertia, weight transfer—so that the recruits can learn how to control the car more adroitly, especially at high speed, in bad weather, and in other difficult driving situations.

They also must learn how to maintain and inspect their vehicles; patrol cops are responsible for checking the revolving turret lights, headlights, brake lights, mirrors, windshields, and side windows. They must look at the body for dents, underneath the car for oil leaks; check the oil and other fluids, and check fan belt, hoses, and air-conditioning. Problems get reported to the NYPD's own mechanics and service stations; repairs take about a week.

An officer should take pride in the appearance of the RMP he drives, says Officer Gambino. This is not only because he has a professional image to uphold, but because the car is, so to speak, his office for eight hours a day. Officers should search for contraband under the back and front seats, on the floors, in the glove compartment, in ashtrays, in the visors. The back seat is the most common area in which contraband is hidden. Caution is essential; a cop could get stuck by a junkie's needle or a perp's knife. Perps may drop weapons not discovered in a frisk somewhere in the back seat. "Some people don't like us," Officer Gambino says, telling them about a cop who once pulled down the sun visor of his RMP and was splashed in the face with acid.

At one P.M. on the second day of driver training, Andy Varga and fellow recruit David Kralick are in an RMP with Officer Nelson Lozano. They drive to Mill Basin again for practice in driving an RMP in a community. They execute U-turns, parallel parks, and other maneuvers. During this mock patrol through the streets, Officer Lozano talks about observations that should trigger a cop's suspicion: a house's open window on a cold winter day, a person loitering suspiciously in a backyard or alleyway, any obvious sign of forced entry. After a cop works in an area for a certain length of time, Lozano says, he or she develops a sixth sense about what's normal and what's not.

While Andy is driving, a woman approaches the RMP and points to an abandoned car near her house. It's been there for months, and she wants it removed. Officer Lozano asks her if she called any authorities when she first noticed it. She hadn't. "I must be honest," she says. "When I do call for things, I get very bad results." Officer Lozano refers her to the 63rd Precinct and tells her they will notify the city agency responsible for towing it.

The New York State Vehicle and Traffic Law states that police must obey traffic regulations just as civilians do if not in an emergency situation. If a violation is committed and is witnessed by a patrol supervisor or someone in a management-level position, there may be a reprimand, a loss of vacation days, or assignment to a footpost. Civilians love to report traffic violations by cops, Gambino remarks dryly. Fire and Emergency Medical Service vehicles must use lights and sirens when responding to calls and can be summonsed if they don't. In responding to an emergency situation, a police vehicle may exercise certain privileges—ignoring parking rules, speed limits, red lights, stop signs, and one-way streets after exercising due caution. On an emergency, for example, a cop may park by a fire hydrant. However, if the emergency is a fire, Officer Gambino says, the Fire Department will put a hose through the RMP if they have to. "Your car will look like an aquarium by the time they're through."

When responding to an emergency call, Officer Gambino warns, the officers may get psyched up. They will forget about their driving and be thinking about what will happen in a few minutes when they are confronting a man with a gun. "You'll be excited, your adrenaline will be pumping, your heart racing, your palms sweating. You'll have tunnel vision, and see only in front of you. Then when you get there, you'll find it's a 90-X, unfounded. You'll have to calm down a bit." Officer Gambino says in his first pursuit, he "lost it." He knew the streets like the back of his hand, but suddenly he drew a blank.

Vehicle pursuits are much different in reality from how they look on television, Officer Gambino points out. When engaging in a pursuit, there are various factors to consider: the nature of the pursuit—was a cop shot, or did a civilian only run a red light?—the time of day, weather, road, location, your familiarity with the area. Most pursuits are terminated on the orders of patrol supervisors and suspects get away. "This may be frustrating," says Officer Gambino, "but you'll still get paid on Thursday."

Of the various exercises the recruits will be tested on, the one that generates the most anxiety for the student officers is the Emergency Vehicle Operators Course (EVOC). Designed in its present form by Detective Edward Unz, planning and training officer of the Driver Training Unit, and retired Sergeant William Feeley, EVOC consists of a series of interconnected "stations," or exercises, that simulate different driving conditions and test different driving skills, using various patterns of plastic cones laid out on the roadway.

The course is demonstrated by the instructors. With two or three recruits buckled up in each RMP, they speed through in rapid succession from the starting line. They traverse the course at top speed, making sharp turns and sudden stops while the passengers hold on for dear life, with nary a cone so much as scratched. After a roller-coaster ride to demonstrate these maneuvers (and their own expertise, perhaps), the instructors have a ho-hum, nonchalant look about them that underscores their final message: "And that's all there is to it."

It is the last day of driver training. After two run-throughs in which Andy launches several cones into frenzied aerial flights, he faces the EVOC test. His mission: to drive his car through the course in two minutes and five seconds or less, knocking down as few cones as possible. Each cone toppled adds three seconds to his final time, and thirteen cones is an automatic failure. If he doesn't pass, he'll be retrained and retested. If he does not ultimately succeed, he will not be permitted to drive an RMP in New York City. That, he thinks, would be really embarrassing.

Andy's radio car is purring at the starting line. Sitting next to him is Officer Charles Gittens, who will time him through the circuit. In case of an emergency, there is a brake on the floor in front of Gittens. Andy is nervous. He is confident he can pass, but he hasn't done nearly as well as he expected during the practice runs. His frustration compounds his anxiety. Waiting for the radio car in front to get halfway through the course before signaling Andy, Officer Gittens sits silently, eyes fixed ahead. Andy's fellow recruits are stationed around the course in safety zones to pick up and replace dislodged cones. They are all standing patiently, staring at his car. Soon the RMP ahead is far in the distance, and Officer Gittens tells Andy to get ready.

Go! Andy presses the accelerator and heads straight toward the single-cone serpentine course, a line of ten cones placed fifty feet apart that simulates driving through normal traffic and moving around fixed objects. But wait—Officer Gittens pulls a surprise. He turns on the turret lights and siren. Andy now feels as though he is really rushing to an emergency, perhaps a 10-13. As he starts the run, his heart is racing, and he has tunnel vision—just like Gambino said. He winds to the left and right, maintaining a steady (required) speed between twenty and thirty miles per hour and avoiding the brake pedal (also required). Andy continues into the double-cone serpentine, six pairs of cones arranged in alternating parallel rows like weaving through heavy traffic and around double-parked cars during an emergency response. He emerges unscathed.

So far so good. He drives straight ahead, following a lane that turns left, then right, which brings the car to the starting point of the cornering exercise. Time is of the essence, and here Andy accelerates, heading into the corner like a bull charging a matador. Accelerating out of the turn, all cones intact, he heads straight up the circuit and turns left, straight into the two most difficult exercises of the course.

The two exercises occupy the complete length of the runway, and required speeds are a factor in entering each. The first, the evasive maneuver station, simulates a radio car encountering an obstruction or having to swerve out of the way of a pedestrian darting into the street. It demonstrates the evasive capacity of a vehicle without relying simply on braking in an emergency. Andy accelerates to thirty miles per hour and enters the cone chute. Directly in front is a row of cones blocking Andy from continuing straight on. To avoid hitting them, he'll have to turn into the right or left cone chute just before the obstruction. The entry chute is short, but Officer Gittens is not giving a signal as to which way to turn. The obstruction grows closer and still no word. Andy feels like he'll be on top of the cones in a second, and a crash is imminent. Gittens shouts, "Right!" Andy shifts his body slightly in that direction, but sees Gittens simultaneously thrust his hand to the left and point in that direction. Andy is confused for a fleeting moment. The car veers slightly off course, and a cone goes sailing. After turning right, Andy travels several yards, then makes a sharp left without braking, following the lane as it curves to the left again and empties out at the center. Emerging from this, Andy funnels into another serpentine drill, which presents no problems.

Now Andy floors the accelerator and enters the longest stretch of the course. The braking exercise is in the distance. Several seconds later, his speed is up to fifty miles per hour, the legal limit in New York City. About two-thirds of the way down the stretch, Officer Gittens tells Andy to take his foot off the gas. The car rolls into the last station at only a slightly slower speed. The braking exercise simulates a near-collision: traveling in a two-lane roadway when the car in front suddenly stops, forcing the driver to change lanes. In the exercise, the driver enters a chute that turns sharply to the left. Heading into the chute at high speed, he must brake to negotiate the turn, but may do so only on the instructor's signal. At what again seems like the last second, Officer Gittens finally signals and Andy pumps it hard for a second. He is careful not to lock his wheels as he turns left sharply or he'll hit an obstruction. As Andy brakes and turns, the car skids with a screech and the rear kicks up a cone.

Andy navigates the vehicle through several additional sharp turns and finally comes to a stop at the end of the station. His time is 1:44. With six seconds in penalties for the two cones overturned, his time is raised to 1:50. Andy did well, and he is now more aware of his own limitations and capabilities. He has a better understanding of what it's like to be on an emergency operation. Of the twenty-four recruits in Company 20, five fail the EVOC test, more than twenty percent. Company 20's failure rate is higher than that of the entire class, about fifteen percent.

After experiencing the EVOC course, normal street driving seems elementary. Perhaps other recruits, like Andy, now imagine rushing off from wherever they are in traffic to an emergency, safely maneuvering around other vehicles and pedestrians, and through intersections on the busy streets of New York.

———13———
INTEGRITY WORKSHOP

As the recruits have already seen, wearing a uniform is a sword that cuts both ways. In some members of the public, it inspires respect and cooperation; for others, it is like a red flag to a bull, causing abuse and contempt to be heaped on the shoulders of the wearer. Whether the reaction is positive or negative, however, there is always scrutiny, and even the rawest recruit soon feels that because he is a cop, in uniform or not, every action, every move is being observed by a group quick to judge and tough to please—the public he or she is serving every day.

The law and the police department also hold police officers to very high standards. What is acceptable behavior by citizens may be unlawful or improper for cops. During Christmastime, for example, some people look forward to receiving gifts from business acquaintances. But a merchant pleased with the attention and service of a neighborhood cop may not legally give anything to the officer. If he merely *offers* a present, he is guilty of giving unlawful gratuities, a misdemeanor; likewise, if an officer accepts or solicits any free gift or service, he would be guilty of receiving unlawful gratuities, a misdemeanor.

Probity is of the highest concern to the NYPD, and certain conduct automatically results in suspension or termination. To avoid even the temptation of misconduct or appearance of wrongdoing, the department discourages or forbids certain actions off duty and on duty. Cops may not work in a bar, for example, nor as locksmiths within the city limits. And an investigation will always follow the discharge of a weapon, any civilian complaint, and all allegations of corruption.

Throughout the term at the academy, integrity is constantly drilled into the students' minds. A lesson on police ethics in the *Social Science Student Guide* includes the text of the New York City Police Department Code of Professional Conduct, and one evening is devoted exclusively to the theme of proper police conduct. Coming at the end of June, two short weeks before the recruits hit the streets and after the Internal Affairs presentations, the Integrity Workshop emphasizes the great weight of responsibility put on their shoulders—to avoid impropriety and temptation, to keep the rights of citizens foremost in their minds, and to enforce the law fairly and with humanity.

The Integrity Workshop is divided into three parts, one for each of the academic subjects. It begins with Social Science role plays, with the instructors playing all the characters in the first skit; recruits play the uniformed cops in the second.

The scene is a bar, the Dirty Bird, a cozy little tavern with the usual trappings of a licensed premise—tables and chairs, a jukebox, neon beer signs. Behind the counter stands a rugged man, working quietly, while waiting for the first customer. A young man enters, orders a beer, and inserts a coin in the jukebox. He returns to his seat and engages in small talk with the bartender, who is now sitting back and smoking. He is asking whether the Dirty Bird gets much business from the precinct cops when another man walks in and orders a drink. A few minutes

191

later an attractive young woman enters and also orders a drink at the bar. The first customer attempts conversation with the woman, but she rebuffs him.

"What's the matter?" he asks mockingly. "Am I going to bite? A little conversation won't hurt."

"I'm just not in the mood to talk. Can't a woman go to a bar and just sit?"

The man asks if she has a boyfriend or husband. She claims she does, and that he will be arriving shortly.

"Is he a bigshot? A doctor? A lawyer?"

Now the other customer, seeing the woman is quite annoyed by the man's persistence, tells him to lay off. An argument ensues, and when it looks like it's about to escalate into a physical encounter, the second customer whips out a police shield.

"Butt out!" the woman tells the cop, and the obstreperous man challenges him too. "So what are you going to arrest me for? Trying to talk? You wanted to be a big hero, right? It didn't work. She's not impressed."

"Can't a woman just come to have a drink without talking?" she repeats.

"Yeah, without cops," says the man. "So where were we?"

"He's a better man than you are."

The man grumbles something about cops trying to prove they're macho and showing up other men.

"So where's your boyfriend?" the man asks the woman again.

"He'll be here!" she snaps, turning her back.

The action is cut, and the players justify their actions. The man who interceded says he became involved because this is his "usual watering hole," and he didn't want to see anything happen there. The first man says he's drunk and a wiseguy, but that the off-duty officer had no right to intervene. The woman says she reproved the officer because she thought she was doing all right on her own and didn't want the situation to flare up.

The moderator notes that if the situation did eventually result in an off-duty arrest, the duty captain would be called down. He'd ask the off-duty officer questions. Was he drinking? How much? Why did he get involved? As far as liability is concerned, would the department back up the off-duty officer? Probably not, says the moderator. An officer who flaunts his shield in such situations risks embarrassing himself and the department. Unless there's a valid arrest to be made, some people will show no respect for the shield and words of an off-duty cop. What the off-duty cop should have done, says the moderator, was leave the bar.

The scenario continues.

> A third civilian walks into the bar, orders a beer, and says he's buying for everyone. "Are you this woman's boyfriend?" asks the first man.
>
> "Maybe, maybe not," the new customer answers, eyeing the woman.
>
> Everybody settles down with the new round of drinks when the last and first men to arrive suddenly pull out a shotgun and a pistol. The first man says, "We've got a cop here." The officer and the bartender are handcuffed and robbed, and there's an even greater surprise when the perps leave with their accomplice—the woman.
>
> "Why the fuck didn't you do anything?" the irate bartender asks the off-duty officer.
>
> "It's your bar. I just came in here to drink."
>
> "Thanks a lot, pal. I'll remember this."

The lesson to be learned from this scenario, says the moderator, is "to keep your mouth shut and don't advertise you're a cop when you're off duty. Don't show your gun and shield."

Two plainclothes anticrime officers bring a prisoner into the 21st Precinct station house. As they lead him past a desk officer, they warn him, "Keep your mouth shut. Just keep on walking." In the interrogation room, the rear-cuffed prisoner kicks a chair over and spews out obscenities. In turn, the cops hit him in the groin.

"I'll get your fucking shield and your gun!" he moans.

More profanities follow, and the cops hit him again. The prisoner calls out to the commanding officer for help as another prisoner is brought in by two uniformed cops. The desk officer yells, "Keep it down in there."

A minute later, one of the uniformed officers comes out of the interrogation room to complain to the desk officer that the anticrime cops are "roughing up" their prisoner. "Oh, yeah?" the sergeant replies. "Here's a dollar. Go get me a cup of coffee."

Back in the interrogation room the action continues. "Don't they teach you this shit in the academy?" asks one of the plainclothes officers incredulously of his uniformed colleague.

He looks at the prisoner and shouts, "What's the matter with you? Don't you learn?" Then he takes off the cuffs to fingerprint him. The prisoner responds that he has phone calls to make and calls out again to the C.O.

A uniformed officer now protects the prisoner from the plainclothes cops. They squabble. "You're lucky you haven't lost your jobs!" the uniform yells at the plain-clothes cops. Then they tell him that the suspect has been brought in for child molestation.

The moderator asks various participants in the skit how they felt. A uniformed officer, played by a recruit, says it was "tough." The desk officer gets a big hand. "I know what's going on," he says, nodding his head, "believe me. But I showed what it's like not to get involved." The two anticrime officers complain that the prisoner "messed up a five-year-old kid." The moderator asks if there are "people out there who deserve a beating," and the class roars back, "Yes!" Then the moderator guarantees that in the first year out, at least one or two recruits will find themselves in the unenviable situation just played out, faced with the dilemma of whether they should "rat" on a fellow officer.

How should an officer handle this? The officer should warn the belligerent officer to stop, or he'll request the desk officer to call IAD. Since he is accountable for the actions of the other officers he works with, a cop should say up front where he stands. "You're stuck, so you have to take the right action," says the moderator succinctly.

Officer Richard Francis, a Social Science instructor, holds up a sign titled OFF-DUTY OPTIONS. Underneath are listed four words, each followed by a question mark:

Arrest?
Mediate?
Observe?
Leave?

The instructor recommends not getting involved off duty. The choice is the individual's, but observing or leaving seems to be the most judicious.

The department limits police officers in exercising certain police authority off duty. The NYPD discourages off-duty cops from using their authority to settle disputes between family, neighbors, and friends; making car stops; becoming involved in traffic altercations; arresting civilians if the cop is the complainant; using a weapon unless absolutely necessary; using physical force unless it can be justified.

The Police Science portion of the Integrity Workshop centers on a film about the Trial Room, which warns against certain conduct that could get the recruits in trouble later as police officers, although civilians wouldn't incur the same penalties. John McKee, a genial twenty-five-year-old instructor, says, "As police officers, you represent to society something different." He advises the students to beware of actions that could get them "jammed up"—leaving an accident scene or smoking marijuana, for example. "What you are about to see," he says, emphatically, "is the most important thing you'll see in the police academy. If I had my way, I'd show it at the beginning and the end of training."

Officer John Eterno reminds the recruits that before they came on the job, they were given a screening that measured integrity. "You should already have that within you," he says, "and this film should enhance that feeling. If you do mess up, lots of things can happen. But common sense should be your guide. You may ask, 'Should I write a summons for this guy, this man who's very influential?' You have the authority." He tells why the *Patrol Guide*, the NYPD manual of rules and regulations for carrying out police action on duty and for off-duty conduct, runs over one thousand pages. "Every time something goes wrong on the street, we write another procedure."

The tape the recruits see on the Trial Room is a speech especially prepared for police academy students by Hugh Mo, at the time he served as New York City's deputy commissioner of trials. Officer Eterno impresses upon the students the importance of the message Mo delivers. "Use your head," he says. "I tell you now there is no place for drugs on this job. We gave you this training, the background. Now it's up to you."

Hugh Mo, an Asian, is dressed in a suit and standing at a podium. He videotaped the speech after he had been deputy commissioner of trials for eight years. In the videotape he covers the disciplinary system of the New York Police Department and the behavior that violates the rules and regulations of the department. Proper conduct, he begins, "requires integrity to the highest order of service."

"The department has always maintained a policy that it will remain drug free," Mo says forcefully. "It is improper to be involved in drugs. It is extremely serious in this department. Any misconduct in drugs will result in dismissal. Cops suspected of drug use will be administered a test."

Mo details potentially criminal actions and situations. An officer will be found guilty of official misconduct if he visits an unlicensed bar or after-hours club or abuses sick leave. It is a crime to drive while intoxicated, to falsify an insurance claim. A cop who makes an arrest may never play judge and jury. "The police officer should be aware," Mo says, "that this department will never tolerate punitive measures on a prisoner in custody or in cuffs."

Mo warns that if an NYPD cop is unfortunate enough to have to make an appearance in the Trial Room, he will find it "a total adversarial process." He says the officer "should not act like a guilty party if innocent, should be composed, and avoid outbursts."

He urges cops to be "moral, courteous, and respectful when dealing with the public," and not to "fall into the pitfalls that may be acceptable to society but not to this department."

After the videotape, Officers McKee and Eterno offer some advice to the recruits. Officer McKee begins with a story.

"I had made a totally legitimate arrest. I ran a plate into Central on a Connecticut vehicle, a Cadillac. It came back 10-16, a stolen vehicle. I put the guy in cuffs and brought him back to the station house. Just another GLA [grand larceny auto]. Two months later I received paper in the mail that the guy's suing me for $250,000. The car was stolen in Connecticut, but after it was recovered, it was never cleared off the computers. Don't think it can't happen to you. The Corporation Counsel (legal division of New York City) told me I was indemnified. It was a probable-cause arrest." He acted lawfully and properly, and the city backed him up.

Changing the subject, he asks how many recruits closed their eyes for just one second during the videotape. A number of hands go up. He points out that they slept on city time.

Officer Eterno: "You are changed individuals. Some of you don't realize it yet, but you are. Soon you'll get a gun, a shield, and the responsibility of protecting society. Along with it should come a maturity."

Officer McKee: "You're about twenty-two years old. In a few weeks you'll be telling people two or three times your age what to do. I treat people the way I'd expect police officers to treat my parents."

Officer Eterno: "It's not easy, all the training. I wish we could give you more tactics. Both on and off duty, you'll be scrutinized. Use common sense and you'll be okay."

Officer McKee: "There is no such thing as a nonconformist on this job. A nonconformist scars the department forever." He recalls a recent drug scandal involving cops in the 77th Precinct. "Do you know how I felt the next day out on patrol? I was disgraced. Everything I had done—from delivering a baby to sending a person to the morgue—was blown away."

Officer Eterno: "If someone comes at you with a gun, don't be so paranoid that you don't protect yourself. Do your job, do it right. Cover yourself. Don't be afraid to protect yourself."

Officer McKee: "In terms of integrity, you'll hear about the guy in the local coffee shop who does the 'right thing' by cops. That's BS. You go there every morning and he gives you a cup of coffee for twenty-five cents or for free. Then one day he has a dispute with one of his customers, and the customer is one hundred percent right. Whose side are you going to take? There's no such thing as doing the 'right thing' by a police officer. Pay the fifty or sixty cents. Otherwise, you as a police officer are guilty of a misdemeanor.

"That's what this workshop is about. You must have integrity at all times. If your radio partner is doing something wrong, you are just as guilty."

Officer Eterno: "Store owners are happy to see you, the cops.

Why? Because it's crazy out there. You're safety from the nuts. Thank God the cop is here. I want him to stay here.

"You're going to have relationships with people you meet. You'll learn about their lives. Use your head. Your training will go further. The lieutenants are still learning, the cops are still learning. Learn from your experiences. You'll get to know some 'hairbags'—cops with experience. Listen to them. Put those experiences in your pocket and gain something from them. So you'll be better able to approach the situation."

Officer McKee: "If you feel a little unsure of yourself, you're not unlike the person sitting next to you. When you're out there, you'll get right into it. But if you're unsure, call your patrol supervisor."

The third element of the Integrity Workshop is Law, explored in three role plays.

> The call comes in from Central: "Look for the perp of a robbery. Fourteenth Street by Union Square Park. The perp is a male white, about six feet tall, wearing blue pants, white sneakers, and a blue shirt." An officer on patrol encounters a man who fits the description.
>
> "Excuse me. Where are you going?"
> "To work."
> "Where?"
> "McDonald's."
>
> Without hesitating, the suspect walks away quickly. The officer, taken by surprise, watches vacantly for a moment, then collects himself and pursues the suspect. But it is too late. The man is gone.

The action is cut, and the moderator says, "That may be the one who got away." The police officer had the legal right in this circumstance to stop, question, and, if need be, to frisk the man who resembled the robbery suspect. The suspect may be screaming that he wants IAD, CCRB, a chief, or someone whose name he read in the newspaper, but the cop shouldn't be intimidated. He should act properly and the suspect will calm down. The man may write a letter to the police commissioner, who will hand the letter to someone to deliver to CCRB, but the case will be investigated and the officer will receive a letter stating that he acted properly. The skit is repeated, this time with a different recruit playing the police officer. A man who fits Central's description walks out.

"Excuse me, sir. May I ask you what you're doing in the area?"

"Sure. I'm going to work."

"In the area?"

"Yes. McDonald's."

"May I see your ID?"

"Yes." The man pulls out some identification.

"Would you stay here while I call for backups?"

"Why? Officer, are you accusing me of something?"

The officer orders him to put his hands up and move against the wall. He requests backups over his radio. Central tells him none are available.

"What's the condition?" Central asks.

"Possible perp of the robbery. Fits the description of the perp of the crime."

"Officer!" says the perp. "You touched me. That's police brutality. I want to make a civilian complaint."

A call comes in from Central. The real perp has been apprehended. Incensed, the man who has been detained and put against the wall demands the officer's shield number.

The role play is cut, and the moderator asks the recruit who played the cop in the first skit how he felt. "Nervous," comes the response. Then he turns to the audience. "What did you think of his reactions?" he asks the other recruits. "How would you have acted?"

The answers are varied: "I think he did well. The suspect fit the description." Another recruit says, "I think I would have called Central and asked for a further description of the perp." The latter response is praised by the moderator. He illustrates a follow-up to Central: "I have someone who fits the description. Is there anything further?"

"Can you detain him for reasonable suspicion of a felony?" asks the moderator. Yes. Under 140.50 of the Criminal Procedure Law, a police officer may ask a suspect for his or her name, address, and a reasonable explanation of his or her conduct. An officer should speak in an authoritative voice, he adds.

The moderator addresses the recruit who performed in the second role play. "You called for a backup. None was available. Is that going to happen? Sure."

Another theme brought out is that cops are human, they can make mistakes. A description came over the air of a man who committed a chain snatch; someone appeared in the vicinity who fit the description. It's logical that that man might be a suspect. What should a police officer do?

Certain things should come to mind: What is the man suspected of? Robbery, a violent crime. Do robbers carry weapons? Generally, they do. So would it be feasible for the cop to do a protective frisk in this case? Sure. If a frisk is conducted but the suspect turns out not to be the perp, the officer should fill out a UF 250—a Stop, Question, and Frisk Form—in compliance with NYPD regulations.

If the person says the cop touched him and wants to make a complaint, how should the officer react? Should he tell him to "go fuck off"? No. He should give his name and shield number and tell him if he wants to make a complaint, to go ahead and do so. The officer was perfectly honest in carrying out his job. Might he apologize to the man? Sure. It was an honest mistake. Saying "I'm sorry" might mollify the man's anger.

The moderator asks for the best method of finding out if a suspect is the person who allegedly committed a crime. One recruit says to put the perp in an RMP and bring him to the victim. Wrong, says the instructor. You almost always must bring the victim or a witness to the perp. Why? A description may be given of a person wearing a hooded black sweatshirt, blue jeans, and white socks, and a few minutes later an officer may actually spot someone wearing similar clothing. But is that positively the perp? It's less an infringement on the rights of a person by detaining him at the location where he happens to be than taking him, possibly by force, to wherever the victim is. If a crime was recently committed, a cop should ask in which direction the perp fled, tell the victim or witness to get in the backseat of the RMP, and notify Central that he has the victim or witness in the car and that they're looking for the suspect. The class moves on to the second role play.

A message from Central is received by two officers over their radio as a man walks by. They ask the man to put his hands up because he matches the description Central has given them of someone who just committed a crime. The man complies and assumes the position against a wall. "I'm a working man," he protests. "I have a deli." One officer frisks him and finds a gun in an ankle holster. The officer makes a call on his radio.

"I just carry a gun for protection," the man cries out. "I've been held up four times in the last four months!"

"Do you have a license for the gun?"

"No."

While the officer attempts to cuff the man, the man says he's the guy who owns the deli down the block from the station house and that many of the cops there know him. They come in and he gives them free sandwiches. He even gives the captain his lunch every day for free. Then a call comes in from Central saying that the perpetrator of the robbery has been caught.

Based on the experience of the first recruit on the stage, the moderator says, the recruits seem to be getting a better feeling of stop, question, and frisk law. He summarizes what happened: A robbery recently took place in which the perp had a gun. A man comes by who fits the description of the perp. The officers frisk him and feel a bulge on his right leg. It's a firearm. Can an officer take out his gun in this situation? "Absolutely, but you don't have to have your finger on the trigger all the time." He adds that in the role play, the two student officers were thrown together; normally they would have had time to plan.

"In stop, question, and frisk situations," he says, "you can use the maximum amount of power needed, which is having your gun drawn." The moderator points out that because robbery is a violent crime, a police officer may frisk head to toe. He warns the student officers not to conclude their frisk after a gun is found. "We carry more than one gun," he says. "So may they."

The officer now has a situation in which he stopped and frisked a man who fit the description of a perp who committed a crime, and has found a gun on his person. But Central broadcasts that the real perp is in custody. What should the officer do? Charge the man with the illegal possession of a handgun.

The officer in the role play is faced with an allegation of police corruption. What should he do? The *Patrol Guide* provides that a member of the service should notify the Internal Affairs Division, and identify himself, give the facts of the alleged improprieties, leave his telephone number, and follow the instructions of the IAD supervising officer. In this situation, the uniformed officer wouldn't want to go to the commanding officer of the precinct because the C.O. is one of the alleged perpetrators.

The moderator commends the two recruits on their performance, and they receive a round of applause. Those in the audience also feel a sense of pride. "Good," says the moderator. "You're thinking like cops."

The third role play is a scene that takes place on a New York City street.

An out-of-towner gets into a cab, requesting to go to 29th Street and Fifth Avenue.

"Where are you from?" asks the driver, a gruff man who fits the stereotype of a New York City cab driver. "Arizona," answers the fare. "Arizona? Where's that?" The driver pauses, then says, "I know a shortcut. Hold on."

At a red light the taxi is hit by another car, and both drivers get out of their vehicles. The second driver takes out a shield and announces he's a police officer. He asks the taxi driver for his papers and pokes him.

An altercation develops between the cab driver and the off-duty cop. Two police officers arrive at the scene and hear out the parties. The taxi driver says he was pushed. "That might have been attempted assault!" he shouts. The off-duty cop, who obviously has been on the force for years, refutes the cabbie's claims, and asks the two young officers who they're going to believe. The officers call for a patrol supervisor.

When the patrol supervisor arrives, the cabbie says to him, "What's going on here? There's three cops against one. I've got rights too!" He asks how he can file a complaint against the off-duty cop, who in turn denies the charges.

The action is cut. "What just happened," says the moderator, "is not an uncommon situation on the street these days. It's a minor situation, but I've seen police officers side with the off-duty cop. They say, 'Okay, we'll take care of it.' Is that how we'll handle it? No."

When the uniformed police officers first came on the scene, what did the off-duty cop try to do? Basically tell them, "Look, I'm a cop. We don't need any reports. Insurance companies don't have to be notified. Don't worry about it. I'll handle this."

Obviously, the moderator continues, this is not the proper way such a situation would be handled. It's the uniformed police officer's responsibility to take charge. He should take each person aside and calm him down. He shouldn't lose his cool, because the other people may lose theirs and the whole scene would become a disaster. The paperwork should be done and the proper notifications made. If there's an allegation of assault, he has to investigate it. If an arrest is warranted, he must make it.

For an allegation of discourtesy or abuse of authority, an officer should refer the complainant to CCRB.

With this scenario, the police academy attempts to dispel the myth of the "blue wall," that cops help their fellow officers no matter what. If a police officer is wrong, he's wrong. "There's no point in you sticking your neck out," says Law instructor Gary Lombardo, "because what happens? You stick you neck out and it gets chopped off and the other cop ends up in the clear."

It was a warm July evening, Andy Varga's first day out on patrol. He walked into a Lower East Side pizzeria to get a soda. A Hispanic man with a heavy accent behind the counter said the soda "is on me."

Andy replied that he could not accept anything for free. He had to pay for it, and pay the full price. No free meals, no discounts. He explained that the department frowns on any special consideration given to cops, and how the Internal Affairs Division seems to be everywhere.

At first the counterman didn't seem to understand why Andy had to pay for the soda, but then he became apologetic. He thought he was "doing a good thing" by offering a police officer free food.

Andy drank the soda in the parlor, but instead of feeling good about himself, satisfied that he just warded off a small demon in the purgatory of cop temptation, the kind which he was warned could lead to progressively greater transgressions and outright corruption, he felt nervous. How could this have happened to him on his very first day out? Maybe, he thought, just maybe, this seemingly innocuous offer of a free cup of soda by an immigrant was an integrity test staged by the ever-crafty, omnipresent, and formidable Internal Affairs Division.

14
CAR-STOP WORKSHOP

On Greenwich Street on the lower West Side of Manhattan, Officer Frank Petit pulled a car over for running a red light. Suddenly, before Petit could race for cover or draw his own gun, the driver stuck a gun out the window and shot him in the leg, permanently disabling him. The driver sped off and the cop's partner, who had been reading a Sunday newspaper in the patrol car, sat stunned.

Officer Fred Bugdin and his partner, working midnight to eight in the Midtown North Precinct, learned that someone had been firing shots out of a taxi. At Lexington and 51st Street, the officers pulled over a cab that fit the description. When Officer Bugdin got out of his radio car, a drunk Housing cop in the back seat of the taxi fired one shot into his chest, killing him.

When a police officer stops a vehicle, even for a minor traffic infraction, he is at a distinct disadvantage. The driver knows who the cop is, but the cop doesn't know who the driver is. Is the man who just ran a red light an "average" citizen who was daydreaming, or is he a perp fleeing from a stickup he just committed? An escaping felon who breaks the speed limit is more likely to think he's being stopped for his crime, not for speeding. The cop may become the unsuspecting target of a shooting or other violence.

Making car stops for routine traffic violations is something a patrol officer does during every tour of duty. If he or she doesn't follow the rules or has a lax attitude, these stops can be lethal. At Floyd Bennett Field in Brooklyn, the student officers are taught the proper way to execute these with the Car-Stop Workshop, a one-day training course broken down into several components: Car Stops, Vehicle Inventory, RMP Tactics, and Footpost Car Stops.

As the students learn, a car stop is not just a matter of pulling over a motorist who ran a red light or passed a stop sign, collecting relevant documents, and issuing a summons. There are tactics and procedures to be used to protect the cop from the car's occupants as well as from other drivers and bystanders. There are instances when a cop should search the auto or a person inside it. What are these and how intrusive may the cop be? How should the officer interact with drivers? What is the role of the patrol car driver (called the operator) and his partner (the recorder) and how are they different? How can a cop conduct a car stop as safely as possible on footpost, when he has neither partner nor patrol car? What about felony car stops, where a car's occupants may have to be taken out for a frisk or arrest? How should prisoners be transported? What does the cop do at an accident scene?

The Car-Stop Workshop was conceived in 1984 as a result of a communication sent to the police academy by the Civilian Complaint Review Board. CCRB had identified a trend; people were complaining that cops were acting discourteously. In response to that communication, the Social Science Department developed a lesson in interacting with motorists. With the assistance of the other disciplines, including physical education, this evolved into an interdisciplinary workshop.

In a classroom training session, the recruits see a videotape of different car-stop scenarios, most based on real-life incidents: a driver pulled over for speeding, plaintively telling the officer that if he gets a ticket, the officer will be "taking the food out of my kid's mouth"; a woman so nervous she's trembling getting a summons for passing a stop sign; a driver in a suspicious vehicle, his right hand lying casually over a gun, who suddenly sticks his arm out the window and fires three times at a cop; a man who just killed a girl in a stickup storming out of the back of a van to kill two officers who pulled the vehicle over for passing a stop sign. Each segment is followed by a discussion and the instructor's critique. While the scenarios have an impact on the students—and the gore elicits moans and groans—it is the outdoor role plays in which the students participate that really drive home the proper tactics to use in such situations.

A professor from John Jay College is driving with his wife, Marion. A patrol car with its lights flashing pulls up behind it. Out of the loudspeaker comes the stern command, "Pull over to the side." Then two officers get out of the radio car. The operator approaches the driver of the car, the recorder the passenger side. The operator glowers at the driver.

"What are you, some sort of asshole? Didn't you see that stop sign?" The man looks up in surprise. "And look at this piece of shit you're driving!" He asks to see the driver's "papers."

The other cop looks at the female passenger, an attractive young woman. "Are you always with that guy?" he asks.

She says that she and her husband are going to the mayor's mansion, where her husband is to deliver a speech on the homeless.

"You're married to that doofus?"

"I'll tell you what," says the cop by the driver. "I'm

209

gonna give ya a receipt for sixty dollars. You tell the mayor it's your donation to the homeless people."

While the cop is speaking, his partner is trying to engage the professor's wife in romantic conversation.

"Where was the stop sign you missed?" asks the operator sarcastically. The driver answers, but then, annoyed by the behavior of the two cops, asks him for his name and shield number. The officer mutters a name and number and walks away.

"Tactically, what did you think of the car stop?" asks straightfaced Officer Robert Keating of the Physical Education Unit. His question is met with laughter.

"Not one thing was done right," he says, adding that the purpose of the role play was to demonstrate a "totally unprofessional car stop so you can see how foolish it looks. We approached the car and insulted and chastised the occupants." He tells how asking to see "papers" could be offensive to Jewish people, who form a large population in New York City. It may remind them of the Gestapo in Germany during World War II, he says. Foreigners might respond by showing their green card.

The correct approach: Tell the driver what he did wrong. Ask to see his license, registration, and insurance card. Keep it short. It's up to the officer whether or not to issue a ticket. When would a cop want to use that discretion? In an emergency, such as when a man is rushing his injured baby daughter to the hospital. "You have to be a little flexible," he says. "It could happen to a member of your family."

Officer Keating addresses the behavior of the partner, who was trying to pick up the driver's wife. Eventually, someone's control will break, he says. "A husband or boyfriend may take a swipe at you, and you'll have an arrest for assaulting a police officer. But the facts may come out, and you'll be penalized.

You're a police officer here to serve the public. People deserve to be treated courteously.''

Officer Keating warns the men not to use their power to get dates. He asks how many men are in their early 20s, and a number of hands go up. "We have a lot of young police officers in the department," he says harshly. "Some may get excited when they see a beautiful woman. But you're not out there to pick up girls!" Some of the recruits laugh, but they recognize the seriousness of Keating's words.

The next tactical error Officer Keating points out was throwing the driver's documents through the window. A proper way to return them is to say, "Sir, here's your license, registration, and insurance card," giving them back one at a time. In closing the summons issuance, a statement must be chosen carefully. "Thank you and have a nice day" could be taken sarcastically. The department prefers a statement like "Sir, if you're ready now, I'll direct you back into traffic" to end the encounter politely.

When the driver asked for Officer Keating's name and shield, he gave a false name and number. "If you have to do this, then you're ashamed of your job," he says. "You should be proud. And people know about CCRB."

Other instructors tell stories, one about a civilian who made a complaint to CCRB because a cop was too polite. Another is about two police officers who stopped a man, circled his car, finding additional violations, and then told the driver they could settle the problem for a "finsky." "You mean a five?" "Yes." The driver, a police captain, whipped out his shield, and soon afterward there were two fewer cops on the force.

Next, a proper car stop is demonstrated. It shows the tactics, the instructors say, that officers use 99.9 percent of the time. It's a routine car stop, and the vehicle is unregistered.

Officers Stephen Collins and George Mastorides are on patrol when they observe a traffic infraction. They turn on their RMP's dome lights and through the loudspeaker issue a command: "The white Chevy, pull over to the right." The two officers get out with their hands on their guns, and slowly approach the car. Mastorides, the recorder, taps the trunk and right side of the car as he advances to the passenger side. Collins, on the other side standing behind the driver, looks forward and tells the driver the violation he made and politely asks to see the man's license, registration, and insurance card. The two officers walk back to the RMP, get in, and make out a summons. They return to the car the same way they previously did, with the recorder tapping the trunk and the side. Officer Collins returns the documents to the driver and escorts the car back into traffic.

Pairs of recruits are then selected to play cops making a car stop. The role plays take place on an open lot with an actual RMP. After each skit, the instructors critique their performance.

After several run-throughs, the students finally master the procedures and techniques in making a car stop:

Select a spot to stop the vehicle that offers some control, like a bus stop. Park behind the stopped vehicle at a distance to allow a zone of safety—six to eight feet between you and the stopped car is good. "Split" the vehicle in half when parking; that is, the patrol car's center should be at the stopped car's left end. Jot down the license plate number and a brief description of the car in case the driver attempts to flee or shots are fired.

The operator (cop driver) and recorder (cop passenger) should approach the stopped car together, with the recorder holding the radio in his nonshooting hand. Unlock the strap over your gun if you sense danger, but keep your hand over it so it won't fall out if you trip. If you take your gun out, keep it along the side of your leg, finger off the trigger.

Push down on the trunk to lock it in case someone is hiding inside, but do not stand behind the car because the driver could slam it into reverse. The recorder taps on the right rear side of the car with his knuckles to distract the driver; the other cop appears by surprise. The driver will turn his head to the right, only to find an officer at his left.

Stand behind the driver so that when bending down and leaning forward you can see into the vehicle but the driver can't see you without turning around. If the driver suddenly throws open the car door, trying to push you into a traffic lane, the door won't hit you since you're not standing parallel to the driver. If people are seated in the rear, stand behind these passengers, who should pass the paperwork to you from the back seat.

You may ask the driver to shut the motor off, but he or she does not have to. Ask politely: "Miss, would you please turn off the engine?" A summons cannot be given for lack of compliance, but the response will give an indication of what kind of cooperation can be expected, whether there may be a problem. Tell the driver what violation he committed and ask for his license, registration, and insurance card. No lectures on what the driver did wrong. Stand sideways with your shoulder facing the person inside. Standing directly in front would make you a larger target and expose your vital organs. During the approach and the operator-driver interaction, the recorder observes the inside of the vehicle and the actions of other occupants of the car. Caution: A person reaching for the glove compartment to get documents could just as likely be going for a gun.

The driver may make a hard-luck plea. A cop may let him go with a warning; traffic tickets are issued at his discretion. But if the driver threatens or offers serious opposition, return to your car or take other cover and radio for assistance.

Returning to the RMP, walk with your shoulder turned sideways. Walking backward could make you look clumsy if you trip. Back in the RMP, one cop, usually the recorder, writes the summons, the other observes the vehicle. Don't bury your head in your memo book. Hold the memo book up to eye level so that you can see the occupants of the car while writing. Sometimes a driver might give an expired insurance card but then find a current one while rummaging through his glove compartment. While the summons is being written, he may run out to hand it over. Tell him to get back in his car. In the event he doesn't, direct him to the sidewalk.

In returning the documents and issuing the summons, approach the car as before; the operator fans out the papers and returns them to the driver one at a time. Don't reach in; the driver should reach out. If he's angry and starts to complain, cut him off right away. Tell him there are instructions on the back of the summons for contesting it if he chooses. Then assist him into traffic. Keep the encounter short and businesslike. Never consider any vehicle stop routine or low risk.

A felony car stop, when the police have reason to believe the driver, other occupant, or vehicle has been involved in a felony crime, calls for much different strategies because of the high potential for danger and the possible presence of guns or other weapons. The recruits see these cautionary measures firsthand in the felony car stop scene that follows. Two recruits play the cops and two the perps.

> Over the loudspeaker, the recorder yells the commands:
> "The white Chevy, pull over.
> "Turn the engine off and throw the keys to the ground.
> "Place your hands on the dashboard where I can see them. You, too, passenger.
> "Passenger, open the door.
> "Step out slowly and put your hands up.
> "Walk to the right front fender.
> "Put your hands on the car and spread them.
> "Driver, same thing."

214

The two officers exit the RMP together with their guns drawn. One goes to the front, the other stays at the rear. The cop at the front holsters his gun, while the other has his weapon trained on the perps. The front cop searches the waistband of the first perp and cuffs him. He then places the perp at the rear side of the car and does a thorough frisk. Then he conducts a brief frisk of the second perp and cuffs him. Then the complete frisk. No weapons are found.

Officer Keating steps to the front and glares at the class. "I'm here so some of you don't get killed!" he yells. The recruits are incredulous, so Keating walks up to one of the "perps," reaches for the gun in her waistband, and waves it at them. When setting up the scenario, Keating had held a deactivated gun with which he gestured nonchalantly. He slipped it to one of the perps to hide when she was getting into the car. Throughout the skit he was holding a nightstick and wondered if any of the student officers noticed that the prop gun had disappeared. In all the classes held that week, only one recruit found the gun, and he was so nervous he dropped it and cuffed the second perp without searching him first. Cops are supposed to be trained observers, says Officer Keating, and should stay in control.

Officer Keating repeats the procedures and tactics to be used in a felony car stop: Give Central as much information as possible. When both cars have stopped, roll down the windows of the RMP and open the doors. Stay in your vehicle at this point. Only the firearms should come out. The engine and the door are your cover. In a firm voice, over the loudspeaker, tell the occupants of the vehicle what to do: Turn off the ignition. The driver's hands go on the windshield while the passenger is told to put his left hand over and open the door from the outside, then go to the front corner on his side. He is not to look at the cops, since he will try to determine whether he can

215

"blow you away," the recruits are told. The driver also gets out the passenger side, even if he has to climb over a console, also not looking at the officers. He should be ordered to put his hands up, then kick the door shut.

Now you get out of your RMP to do the search. Walk together to the car. The recorder stops diagonally to the front right of the vehicle, the operator diagonally to the rear right. Point your guns. Order the perps to go around to the hood and to spread their legs and arms so they're leaning off balance. In the role play, Officer Keating notes they were standing straight up and looking at the officers. The recruits also forgot to tell the driver to kick the left door closed with his foot. "Thirty people will watch you make a car stop," says Officer Keating. "Twenty-nine may root for the bad guy. Don't give anyone ammunition."

The operator comes up to the perps, does an initial search, including the waistband, and cuffs them. Then the perps can be separated, and a systematic search can be done. When the perp has been cuffed, you have much more control, and your guns may be holstered. A thorough search may reveal something previously missed. When the perp leaves the car, search it again. He could have left contraband behind. "If you have a gut feeling that it's a bad car stop, wait for backups!" the recruits are told.

Be confident, Keating continues, for it might throw the perps off balance. "Yes, I might be scared to death," he says, "but so should they be. If there's three, four, or five perps, nothing says you have to go up to the car. You can wait for backups."

Officer Keating issues a final warning: Women can hide guns anywhere. He tells of a cop who brought a woman clad in a bikini to the station house, where a .22-caliber pistol was discovered in her crotch.

When you can't see inside a vehicle when stopping vans or cars with tinted windows, a slightly different set of tactics is called for. Because of these vehicles' characteristics, the chosen location for the stop should offer the officer an optimum vantage point. If the situation looks suspicious, the recorder should relay the license plate number to Central to determine if the vehicle is stolen—a "10-14."

A final role play is set up. Andy Varga and another recruit play the cops.

It's roll call at the station house, and the sergeant says there has been a robbery in the area. The perps are two male Hispanics and are armed. They are driving a stolen white Chevy Citation; he gives the license plate number.

Andy and his partner get into a radio car and circle around. When they are out of audible range, the instructor, Officer Maniscalo, says that a twist will be added to the role play; when the officers stop the car, two women will be in it.

The two officers spot a car that matches exactly the description given in roll call, including the license plate number. As Officer Maniscalo predicted, they are surprised to find the occupants to be two women—Lissette Sierra-Solis and a companion. Andy Varga frisks Sierra-Solis, and she protests she wants a female officer but is cuffed anyway. The same thing happens with the second woman.

The Law instructor asks if the officers, who found nothing illegal on the women, can legally search the car? The courts have said that police may search a car if they have probable cause to believe that weapons or evidence from a crime are in it. The two recruits find the case before them perplexing. Although they seem to have the right car, clearly, they do not have the perpetrators of the robbery. Yet they decided to arrest the women.

Officer Maniscalo now raises the question of whether it is a valid arrest. The answer is no, as the recruits, when they

217

have time to think the matter out, admit. But the question Officer Maniscalo now asks is, if you have probable cause against the car, then why don't you search it?

The officers agree that based on all the information provided them, this is the car from the robbery. Now, when they search it, they discover two revolvers in the glove compartment. At this point the officers may validly arrest the two women for possession of illegal weapons.

When the officers arrive at the "precinct," Lissette protests Andy's frisk, which raises the question: May a male officer frisk a woman? Yes. If a police officer reasonably suspects that a female perp has a weapon, he may frisk her. A woman is quite capable of killing, and frisking her is for the cop's protection. Now that the women are in custody at the station house, a search more thorough than a frisk may be done by a policewoman.

Sitting on the lot is a scabrous old Eldorado, green on the bottom, white on top. It was seized by the NYPD and is now department property. For the Vehicle Inventory Workshop, part of the car-stop training, Officer Daniel Albano has planted fake guns, drugs, and paraphernalia in it to demonstrate the kinds of places criminals hide contraband. He selects some recruits to search the car under a hypothetical auto exception (which allows cops with grounds to suspect evidence is hidden in a car to search the car and its contents without a search warrant) or during an inventory at a station house. He warns the student officers that in this age of AIDS, they must be careful not to get stuck by a hypodermic needle. Leather gloves should be worn. If an officer does get pricked, he should notify his patrol supervisor.

The recruits begin their search, but they are quickly interrupted by Officer Albano for not designating someone to list the items found. Then the students renew their search, with their fellow recruits shouting encouragement from around the car.

Contraband is found under the headrest, armrest, dashboard, and seat, as well as in numerous other places. Hypodermic needles are found inside an umbrella, an eyeglass case, and a flashlight barrel; crack is discovered inside a toy shoe, white powder in an oilcan. The trunk is full of objects in which weapons and drugs are hidden. The students greet some of the less obvious hiding places with laughs, but learn that mundane objects can be used creatively to conceal almost anything, and that a search cannot be too thorough.

Tactics in cuffing and transporting prisoners in a patrol car are covered in another set of role plays.

> A 10-31 call comes over the radio, a burglary in progress at a factory. Two officers in the vicinity drive to the scene and get out of their radio car with their guns drawn. They see a suspect off to the side and order him to turn around and get against a wall, with palms held out toward the cops. One officer frisks the suspect while the other trains his gun on him. The perp is cuffed and led to the back seat of the RMP.

The role play is critiqued by Officer George Mastorides, a seven-year veteran. "With only one suspect," he says, "it doesn't make sense for one of you to search him while the other has a gun on him. If he runs away, you can't shoot him. Why don't you both come up and search him? He is less likely to run away. Holster your radio and your gun."

He also criticizes the way the officer escorted the perp to the radio car: too mildly. He talks about "hard rocks," perps who have been through the system before. How the officer holds the perp communicates whether he means business or not. If the suspect is held lightly, he'll break away. "You can

219

lay him over the trunk, but don't stand directly behind the perp." Officer Mastorides tells of a fellow officer who once brought a prisoner into the station house. The officer let down his guard and stepped behind the prisoner while conducting a search. The prisoner butted his head backward and broke the cop's nose.

The perp gets into the radio car first, not the cop. "Just because the perp is rear-cuffed," Officer Mastorides adds, "that isn't the end of the story." He tells of a rear-cuffed perp who shot the two cops driving him back to the station house. After the recorder follows the perp into the back seat and closes the door, he should not forget to lock the doors. Once a drunken driver, he continues, arrested and rear-cuffed, managed to get out of an unlocked car and belly up a fence in a schoolyard before being caught.

The operator waits for the recorder to get in, then enters the car himself. The perp always sits behind the front passenger seat. Officer Mastorides advises the recruits to cuff as quickly as possible to avoid a crowd. "It's entertainment for people," he says. "And they can become rowdy or hostile."

Officer Mastorides asks the recruits what they should do if they have the perp in the car, and he's biting, kicking, or ranting. "Do you give him a squirt of Mace? No. Take him out of the car? No. Sit on him? Perhaps. The city gave you a nightstick. It's authorized equipment for you to use if you need it. First, give a loud, firm command: 'Shut up and close your eyes!' Call Central when you start transporting the prisoner and document the times when you use force, so no false allegations are made."

One-man footpost car stops are covered next by Officer Mastorides, who cautions the recruits about their danger. There are two basic vehicle summonses the footpost cop issues: a parking summons put on the vehicle requiring only a license number, and a moving-violations summons served personally to the driver and requiring a license, registration, and insurance card. A police officer on foot is at a disadvantage in trying to order a vehicle to stop. The driver knows he'll be found or arrested if he has outstanding summonses or if he's in trouble. The car could be used as a weapon. The instructor tells the recruits that if they feel a particular footpost car stop is too dangerous, they should call for backups.

In doing a footpost car stop, the officer needs to position himself at a corner where people slow down, like an intersection, or a place where he can pull a vehicle out of traffic, such as at a bus stop or by a fire hydrant. The officer should have a cover, a pole or mailbox, while writing the summons. "If you don't have these on your post," says Officer Mastorides, "it's not wise to do car stops on that tour! You don't have an RMP to create a zone of safety, or a partner." People will also throw things out of buildings at a cop, so the officer needs to keep a careful watch around him.

In demonstrating how not to make a car stop, Officer Mastorides walks in front of a parked car and asks the hypothetical driver to pull over. The recruits laugh. Now, off to the side, he whistles and gives a loud, clear command: "You in the blue Chevy, pull over here!" Most people will respond to the uniform, he says. "Think of how your aunts and uncles would respond."

Months later, when Andy Varga found himself doing car stops as part of his field training, he had good cause to remember Mastorides's words. On footpost patrol, one day Varga saw a late-model car run a red light at East Houston and Second Avenue and motioned to the driver to pull over. He told the driver to turn off the engine and asked for the keys, noticing a woman in the front seat and a child in the back. Then he asked the driver for his license, registration, and insurance card. The driver leaned forward and reached to his back pocket with his right hand, and Andy glimpsed a revolver sticking out of his left rear pocket.

221

A sudden wave of fright overtook him, but acting on instinct, Andy reached in and put his hand over the gun, telling the driver not to move. Quickly regaining his composure, he ordered the driver to put his hands on top of the steering wheel. The man complied but Andy was still upset with himself. He had made a mistake reaching into the car with his hand. The driver could have grabbed his arm and overpowered him. Thankfully, the driver seemed to be a decent sort of fellow.

Andy radioed a 10-85 to Central, and within seconds the first unit arrived. It turned out that the driver was a diamond dealer who, having been robbed several times, applied for and received a valid license to carry a gun. After all the man and his family went through in those few minutes, Andy made a final munificent gesture: he didn't issue a summons to the driver. Seeing the expressions of fear on the faces of the driver and his family, Andy didn't want to put them through any more distress.

After having made countless car stops, Andy divides drivers into three different groups: those who are polite, those who sit quietly but at the end say they'll fight you in court, and those who argue no matter what. Andy encounters people who fit into this last group several times a week.

One day a car ran a red light, and Andy and his RMP partner pulled it over. The two officers approached the car.

"What'd I do?" the driver, nineteen years old, snapped at them. There were two young women with him in the car.

"You passed a red light back on First Avenue and First Street."

"No, I didn't," the young man bellowed, getting out to confront the cops.

Andy asked the driver for his documents, and the teen started yelling, "You know, I had my car parked up by a school and I came out and found my radio missing. Let me tell you something. You guys are doing a real great job stopping people for going through red lights. But to find my radio, you guys are doing a shitty-ass job. My girlfriends could do a better job than you!"

Andy repeated his request, and as the driver went through his wallet Andy noticed an ID card from John Jay College and a Lieutenant's Benevolent Association card. Andy asked the driver to get back into his car and wait there, then returned to the RMP, thinking maybe he would cut the kid a break. Andy was also a student at John Jay, studying police administration. The kid was only acting tough, he thought, showing off in front of his girlfriends. Still, he had already started writing the summons; once begun, you have to have a pretty good explanation for not completing it.

Suddenly the officers looked up. The driver was gesturing and ranting beside the patrol car.

"What the hell's going on here?" the driver screamed. "You guys aren't doing your job. My uncle's a lieutenant on the job."

Andy looked at his partner. "I already started the ticket."

"What's your shield numbers? I want your shield numbers. I want to tell my uncle what kind of treatment I'm getting here."

"Fine," said Andy. "Here's my shield number." As he wrote it down for the teen, the other officer asked him where his uncle worked.

"He's in the Terrorist Task Force and he's a lieutenant."

"If you told me this at the car I would have given you a break," Andy said. "I already started writing the summons. You're getting the summons."

The teen continued to be abusive and Andy's partner rolled up the window, saying they were going to write everything they could on the kid. He got out and checked the kid's car over—the lights, high beams, directionals, and other parts. He returned, telling Andy to write two more summonses—no front plates and the driver not wearing a seat belt.

Andy wrote the tickets and got out to issue them. The kid was sitting in the back seat now. Andy told him to get out of the car. He wanted to stand face-to-face with him as he handed over the summonses, explaining the procedure for handling them. He also told the kid to go back to his uncle and tell him what happened. "Tell him why I stopped you and why I issued you more summonses," he said. "If your uncle had respect for you and the police department, he would have told you how to act in front of a police officer if you were stopped. If your uncle wants to call me, he can."

Several months had passed, and he never did get a phone call from the lieutenant.

───15───
FINAL POLICE
ACADEMY DAYS

It is early June. Officer Battista's Police Science class, Company 20, is on Lesson 62, Tactics. "Thirteen lessons from now, we're done," he says, giving the students the gimlet eye. "Does that make you a cop? Technically, yes. But you haven't had any real experience yet.

"Let's look at where we are. You've been in the police academy for four months. You've grown comfortable. But when you see a couple of officers drive by in a radio car, you compare yourself to them and wonder how much of a cop you really are.

"Everybody's very comfortable here, relaxed. The police academy is like a security blanket. But before you know it, this security blanket is going to be ripped off and you'll be naked. It will happen your first day on patrol.

"It's a tough job. There'll be times when you won't feel like going in. Your biggest problem here is, 'Will I make the two-mile run?' or 'Will I get yelled at in class?' Your buddy calls up and says he heard you're a cop, you say it's great. They don't know you're sitting down eight hours a day. They say they wish they were cops, and you say, 'Yeah, maybe one day you'll pass the test.' Your friend could be making $50,000 a year as a CPA, but who cares?

"So you wake up in the morning, you shower, you look in the mirror, and you think, 'I'm a cop. I can't believe it!' You get this big attitude. You go downstairs, get a cup of coffee if you have time. Your car pool may be there. If you live at home, your mother will say, 'Be careful.' You say, 'Don't worry.' " The class roars with laughter. "You know you're in the police academy for eight hours. You copy your homework on the way to work. You think about what you're going to do on the weekend.

"You sit in class and wait for meal. Your big decision is what you're going to have for lunch. You meet your buddies. In the diner everyone turns around and stares at you. You're probably thinking, 'They're impressed because I'm a cop,' although they might just as well be laughing at you.

"You don't worry that anything is going to happen to you. At the diner the recruit's attitude is if anything does happen, we'll all get them.

"But a month from now you will graduate. It'll be a great ceremony. The mayor will be there, the commissioner, TV stations, the media. You'll get your Field Training Unit assignments. You'll want to know who's going with you.

"That's when reality starts to set in. When it hits you in the face. Two days later, they'll say, 'Officer, take your footpost.' It's four to twelve, and it's pouring out. You have three blocks—two vacant blocks, and one with two burned-out storefronts and one candy store. You're there for eight hours. You thought you were going out in the radio car. It's freezing, it's dark, it's depressing. You ask yourself why you became a cop. Then meal comes. There may be only one place to eat. You have no choice. The guys in the precinct don't know you to come and pick you up. So you go to that candy store. There may be no one there you know or who speaks the same language, depending on where you work. Your academy buddies are no longer around.

"Then a guy comes in with a shotgun. Can you call time out? Can you call your buddies? It's you alone. What are you going to do? Reality sets in. All the fun you had may be over for good.

"The experience I just described is that of an officer from the last class, out for less than thirty days. If you get into a confrontation, you may have to call for help. If you get into a shootout, shoot until you stop them or they go away. The most important thing is cover.

"If you get hit, don't you dare give up. When you give up, I guarantee you, that's the minute you're going to die. Never give up! If you see your partner go down, don't give up. Don't run away. Otherwise, you leave him for dead. Help him.

"If you get hit, keep on firing. Never give up!

"If there ever comes a time, God forbid, that I have to read about my recruits having been involved in some type of confrontation and they died, I want to read that they died fighting. Not that they threw their weapon down and gave up. Because I'll come to your wake and tell your family how sorry I am. And I'll go to your funeral. And when everybody walks away, I'll spit on your grave. Because you were a loser."

An electric chill seems to run through the bodies of the student officers, and they turn toward one another, discomfited by the provocative words of Officer Battista. As if on cue, the room suddenly goes dark and a videotape plays. A number of scenarios are presented, and the students critique the tactics used by the officers in each situation, any one of which could be deadly.

A woman comes out of her apartment building and looks out into the street. She sees a taxicab driver being robbed by his passenger. She runs down the street and tells a man, who turns out to be an off-duty police officer although he does not inform her of this. He instructs her to notify the police and give a description of him, as well as the perp. Proceeding to the scene, the off-duty officer sees a man get out of the cab. Taking cover behind a parked car across the street, and with his gun drawn, the off-duty officer tells the suspect to raise his arms and then to put them over the hood of the cab.

The videotape stops, and Battista asks the class to enumerate both the good and bad tactics of the off-duty police officer. Good: He told the woman to give the police a description of him so he wouldn't be mistaken for a perp, he thought out a plan before he acted, he approached slowly, he used a car for cover, he made observations, he waited until the suspect left the taxicab before taking action. Bad: He did not identify himself as an off-duty police officer to the woman, he didn't check to see if the perp had accomplices nearby (violating an unwritten rule, "When we find one bad guy, we look for others").

Officer Battista points out that the woman thought she was talking to a civilian. An off-duty cop who acts like he's on the job risks getting hurt by on-duty police officers. When uniformed officers respond to a call and see a man with a gun, they'll think he's the bad guy. The off-duty cop's alternatives were to follow the perp, or to dial 911 himself. "We don't want to second-guess," Officer Battista says. "When you're off duty, no one should know you're a cop. Don't walk around with your gun or shield sticking out."

Another mistake was that the off-duty officer shouted instructions to the perp from across the street. A car could have driven by, giving the perp time and opportunity enough to pull out a gun and hide it. As the off-duty officer approached, the perp could have shot him down. Or the perp could have taken cover underneath the car. "Remember," says Officer Battista, "you act and don't react. If you're off duty and there's a need for a cop, call one."

Other scenarios follow. Two cops responding to a domestic dispute listen in front of the apartment door and hear a disturbance. One knocks on the door, announcing "police," and a woman quickly opens the door and throws a noxious chemical in the officer's face. A man is pulling the door handles of cars in an obvious attempt to get inside and steal radios or the cars themselves. He is spotted by two police officers, who get out of their radio car and shout, "Police! Don't move!" The man turns around and shoots at one of the officers. Someone rushes up to a cop and says that a man who tried to rob him is being held in a building around the corner. Rushing to the location, the cop encounters two men fighting—one is well dressed, the other appears slovenly. He orders the ragged man, who protests that he is the superintendent, against the wall as the real perp escapes.

Officer Battista issues advice and warnings to the recruits based on the tactical errors made by the cops in the scenarios. Be cautious. For instance, stand off to the side of the door and listen to try to get information that could help in a safe tactical approach. Overheard threats like "I'll cut your guts out" or "I'm gonna blow your head off" will obviously tip you as to the kind of person you'll be dealing with. And just because the call is for a family dispute, it doesn't have to be that. There could be a guy inside with an Uzi machine gun who has nothing to do and wants to kill cops.

Create a plan when responding to a family dispute or any other job. At the scene, put the plan into action. And once someone is in custody, don't let your guard down. A perp in handcuffs can still cause injury.

Be prepared for the unexpected. Do you think a shootout could occur when stopping somebody who was just trying car door handles? In New York City, anything can happen.

Be open-minded. One of the pitfalls cops can get into is holding on to stereotypes. The officer in the fight scenario made the mistake of automatically assuming the well-dressed man was an honest citizen and the bedraggled one was the perp. "Criminals are clever," says Officer Battista. "Some will put on a suit and go to tourist areas like Fifth Avenue, where they'll blend in with a crowd and pickpocket tourists. We catch them because they keep doing it."

Throughout the month of June, the student officers have but one mission: to pass the third and last trimester exam. After four months of academy training and with the balmy weather now revivifying New York, they're eager to break out of the confines of 235 East 20th Street and get onto the streets.

With training nearly over, mild disciplinary action is sometimes meted out in ways that have an immediate impact on recruits since pulling a Star Card at this point may have little effect. For example, just after midnight a company is seen standing silently in formation on the Campus Deck, a peculiar sight at that hour. It turns out that some recruits were told to quiet down earlier in the day and didn't, so the instructor ordered the entire company to assemble after the tour. An instructor chews them out just long enough to make some of them miss their trains. The instructors call this "return roll call"; the recruits have their own name for it—"Midnight Mass."

Finally—the weeks seem like months—the third trimester and gym final are done. Although the academy is in session for another two weeks, it is over as far as the students are concerned. Until graduation they merely need to show up and let the instructors baby-sit them. The students want more than anything just to relax, but the academy doesn't let them sit idle.

During the week before graduation, the main order of business is to keep the students under control. They are excited that they are going to be cops, restless to break the onerous bonds of the academy after twenty-three long weeks. Yet they are uncertain that they are prepared to handle the formidable job ahead, anxious about their survival in the insanity of the city. The instructors can barely contain the rowdiness, the students as frenzied as adolescents about to burst into adulthood.

With the last trimester exam taken and all the exhortations given one last time, it is a week of special classes. All the squads assemble for these in the auditorium, where it is so brutally hot and stuffy that walking outside in the ninety-degree-plus air is a welcome relief.

Detective Lieutenant Edward F. Clark of the NYPD Hostage Negotiation Team describes the special training and years of experience his unit brings to hostage situations. Which techniques work and which don't has generally been determined in actual hostage situations through the years. "If you people find yourself in a hostage situation," says Detective Lieutenant Clark, "we'll be negotiating for you."

The Hostage Negotiation Team, 125 trained detectives, responds to between 175 and 200 hostage situations every year. In the first six months of 1988, it has recovered thirty-two people. Since the unit began in 1973, it has lost only a single hostage.

The students learn what they can do to isolate and contain a hostage situation—cordon off the area, cover escape routes, evaluate the situation, take cover, and operate from that safe location. Cops do not exchange themselves for hostages. Weapons are not negotiated for, nor is nuclear material. Nor are hostages exchanged for the release of persons held in custody.

Time is a key element, and time is on the side of the police. Immediately after taking hostages, the perp is in a volatile state of mind. If he can be gradually calmed down by patient negotiation, he will realize there is only one viable way to get out.

231

If a cop becomes a hostage, he has no obligation to get himself killed. "If you're alive," says Detective Lieutenant Clark, "we can get you out. If you're dead, we can't." If a cop finds himself on the inside, the best thing he can do for himself and the hostages is to try to calm everyone down.

Political discussions with hostage-takers should be avoided, as well as any touchy subjects. A cop should try to establish a rapport, to make the perp see him as a human being. On the street, people don't see the cop's face, only the uniform; he is seen as a representative of the government, as a soldier. But it may be difficult, even for a terrorist, to execute someone with whom he or she has established a rapport.

What kinds of cops help in hostage negotiation and are recruited by the team? Young ones who can talk about the people the team has found hostage-takers want to talk about—Madonna, Prince, Sean Penn, the Grateful Dead. Women officers, because the soothing voice of a woman may snuff out the lit fuse of a volatile person.

Food is also a useful tool; it can make the hostage-taker drowsy. Sleep-inducing drugs are never given, because the last thing the hostage-taker may do before he dozes off is kill the hostages. Other tools used to help deal with hostage-takers are listening devices that permit conversations in a distant room to be heard and recorded, and special telephones through which the perp and the authorities can communicate. Fiber optics, special cameras, night-vision goggles, walkie-talkies, portable telephones, surveillance trucks with periscopes, and Bell Jet Ranger helicopters are also used.

Dealing with the media is addressed by Captain Tom Fahey, who works for the deputy commissioner of public information. Sooner or later, he says, all those present will be involved with the media. Citing Andy Warhol's famous proclamation that everyone will be famous for fifteen minutes, he tells the students: "What you want to avoid is becoming infamous."

The first cop on the scene of some exotic homicide may face

people from the media who get there before the sergeant. A reporter will stick a microphone in front of his mouth and ask what he thinks happened. "You're wearing that blue suit," says Captain Fahey. "You're representing the police department. You will be held responsible for your statements." There's nothing wrong with a cop responding, "I don't know," he says. Reporters can be referred to the sergeant, the duty captain, or deputy commissioner of public information.

Captain Fahey tells the students that the public and the press will ask them questions about department policy: Why is the police department not enforcing drug laws? Why aren't there more cops on the street? "You're going to get caught up in situations out there, times when you feel at odds with the department, and you may feel like you want to express yourself. I'm not here to take away your constitutional rights. Just do it off duty, and say it is your personal opinion.

"I'm not here to defend the media, either," adds Captain Fahey. "There are many things wrong with the media, but the last time I looked, the NYPD wasn't perfect either. There are some excellent reporters out there, and some dirt bags.

"I would love to be in the position of some of my counterparts in foreign countries," Captain Fahey says with a wry grin. "I'd come in in the morning and say, we'll let the press know about A, C, F, and G. That's not the way we work in this country, and certainly not in New York City. Sometimes information is embarrassing to the department and we'd rather not let go of it, but it goes out. If I ask myself as a citizen of New York City, 'Am I happy the media have access to this stuff?' I say yes. The same media that embarrass us stick up for us."

Dr. Alan Wikler of the NYPD's Psychological Services Unit talks about suicide among members of the force. Cops should seek help early if they need it, or urge others to get it if they notice any warning signs. Depression and inability to concentrate are symptoms. The popular idea that people who talk

233

about suicide don't do it is a myth. And attending counseling sessions at Psychological Services won't hurt an officer's career.

The Psychological Services Unit also screens 911 operators and the civilians who guard prisoners at the precincts. It conducts psychological evaluations of officers selected for special units (Bomb Squad, Emergency Service). Psychological screening is also required for certain promotions of detective grades. Whenever cops are involved in a shooting or in a personal tragedy, it's mandatory that they see a psychologist in the unit's debriefing program to determine whether they are fit to carry firearms. They may then be referred to psychologists, social workers, or psychiatrists.

The speeches that draw the deepest response from the students are made by officers from the Police Self-Support Group, formed to help cops who are seriously injured in the line of duty.

Blinded on New Year's Eve 1982, when the terrorist bomb he was trying to dismantle exploded, Detective Richard Pastorella describes his agonizing experience in unnerving detail. He stresses safety on the job.

Detective John Snidersich, a former member of the Street Crime Unit, broke up a bank robbery on August 3, 1979. He was shot three times; one bullet is still in his chest. Bulletproof vests may be uncomfortable, he says; they may restrict mobility—but not as much as being shot when you're not wearing one. A cop wouldn't think of going out on patrol without a gun, so why go out without a vest?

Before Officer Dennis Brennan speaks, he plays an audiotape. The recruits are chilled to hear his voice crying for help on his radio after he was shot at a traffic light while on his scooter on January 27, 1984. A sniper on a rooftop, showing off his gun, had picked out a cop at random for target practice. Officer Brennan cites himself as an example of the sobering fact that a police officer doesn't have to be responding to a bank robbery, a family dispute, or a hijacking to be injured; tragedy can strike at any time. On the street everyone knows who the cops are—they can be spotted a block away. But a cop doesn't know who his adversary is. It could be a young boy on a bicycle, or a man dressed in a business suit, or a middle-aged woman pulling a grocery cart. It could be anyone.

Running through Tom Ramos's mind are thoughts of what his family would go through if he were shot on the job. The natural tendency, he knows, is to think it could happen only to the next guy, but he is realistic enough to realize that at any time he could walk into a situation that would change his life for the worse. He looks around the auditorium and asks himself, "Which one of us will be injured?" For a moment the sight of the injured officer onstage makes him question whether the job is worth it. There are risks in all jobs, he reasons, but the challenge and rewards of law enforcement more than compensate.

Use your heads, the officers tell the students. Apply the information given to you at the academy. Don't ever become complacent. "Look what happened to us, through no fault of our own. At any given moment you could become one of us. We prefer that you *don't* become one of us." Swept by the courage and conviction of Detectives Pastorella and Snidersich and Officer Brennan, the students greet their last words by standing unanimously for a long ovation.

A block of time is set aside for recruits to join fraternal organizations of the NYPD. Fraternal organizations are groups whose members have a common ethnic, religious, or other bond, although membership is typically open to all brother and sister officers. In classrooms on the fourth and fifth floors of the academy are representatives of the organizations, eager to discuss with the students the purpose of their groups. Lissette Sierra-Solis and Tom Ramos meet with the Hispanic Society; Andy Varga with the Emerald Society, the Holy Name Society, and the Pulaski Association; Stefanie Hirschhorn with the Shomrim Society.

The Shomrim Society, like the other fraternal organizations, is basically a social group, as opposed to the Patrolmen's Benevolent Association, which represents police officers in contract negotiations and disciplinary hearings. Shomrim offers certain services such as death benefits, but if Stefanie is interested in meeting other Jewish officers on the job, she might attend any of the group's social functions: its annual January dinner-dance, Father's Day picnic, or summer weekend getaway at an upstate hotel.

A fraternal organization provides moral support and advice. Although there are department channels for a cop to go through if he is the victim of disparaging ethnic or religious remarks or actions, the society can also help to guide him through the problem. "We're a small minority and we will not stand anti-Semitism," says Sergeant Gerald Mines, who is representing the Shomrim Society at the academy. "If you tolerate that, you're just as bad as the people who perpetrate it." All of these organizations look out for their own over whatever hurdle needs to be cleared.

The last gym classes, held the week before graduation, are affairs of sweet vengeance. After all the verbal abuse and merciless workouts, the student officers get to let the instructors know just what they think of them—in front of everyone.

On June 7 at four P.M., six B Squad companies pour out onto the gym floor. Fifteen minutes later their workout begins, this time led by the recruits in riotous parody of their tyrannical instructors.

Wild cheers greet one recruit's imitation of an instructor whose physique would turn the Incredible Hulk even greener with envy. A solid, rugged young man puts shoulder pads underneath a black sweatshirt and begins the exercise by ordering the recruits, "Get your butts down!" Pacing back and forth on the stage, he points menacingly at the student officers. "I know some of you are going to hate me," he growls, "and some will love me. It doesn't matter to me." There's applause and laughter, and he jumps off the stage with a wicked smile.

One student squats, grabs his heels with his hands, and extends his buttocks up in the air. Some of the recruits have trouble following, and he screams at them. Another recruit mounts the stage and says with a sneer, "Remember, there's only two things that touch me—my wife, and soap."

One student officer conducts a beer-drinking exercise by raising and lowering his hand. Another recruit, instead of leading the class in push-ups, leads in eyebrow lifts. Another extends his right hand out and his left hand across it in an obscene Italian gesture. All these get strong hands. An unimaginative recruit who leads the class in straight leg lifts gets booed off the stage.

The recruits are not beyond mimicking their comrades either. Two male students imitate some of their female colleagues in a series of push-ups by moving their rear ends up and down but not bending their arms.

The instructors are watching from the side, smiling goodnaturedly, accepting the roasting as coming with the turf. "It's a way of getting it all out," one female instructor says with a smile. At the end of the class the recruits rip one another's gym shirts off their backs.

The week before graduation is also when recruit evaluations are completed and presented to the student officers. On July 7, Company 19 is sitting in Room 413. Officer Frank Dwyer gives the class basic information: High grades don't necessarily mean a very good report since class participation and other factors are also weighed. The students are then called, in alphabetical order, to a table outside the classroom, where they see their evaluation and get an explanation of the various reports that go in their personnel file at One Police Plaza. Consulting with the students are Officer Dwyer, Company 19's official company instructor and Law instructor, and Officers Annette Bagley and Jeri Kocik, their Police Science and Social Science instructors.

Lissette Sierra-Solis is eager to get her critique over with, but she has a long wait before she is called. When the first recruit returns to the classroom, he tells some of the questions he was asked. "Where do you see yourself in the department in a few years?" is one that strikes Lissette. Her first reaction: "I don't know what I'm going to do tomorrow, much less three years from now."

About forty-five minutes later Lissette is called. She waits in the doorway for a few minutes as the instructors discuss her file. When she is signaled to come to the table, Officer Dwyer asks, "How do you think you did?"

"I think I did pretty well."

From five possible overall evaluations, ranging from "Well above standards" to "Well below standards," Lissette receives the second highest evaluation, "Above standards." She reads each instructor's evaluation of her general performance in numerous categories: appearance, communications skills, human relations, self-image and discipline, judgment and decision-making, and police ethics. There are categories for the student's academic record, discipline record, and absence, and finally, spaces for instructor comments and the overall evaluation.

Lissette's instructors wrote that she should adjust well to the streets, especially because she has a husband on the job and has shown that she has learned much from his experiences. Officer Kocik stated that if she handles herself on patrol as well as she performed in the role plays, she'll have no problem. Officer Bagley asks Lissette if her husband helped her while at the academy. "I hardly got to see him," Lissette answers. With the conference over, all the instructors shake hands with Lissette, welcome her to the job, and wish her the best of luck.

Although officially sworn into the NYPD as police officers, gun and shield day marks the recruits' first real rite of passage into the city's elite law enforcement brotherhood. For disciplinary, physical, emotional, or personal reasons, some do not make it through the academy; training is an ordeal that has its casualties. Of the approximate 860 recruits to enter training, the graduating class totals 760: 577 NYPD officers, 160 Transit officers, and 23 Housing officers. Men compose 85.6 percent of the total class, women 14.4 percent.

News about student officers at the academy travels fast, even between the A and B Squads, who rarely see each other. The names are often unknown, but the stories and the people are real. During the term of this class at the academy, one recruit was arrested for committing a burglary; a few were forced to resign after failing the urine test for drugs; some saw crimes being committed, called the police, and were credited with the arrests. One recruit returned from a tour one night and found a burglar in his home. In self-defense, he shot and killed the burglar with his hunting rifle. He was found justified in shooting the man and was allowed to continue at the academy.

During training the recruits were told not to take any police action or become involved in any altercations; instead, they were to dial 911. They were told they were cops, yet they felt only a notch above civilians. When they first faithfully swore to serve the people of New York City, it was essentially a promise that the city would make them police officers. It certainly wasn't a guarantee.

With a gun and a shield, their lives will always be different. Guns and shields are more than diplomas. Most high-school and college graduates stuff their diplomas in desk drawers; some joke they're not worth more than the paper they're printed on. But a gun and shield are symbols of authority as well as the instruments with which the law is enforced. The bearers have, in their own eyes and in the eyes of others, an exalted status, but with that also comes a responsibility, and sometimes a terrible one.

It is 6:30 A.M., July 11, two days before graduation. It is bright and sunny, and soon the thermometer will climb to ninety-eight degrees. B Squad student officers start drifting in, and there is one notable difference about them. They are dressed as New York City police officers, real cops, with the blue uniforms, eight-pointed hats, regulation shoes, and the panoply of gunbelt gear, minus revolvers. They look spit-polish sharp, move with poise, and exude an aura of professionalism. Are these the same recruits who only six months before were so gangly and awkward, so frightened to death about what lay ahead in this job? Who feared they might be thrown out for the most frivolous of reasons, or might not measure up to the stringent standards of the department? Gone is the pale innocence of the idealist; now one sees only the uniform.

As the officers wait for muster on the Campus Deck, Sergeant Lindsay Eason of IDU watches. At the academy for seven years, Sergeant Eason has always been amazed by the impact the street uniform has on the recruits. Their personalities change; their behavior is different. "You would think I'd be used to it by now," says Sergeant Eason, "but I still marvel at the expression on their faces. I wish the present state that the uniform has brought them to lasts for their entire careers."

The recruits are eager to make collars, rid the streets of crime, earn gold shields, and advance to specialized units. But the anxiety of going into the streets now as police officers, hopefully saviors but maybe victims, manifests itself in different ways. Some are possessed by nervous excitement. For others, like Lissette Sierra-Solis and Andy Varga, it comes out in their sleep.

Transit Officer Sierra-Solis dreamed she was in a train and

asked someone to put his hands up on the wall as she learned in gym. Ignoring her, the man looked her straight in the eye and reached into his pocket, as if to grab a weapon. Feeling her life was in danger, Lissette opened fire on him, getting off four shots. But the gun wasn't firing bullets. She looked for holes in the man, but there weren't any. In another dream, corrections officials were transporting prisoners in the subway. When the train pulled in and the door opened, people on the platform began screaming, "It's Corrections, it's Corrections!" and ran away. Lissette looked through the subway door and saw a train full of large, vicious-looking prisoners, and they weren't handcuffed. Overcome by fear, she started running away too. Then she stopped in her tracks when it hit her: "Why am I running? I'm a police officer."

In Andy Varga's dream, he arrived late at the police academy on gun and shield day. He ran to his company, and some friends told him that he wasn't supposed to be wearing the academy pin on his collar. He fumbled to get it off, and the next thing he knew he was traveling uptown to meet his girl-friend. On the way something happened, and he had to make an arrest. He thought to himself, "No, I don't want to make this arrest," and then suddenly awoke.

There are those like Henry Ramirez who are entirely psyched up about the job. "In eight and a half hours," he says, "you'll go through more than anyone else. Anything can happen. You can make an arrest, get into a gun battle, help someone who is sick, save somebody's life. You're constantly in the lime-light. It's a rush!" Henry has adapted and modified a slogan of the U.S. Rangers: "I eat lightning, crap thunder, and have gasoline running through my veins. I'm one of New York's Finest." Another of Andy Varga's Breakfast Club members, Frank D'Elia, says, "I want eventually to work undercover in a narcotics detail and collar big drug dealers. I want to clean the city up. Everybody says it, but I really mean it."

* * *

Soon the recruits will be out on the streets as rookie police officers, transforming book information and theory into practical action. There was an overwhelming amount of complex material for the student officers to learn and remember in a very short time. Now they are to draw on their lessons and apply them to real-life situations.

Not only is remembering and applying all the information hurled at them in the last six months intimidating, but equally as daunting is the question of how they'll actually react to various kinds of offenses on the street. There are so many unanswered questions, from the most mundane to the grimmest. How will they respond to an unlicensed pushcart vendor? A robbery in progress? A week-old bloated corpse? Infractions, violations, misdemeanors, and felonies, each of which seemed so clear-cut and manageable on paper, now confront them like a nightmare. Each glance must be an astute observation. Crime happens so fast that perceptions must be snapshot-quick, and action immediate and intelligent. Is the officer acting within the law? Within regulations? Safely?

There are the larger questions, too, equally as troubling. Will their ideals and ethics in a city of crime be confounded by the limitations of the system, eventually to be washed away in a sea of cynicism? In just two years' time, will their personalities have metamorphosed to such a degree that they complain constantly, make wholesale condemnations of people for frivolous reasons, become the proverbial salty cop on the street?

The public perception of cops often seems to be that they are self-righteous, macho muscleheads who are on a power trip, seeing only black and white in their quest for law and order. In the academy, however, recruits are taught compassion and kindness, understanding and patience. They learn that cops are human beings first, cops second.

If the recruits can apply the self-adjustment techniques of their training, they should do well—even in New York City, where there is cause for despair on nearly every city block, where the legal system is so backed'up that apprehended criminals may be out in a matter of days, where all too often hopelessness seems the most prominent psychological landmark.

By 7:35 A.M., the student officers are in assigned classrooms. Lissette is in Room 413. Several minutes later Officer Dwyer comes in the room and hands out photocopies of a newspaper article. The headline reads: BOY ACCIDENTALLY KILLS HIS BROTHER WITH GUN. It is a warning to the officers to keep their guns secure and out of the reach of children, relatives, and friends.

Officer Gary Lombardo, the OCI of Company 32 and their Law instructor, later reveals a secret. It is customary that before classes begin, the instructors write their name, subject, and lesson of the day on the upper right corner of the blackboard. To this information Officer Lombardo has always attached a number—1, 2, or 3. The students, Stephanie Hirschhorn and Tom Ramos among them, have never questioned this practice or known what it meant. The numbers, Officer Lombardo now tells them, have represented his mood: three being good, two being fair, and one meaning "Don't mess with me."

For the next six months the recruits will be in Field Training Units, in which they'll patrol the streets under the supervision of experienced officers. They'll have radio car tours and work in the station houses, but most of the time they'll be out on foot patrol.

There are nineteen FTU squads throughout the seven patrol boroughs—Manhattan South, Manhattan North, Bronx, Brooklyn South, Brooklyn North, Queens, and Staten Island. Many students have individual preferences, usually based on the area of the precinct. Some want a precinct geographically close to where they live; others want high-crime areas so they can get experience right away. The instructors read aloud the FTU assignments and comment on the nature and reputation of each precinct. One student is assigned to an FTU in the relatively placid, suburban area of Bayside, Queens, and the class laughs.

When the assignment is in some particularly rough area, the instructors emphasize the learning benefits and the opportunity to work with good cops there. Andy Varga wanted FTU 3 but is assigned FTU 2 on the Lower East Side. Stefanie Hirschhorn gets FTU 6 in Manhattan North; Tom Ramos, FTU 11 in Brooklyn South. Lissette Sierra-Solis doesn't get an FTU. As a Transit officer, she'll have three more weeks of training at the Transit Academy, and then go straight into a tactical patrol force.

As the students get their FTU assignments, they talk about fellow recruits whom they'd like to work with and those they wouldn't. By this time the recruits are able to assess the capabilities and shortcomings of their colleagues. They've seen them perform in class and in gym, they've talked to one another and know their outlooks.

Andy Varga says there are certain recruits who don't know their job, who will either get hurt or end up inadvertently hurting somebody else. He doesn't want to be their fall guy. Frank D'Elia adds: "If I run up six flights of stairs or go through a door, I want somebody behind me I can trust. We hear stories from the instructors, and we draw our own conclusions." One story Andy heard from a friend, a city cop, sticks in his mind. The officer and his partner answered a call for a disturbance, and the officer got into a fight with a man. The partner, a woman, was afraid she'd get hurt and locked herself in the radio car. Andy's friend sustained a black eye, and he was furious.

There are mixed feelings among the male recruits about having women on the job. Some say they don't mind as long as they can handle themselves, while others think it is a man's job. Still others think some of the men are unqualified, not knowing when to keep their mouths shut or when to back down in particular situations.

Andy Varga feels gender is irrelevant; it's street smarts that count. He grew up on the streets, saw many fights, and he feels he has a gut instinct on how to behave out there. "You also have to be mature," he says. "You can't be acting like you're still hanging out with the boys on the corner and thinking, just because you're a cop or have a gun, you can do anything you want."

When Andy gets his gun, he intends to look at it, touch it, and get it out of his system. He realizes the consequences of careless behavior by someone who owns a gun. Indeed, for weeks the instructors have joked that on gun and shield day, they'll be hiding in their basements or in Connecticut, as far away from the recruits as they can get.

When Driver Training instructor Charles Gittens received his gun five years earlier, he knew his six-year-old son would be very curious about it. He jokes that if he hid the gun, his kid would be able to find it, take it to school, show his class-mates, and restore it to its hiding place before he got home. So he let his son examine the revolver unloaded and then issued a stern warning that the boy was never to touch it again without asking him.

Unfortunately, not all gun stories have such happy endings. Three classes earlier, the valedictorian proudly went home and showed his girlfriend his new revolver. Then he took a shower and his girlfriend, thinking there were no bullets in the gun, began to play with it. She accidentally shot and killed him.

For cops who have had family on the job, shield numbers may have personal meaning. When Officer Michael Wilson of the Social Science Department graduated, he requested the shield number of his great-grandfather, an Irish immigrant who had retired as an acting captain on the NYPD. He called the Shield Desk but ran into a snafu when he was told there were several Michael Lanes on record, and further information would be needed to zero in on his relative. Did he have a social security number? There were no social security numbers when his great-grandfather was on the job. An address? He managed to locate an address, and indeed his great-grandfather was

245

identified in the police records. Today Officer Wilson is the proud bearer of a bygone two-digit NYPD shield number: sixty-eight.

At ten A.M. Sergeant Willie Freeman of Recruit Operations comes into Room 415 and tells Andy to bring the students to the sub-basement to get their guns and shields. Andy lines up Company 20 and marches them single file through the corridor and down the main staircase to the sub-basement. Several other companies are there, and the students join the end of the line.

Andy waits patiently, nervously. It's really happening, he thinks. He's becoming a cop. He comes to a table, where he is given a box of ammunition. Then, at another table in the corner of the hall, he is given a shield, number 31743. He tells a man behind the table he is City; the man gives him a cap device. He continues along the line that snakes around to the academy's disused indoor firing range. The guns the recruits selected at the outdoor range months before are distributed to them from a storage room along the way. Gradually, Andy makes his way to the front. After a group in front of him has received their guns, Andy is called with nine other recruits to stations along the firing range.

An instructor from the outdoor range prepares them for the street step by step. He has the group draw and present their revolvers, combat-load six rounds, and lock the guns into their holsters. Then the recruits unlock their guns to make sure they can be withdrawn without difficulty, and then lock their guns once more. Andy feels like a soldier during wartime, being armed to fight the enemy.

The mood in the sub-basement is jubilant. Andy can't believe the New York Police Department has given him a gun! Henry Ramirez is on a high too. He says he gets a rush looking at his uniform and the patch on his shoulder. Frank D'Elia is ecstatic, having made a dream real, and he welcomes the big responsibility that comes with it. They all feel part of the "family" now, even if they are neophytes not yet embraced by the legions of cops in the department.

Tom Ramos feels the scene is anticlimactic. He's rehearsed gun and shield day over and over in his mind, exhausting all the emotions he could possibly feel. His fantasies about this day, he says, were better than the reality.

After the students receive their Mace canisters, they proceed to the auditorium, where the B Squad is congratulated by Chief Burke.

A perspicacious, authoritarian-looking figure, and ruggedly handsome with a square face that bears a resemblance to John Wayne, Deputy Chief Robert F. Burke, commanding officer of the police academy, oversees all its units. He wears button-down open vests and ties, chain-smokes, and chews on tooth-picks. With his husky physique he looks like a tough cop. But when one gets to know him, he is affable and warm, not to mention garrulous. Indeed, he is an eloquent speaker and he has acted in plays at the academy. Dr. Jess Maghan, the acad-emy's Director of Training and an articulate scholar, pays Chief Burke the ultimate compliment, calling him "the persona of a New York cop."

"You've come a long way," Burke tells the recruits warmly now. "We're proud of you." He speaks of the power that comes with the shield, warning them not to be arrogant. A cop never knows with whom he's dealing. He recalls once waiting for a parking spot when a rude man pulled in and took it. "I'm a cop," the man told him. "I'm a sergeant," answered Robert Burke.

More advice. Ask the hairbags (old-timers) questions. Think like a cop. Make friends on the post. Get to know the Anticrime cars. Stay out of trouble.

Captain Charles D. DeRienzo, commanding officer of the recruit training school, urges the students to keep their sense of humor. They'll see human beings living in places they never thought it possible to live. Have heart and a good attitude.

"You've come a long way since that cold day in January," he says, the corners of his eyes crinkling. "I hardly recognize you."

Students with an overall average of ninety-four or better are called to the stage to receive a tassel. Among them are Stefanie Hirschhorn and Tom Ramos of Company 32.

After the ceremonies in the auditorium, the officers return to the classrooms, where they place six bullets in each of their two speed loaders. Shortly afterward they leave the academy. It is the first time they have ever walked in public as cops carrying loaded guns.

And so this January–July class gets set to graduate, to take its place on the streets of New York and play out whatever hand fate deals them. It seems much longer than twenty-three weeks ago that these young men and women took an oath to begin a new career.

On Wednesday, July 13, graduation is held at St. John's University in Queens. By 10:45 A.M., the cavernous gymnasium of Alumni Hall is filled with eager celebrants. Local television crews are there, and reporters and photographers from the city's major newspapers. As everyone waits, the graduating class lingers in a large room and in corridors sealed off from the public. It is the first time the A and B squads have assembled together since orientation. The officers, like the academy staff serving as ushers, are dressed not in regular police uniform but ceremonially—dark blue uniform suits with gold buttons down the center.

The main floor of the gymnasium has two sections of blue chairs for the two squads. Flowers adorn the red-carpeted stage, and on the red and blue backdrop is a green banner, against which "Police Academy" is spelled out in white letters. On the red section of the backdrop are large shields with the names of the three divisions of the New York City Police Department.

Soon after eleven A.M. the ceremony begins. First come the dignitaries—Mayor Edward Koch, Commissioner Benjamin Ward, Chief of Department Robert Johnston, Jr., Transit Police Chief Vincent Del Castillo, Housing Police Chief Louis G. Raiford, Jr., and many other high-ranking career officers in the NYPD. They are welcomed by Chief Burke and take their seats at the dais.

Captain DeRienzo is standing in front of the stage at the center. In a stentorian voice he initiates the proceedings. "Class. Ten hut!" All heads turn to the rear of the gymnasium to capture a very happy moment.

With the familiar instrumental opening of Frank Sinatra's recording of "New York, New York" blasting through the gym, the class begins filing in. They are greeted by cheers, sighs, and screams. These are the families and friends of the about-to-be-christened police officers—mothers and fathers, wives and husbands, girlfriends and boyfriends—who patiently sweated through the six months of training with them. As the officers fill the aisles marching in neat rows at snap-crack pace to their seats, the emotion in the audience is deep. Eyes are wet, and parents beam wide smiles. Sisters and brothers shake their heads with tremendous pride. The newest of New York's Finest take their places to the thunderous applause of their loved ones.

The ceremony runs smoothly. There's the national anthem, introductions, an oath, the presentation of awards, speeches. There's humor, political statements. Warnings and congratulations to the new officers. Commissioner Ward points out that among the graduates are a husband and wife, twin brothers, a former member of the police department of Italy.

Mayor Koch says being a mayor and being a cop are similar: "Everybody expects you to be everything—doctor, lawyer, peace officer, priest, social worker. They expect miracles, but we're all human. Some fundamentals that apply to you as to me are: never panic, never do what's wrong because it's pop-

249

ular, never flinch to do what's right because the crowd is yelling at you to do your duty." He cites the escalation of crack and drug use in general and cries out for more judges, more jails, more help. Inevitably, he says, some officers present will be injured in the line of duty. Mayor Koch promises to come to the hospital to "tell you I love you, admire you."

At the end of the ceremony the graduates file out to the strains of "Stars and Stripes Forever." They meet their families and friends outside Alumni Hall, and there is much hugging and kissing, taking of snapshots, and exchanging of best wishes with fellow officers. There is also a sadness. Many of the officers will never see one another again. By 1:30 on this hazy afternoon, the crowd has cleared, the hoopla has dissipated into the steaming summer air. The new officers have the rest of the day off to prepare themselves for their first tour of duty—the next day.

──── 16 ────
FIELD TRAINING UNITS

On Thursday, July 14, the city of New York is fortified by the placement of more than 750 police academy graduates in its precincts—rookies whose practical education is just now to commence on some of the meanest and most despairing streets of America. Just how badly these new officers are needed is obvious from the city's grim crime statistics and the loud public outcry for more police protection. For the rookies the honeymoon is truly over. They are about to confront scenes of human depravity, poverty, and hopelessness that no academic instruction can prepare them for: utterly squalid slums, appalling living conditions, and amoral, cruel, and insensitive people.

Six months earlier these rookies were civilians turning out for orientation on a bitter cold winter morning not knowing what to expect. Now on this hot and hazy summer morning they are doing the same, albeit for real-life street patrol. It's daunting for someone harboring glamorous and idealistic notions about a law enforcement career to be suddenly thrust out into the jungle. The uniformed officer, inexperienced as he is,

251

is now a sentry to protect the good citizens from harm and a sitting duck for the crackpots of society.

Just before 7:30 A.M. Police Officer Stefanie Hirschhorn walks through a side entrance of the 25th Precinct in Spanish Harlem, feeling, as she says, "scared of my own shadow." The "two-five" is a four-story gray building on 119th Street between Lexington and Park avenues. It is undistinguished as NYPD station houses go—sedate, drab, and nondescript. On the first floor is the front desk, a muster area, a community affairs office, cells, and an arrest processing room. Upper floors hold more offices, a detectives' squad, locker rooms, lounges, and a minigym.

In uniform, Stefanie is carrying her .38 revolver. Amazing, she thinks. There's life and death in her pocket. Six months before she was just an ordinary citizen, afraid to walk in certain sections of the city. Now she's about to saunter through some of these very ominous neighborhoods as The Law! She hasn't done any patrolling yet, but she's cautiously aware she's a cop, representing the city of New York and striving to protect and defend its residents.

Stefanie stops at the desk to find out where the Field Training Unit Office is. She ascends the stairs to the second floor and veers left, into a room directly ahead. Soon the room fills up with twenty-two freshly minted police officers, alumni of both the A and B Squads at the academy. Four sergeants and a lieutenant enter a few minutes later and commence the FTU program with the customary orientation protocol: a welcome and an explanation of policies and procedures, including such basics as walking a post, using a radio, making arrests, overtime. There's paperwork and roll call. And especially, there are warnings—don't go on jobs alone no matter how menial they seem; don't stay too close to certain buildings because people might throw things down; don't be lax on duty because bosses—borough chiefs, duty captains, ICOs, deputy inspectors, and zone commanders—check footposts. Keep your eyes open; observe, and if you see anything, put it over the radio. The sergeants spell out the FTU itinerary. For the next six months it will be mainly footpost work, but there will be about fifteen radio car tours, a day with detectives, a day with the desk officer, and a day at traffic court.

The group is divided in half for a tour of the FTU confines in a blue-and-white police van. The trip through the area is a little like riding through a war zone. Desolation and decay are ubiquitous. People look sad or desperate. "What have I gotten myself into?" Stefanie wonders as she surveys the precinct.

Around East 118th Street there are numerous abandoned buildings—one deserted structure is an enormous old school. There are open lots strewn with garbage. One building in particular captures everyone's attention, an abandoned building whose fire escapes and dozens of window openings are filled with large stuffed animals. It is a comical sight on an otherwise sordid block. "F.A.O. Schwarz, Harlem style," Stefanie remarks dryly.

The training officer points out corruption-prone locations— drug buildings, numbers joints, and social clubs where illegal activity is practiced. A visitor, struck by the poverty, wouldn't be able to distinguish a problem location from a benign one, but the cops know. One decrepit building on St. Nicholas Avenue is an active drug den frequented by dealers, buyers, and "skells" (lowlifes). The precinct cops sometimes respond to more than five jobs there on a single night. As they drive, calls come over the radio from Central for "Shots fired," "Man with a gun," or a 10-13 ("officer needs assistance"). Already the police academy seems a million miles away.

One small section comprises Old World Italians who, it's said, don't call the cops when there's a problem. They take care of it themselves. About six years earlier a nun in the area was raped and brutally murdered. Rumor had it that the Mob put out a contract on the perp. He gave himself up to the police shortly thereafter.

Stefanie's FTU covers two precincts in central Harlem—the 28th and the 32nd—and one in East Harlem, the 25th. Her footpost turf is part of Operation Pressure Point (OPP)—an NYPD program in which cops are placed in the worst drug areas to establish a highly visible, active presence to deter street-level drug activity. Loiterers are to be dispersed, double-parked cars in front of known drug locations ticketed, and arrests made when appropriate. The rookies, however, are told emphatically that they are not to start aggressive one-man campaigns against crime. This is to prevent or minimize trouble, injury, or civilian complaints in the first stage of the rookie's career.

Working in OPP, the rookie officers might come across plain-clothes narcotics cops involved in "buy and bust" operations. Their work is so dangerous that they don't carry IDs, don't wear bulletproof vests, and may carry different weapons than city cops. Their protection is nearby backup units. If a bust is about to go down, a detective in an unmarked car might come up to a footpost cop and ask him to stay off the block. But caution is to be exercised in dealing with anyone claiming to work undercover, since perps say they're cops too. And not arresting a real undercover cop as if he or she were a real criminal could blow their cover. Undercovers are to be taken in to the station house, where everything can be settled.

Tuesday, July 19, is a monumental day in the law enforcement career of Stefanie Hirschhorn. It is her first day out on patrol on the streets of New York as a professional police officer. The tour begins with roll call, where footposts and meal time are assigned. Next comes unit training, a regular part of every tour during which updates of the *Patrol Guide*, tactics, paperwork, and other areas of the job are covered. The first unit training class includes a film about street weapons and instructions on how to respond to a 10-13. The rookies are told not to be in a hurry to make arrests or issue summonses.

FTU tours run eight hours and thirty-five minutes. An eight-to-four tour usually runs from approximately seven A.M. to 3:35 P.M., with the FTU officer on post by 8:10 after roll call and training updates. Approximately six hours of the tour are spent walking a post.

The rookies sign out their radios and make calls to Central from outside the station house to check their operating ability.

A radio may be the cop's most valuable tool. There are sundry scenarios—facing an angry crowd, being challenged by several perps, stopping a suspicious vehicle—in which a pipeline to reinforcements may mean the difference between life and death. Stefanie knows the codes fairly well, but now that they have become of immediate importance to her, she needs to be able to use them fluently. She remembers what she learned in the academy—if you're panicking and can't remember a code, just say what you have to in plain English.

Stefanie and the other neophyte officers leave the station house and walk to 116th Street, where they separate to take their posts. Stefanie and her partner each have three blocks along Eighth Avenue from 113th to 116th streets, Stefanie on the east side, her partner on the west. This stretch of land is mostly barren, but that doesn't mean it's empty: Junkies and winos abound, and some of the stores may not be what they seem.

Pounding a beat means being outdoors, standing and walking, observing, conversing, ruminating, giving directions, and becoming acquainted with the people in the area. You sweat or freeze, quickly learn the value of a nearby bathroom, seek out refuge from rain under awnings or in doorways, get bored and tired of standing for so long. Occasionally, there are moments of excitement.

After several weeks on the street, the contrast between the reality and the ivory tower police academy becomes apparent to Stefanie. In gym, for instance, self-defense and the blows and holds to control perps are practiced gingerly, but what's a new officer to do when she's trying to arrest a huge perp who's acting belligerent? On the streets anything goes. Often these experiences are the rookie's first real lessons on survival.

The day before Election Day, the FTU lieutenant in the 28th Precinct tells the rookie officers not to make any frivolous collars. The next day is Election Day, when officers will be detailed to voting sites, and he doesn't want any cops hung up in the arrest process. Stefanie Hirschhorn is on a four-to-twelve tour, driving her FTU sergeant. After getting gas on Randalls Island at the Street Crime Unit, they return to the confines of the 28th Precinct. The streets seem peaceful, calm. They are driving west on 119th Street and pass Lenox Avenue when an elderly man flags them down. He says a huge man in a beige leather jacket snatched a $20 bill out of his hand. He's around the corner. Stefanie and the sergeant exchange glances. "There goes a quiet night!" the sergeant mutters.

Stefanie backs the RMP up on Lenox Avenue, between 120th and 121st streets. While the car is still in motion, the sergeant spots the suspect and jumps out, leaving the door open. He approaches the man, a hulking black six-foot-four three-hundred-pounder. The sergeant, a twenty-year-plus veteran in his midforties, grabs the suspect's arm, but he just shrugs it off. "Uh-oh!" Stefanie says under her breath. She throws the car into park. Leaving the doors open and the motor running, she snatches the radio and runs to the man, grabbing his other arm.

By now a crowd has gathered. "I didn't do nothin'," the man protests while the elderly man accuses him of taking his money. The sergeant tells him to put his hands behind his back. "I'm not coming with you," he says. With the two officers holding his arms, the man walks away. Stefanie is disconcerted by the perp's considerable strength. If he picked her up and slammed her to the ground, she thinks she might wake up five blocks away in need of plastic surgery. She tries to break his concentration by bending his pinky to his wrist, but there is no reaction. Then she feels the ground disappear from under her. The man just raised his arms and lifted her. Now he decides he wants to cross the street. With the sergeant on one arm and Stefanie tucked into his side like a football, he makes his slow flight with little difficulty.

A driver just pulling into a parking space on 121st Street west of Lenox is startled to see a huge black man with two police officers attached to his arms come crashing down on the hood of his car. He watches, unbelieving, as the sergeant grabs the man's crotch and twists his testicles several times with all his might. The man speaks evenly: "I'm still not coming." The suspect is leaning on the side of the car now. Stefanie backs up two feet, then leaps forward, using all her weight to push her foot into the man's testicles and grind them into the car. The man smiles at her. "I'm not coming with you, Miss Policeman." The sergeant looks at Stefanie and says calmly, "I think we need some help here."

Stefanie radios an "85 forthwith" to Central. Then she pauses for a moment. "Where the fuck am I?" She has momentarily blanked out on the location and has to look at the street sign before giving the address. In moments radio cars arrive from all over. Stefanie's best friend in FTU bursts out laughing when he pulls up and sees her ramming the guy like a body check in a hockey game, to no avail. The man is high on something and oblivious to any pain. A dozen cops show up, and several pick the man up by his legs and maneuver him to the ground, where he is cuffed.

At the station house the man is found to have three one-dollar bills and one twenty-dollar bill. He is charged with grand larceny, a felony, and resisting arrest, a misdemeanor.

The prisoner's mother later comes into the precinct. Almost as big as her son, she is irate. As the arresting officer, Stefanie goes to talk with her.

"I gave my boy five dollars to get something to eat," she screams. "He had no money!" Then where did he get the $20 bill? Stefanie wonders.

The mother looks at the old man filing the complaint. "Your ass is mine for getting my son locked up," she growls. "We know what you look like now. We'll get you." Stefanie orders the woman to leave the station house.

Stefanie enters another world when she brings her prisoner to Manhattan's Central Booking, a starting point for putting the perps into the criminal justice system. It is a depressing place to be, a pit stop to incarceration, temporarily at least, that has the musty odor of stale sweat.

The next day Stefanie goes to the Police Complaint Room to see an assistant district attorney, missing her Election Day detail. It is an unpleasant brush with the bureaucracy, the first of many that are likely to frustrate her during her career. The A.D.A., a young woman, asks why it took so many cops to catch the man. Stefanie slaps a Polaroid that an officer back at the station house took of the man and exclaims, "You decide for yourself!" The A.D.A. stares at it for a moment, then picks it up and walks into her supervisor's office. All Stefanie can hear from the room is laughter.

What isn't so funny to Stefanie is that the A.D.A. doesn't charge the perp with the felony, but lets him plead guilty to a misdemeanor. The A.D.A. doesn't want to push the felony charge—grand larceny for stealing the $20—because, she says, the perp had no prior arrests. But Stefanie saw a document on her desk containing several pages of priors. Why did the A.D.A. reduce the charges? Perhaps, Stefanie speculates, because she feels overworked and underpaid.

Indeed, many cops are frustrated with a legal system that they perceive undermines their efforts to bring criminals to justice. They appreciate that the D.A.'s office is backlogged with cases, but they see plea-bargaining as a means more to get a high conviction rate than to reduce pending cases. As an extreme example, if someone is arrested for murder but cops a plea for possession of marijuana, it's still a conviction on the A.D.A.'s record. At election time, the D.A.'s office can claim a high conviction rate. "Yeah," says Stefanie, "on bullshit charges." Not long after Stefanie brings her collar into Central Booking, she sees him on the street.

Despite the uniform, the badge, and the revolver that make police officers intimidating to so many, not all people show cops respect. Of course, there are hard-core cop-haters—felons, drug dealers, organized crime figures—but cops lament that many average citizens have the same attitude. Many cops remember how when they were growing up, neighborhood police officers were icons of respect; sometimes they would discipline a kid who gave them a hard time, and tell the kid's parents, who usually supported their action. Cops today can't administer discipline to young people. Often they have to take what the public dishes out.

Manhattan's Tompkins Square Park runs from 10th Street to 7th Street, and from Avenue A to Avenue B. On a warm Saturday in September, Andy Varga is assigned to patrol the southeast and southwest sections.

At one P.M., Andy returns from meal and meets his partner, Officer Vincent Stella, at the Tompkins Square Park entrance at St. Marks and Avenue A. Officer Stella patrols the northern half of the park. The two enter the park together. Walking toward them are three women, one of whom is carrying an open bottle of beer, a violation of the New York City Administrative Code. Police officers have discretion in issuing summonses for these violations. Twice earlier in the day, Officer Stella had seen the woman—about twenty years old, wearing a tank top and blue jeans and looking like a punk rocker—holding the beer, and had told her to put it away. She disobeyed him each time.

As the two parties get closer, the woman gulps down the beer in full view of the officers and chucks the bottle in a garbage can. "That takes balls," Andy thinks. Officer Stella is glowering at the woman. One of the others calls out, "Say,

259

man, give my friend a break. She just broke up with her boyfriend."

Since going on footposts, Andy has frequently observed people standing in the streets or sitting on stoops drinking beer. He tells them he enjoys a beer now and again, too, but that he'd appreciate their showing him some respect. "If you see me coming, hide it or put it away," he says. In such instances, he's found, people are usually apologetic.

As the groups pass each other, the beer-drinking woman grabs Andy's left arm. In the police academy the recruits were told not to let anyone touch them.

"Don't touch me!" Andy says, pulling his arm away.

"Fuck you!" the woman snaps back.

In his Law classes at the academy, Andy learned that the U.S. Supreme Court has held that people can say anything they want to cops as long as their behavior doesn't constitute a course of conduct. Following a cop around screaming, for example, would be harassment. Otherwise, the court expects the cops to be thick-skinned and withstand public abuse.

Andy is not insulted by the woman's curse. He *is* bothered by her lack of respect. He and his partner just crack momentary smiles at each other as if to say, "Come on, let's not waste our time." As they walk away, they hear the women laughing. A safe distance away, just before separating for their posts, they break into laughter also.

It's not long before the neophyte police officer witnesses man's inhumanity to man. Trying to comfort and help people who have been severely beaten, knifed, or otherwise assaulted is part of a cop's daily life. What can frustrate a cop as much as a heinous crime is a victim who does not cooperate in bringing the attacker to justice. Within a couple of weeks after graduating from the academy, Henry Ramirez is introduced firsthand to this aspect of the job.

On a hot Sunday morning late in July, a group of rookies

emerge from the 52nd Precinct, at Webster Avenue and Mosholu Parkway in the Bronx. They are headed for their assigned footposts, which for most is not within walking distance. Henry Ramirez naturally assumes a police van will take them to their stations, but instead receives a quick dose of reality. "The bus is on Webster Avenue," notes Sergeant Mike Joyce.

Henry is assigned BAND (Bronx Anti-Narcotics Drive) Post Five in the 46th Precinct. BAND is the Bronx equivalent of Manhattan's Operation Pressure Point: a police presence in drug-prone areas to deter buying and selling.

Heading to his post, Henry walks down Anthony Avenue, off Tremont Avenue, where a festive block party is going on. The music is loud; Henry has difficulty hearing his radio, and this annoys him. He's new on the job and doesn't want to miss any urgent calls broadcast by Central.

The morning is for the most part uneventful, and Henry is glad when his meal hour comes. The selection of places to eat is, he discovers, remarkably limited. A pizzeria on Tremont is closed on Sundays. On Webster Avenue there's a fried chicken take-out place whose food is of dubious quality. Particular about what he eats and who handles his food, Henry declines. He'll settle for an apple juice at the station house.

The police station is almost empty; most of the officers are at a fire that broke out at an after-hours club at 175th Street and Jerome. At the end of meal Henry leaves to return to his post. Thinking the sergeant won't mind if he comes by the fire scene, he contemplates whether he should walk down Anthony Avenue. "I'll probably run into something," he muses. A different route would diminish the chances of encountering a confrontation. But he changes his mind. "Don't be scared," he thinks. "It's your job to be out here. Go down Anthony."

He traverses Anthony, which is landscaped with skells along the sidewalks, on cement stoops; and on parked cars. As he approaches number 1911, a tenement building notorious for drug trouble, two women run out. Both are wearing jeans, shirts, and sneakers without socks. They look unkempt; Henry's first impression is that they look like they were playing in Quaker State motor oil. One is about five feet six; the other is an inch shorter.

"Officer, officer," one woman screams. "She took my money. She took my money! She's in there."

"Calm down." The women are excited, and Henry wants to find out what really happened. He also realizes that for many people in this area, their entertainment is on the street: firemen in hats and long coats whizzing past in their bright-red trucks, and police officers in patrol cars racing into action with sirens screaming and lights flashing. They stop whatever it is they're doing and run outside to watch. Before long, while the women are hurling accusations and Henry is trying to understand what happened, a small crowd has formed around the three.

The door of 1911 Anthony Avenue swings open, and a young woman steps out. She is pulling down her cotton blouse over a belly that is obviously nurturing a life. Her mouth is covered with blood.

"What happened?" Henry yells.

"These two beat me up," she answers, pointing to the same two women who were screaming about the money.

Henry pushes through the crowd to reach the bloodied woman. He grabs her by the arm, and leads her to an empty stretch of pavement. "What happened?" he repeats.

As the woman begins explaining how the two beat her, Henry, concerned about her condition, interrupts the conversation to radio Central: "I need a bus [ambulance] forthwith. Have a pregnant female who's the victim of an assault. She's bleeding from the mouth."

By this time the crowd has grown larger. The first two women Henry encountered are screaming; he tells them to quiet down and wait for him.

Talking to the victim, Henry is able to piece together the story: The three women knew each other and went into 1911

Anthony Avenue to buy crack. Two of the women went to make the buy while the pregnant woman waited in a corridor and was given a canvas bag by one of the others to hold. Inside the bag was a pack of cigarettes, with a ten-dollar bill tucked away inside it. During the women's absence, a Hispanic man came into the building and asked the pregnant woman for a cigarette.

"Sure," she said.

The woman pulled out the cigarette pack, and the man reached in. He obviously spotted the $10 and stole it, then left hastily. Soon the women returned. One went for a cigarette and saw the bill was missing. She asked where her money was, and her companion said she didn't know. She could explain only that the man to whom she gave a cigarette must have stolen it, but the women thought her story was bogus. They grabbed her and took her to the first-floor landing, where they began to beat her.

One of the two suggested they take her one flight up and throw her out a window. While the pregnant woman was kicking and screaming furiously, the other two women located a bedsheet and tied it around her throat to hang her out a window. One of the women picked up a piece of concrete lying in the lobby and smashed the pregnant woman on the head with it. Then, figuring she had hidden the money in her vagina, they stripped her. When she was naked, one of the women grabbed a broom from underneath the stairs, and, while the other held her down, shoved it in the woman's vagina. Then they decided to throw her off the roof. As she was being pulled up the stairs, the woman grabbed onto the banister and started to scream. All the commotion brought a man who lived there out of his apartment. Seeing the brouhaha, he yelled at the two women to leave the third alone.

"She's got our money," the two women protested.

At this point someone saw Henry walking down the block and called out that a cop was coming. So the women, obviously

263

thinking they'd be slick, ran out to Henry to beat the other woman in relaying the story.

Finally, an ambulance arrives, and Henry helps the pregnant woman into it. In the ambulance are two EMTs, a man and a woman. Henry and the man leave the ambulance so the female EMT can check the injured woman's groin for injury. Henry explains to the male EMT that because of the major fire, it will be some time before backups arrive. "Buy me some time," he tells him, meaning to keep the ambulance there until a sector car arrives.

The two women across the street see Henry outside the ambulance and approach him to inquire as to the whereabouts of their money. Henry says his only immediate concern is the woman's physical condition. "Stay here," he says. "As soon as she's finished being treated, I'll find out where your money is." He then goes back into the ambulance and asks the injured woman to point to the people who injured her. He wants a positive ID. She points to the two women Henry just spoke with, who are now sitting in a car across the street.

Henry calls Central: "Eighty-five. I'm about to have two under. Have the unit pull up on Tremont Avenue." A few minutes later a car pulls up. Henry approaches one of the cops and says he's about to lock up the two women, only they don't know it. "I'll grab the one in the brown, you grab the one in the red."

Henry takes his handcuffs out and puts them behind his back as he walks toward the women. One looks at Henry as he's approaching and asks about her money. As he gets nearer, her eyes widen as she realizes what's going to happen.

"I don't know about your money, but you're under arrest." Henry throws the cuffs on her while she protests loudly and angrily. By now there is a huge crowd.

"You got any drugs on you?"

"No."

"Needles?"

"No."

"I'd better not get stuck with one. You'd better not be lying to me!"

"I don't have nothing!"

Henry turns her bag upside down and dumps the contents. A couple of empty crack bottles fall out, along with a razor blade.

The women are cuffed and put in the sector car for transport to the station house. Henry is told to stay with the injured woman.

In the ambulance she says she doesn't want to be bothered pressing charges. "We've gone this far already," Henry protests, not believing his ears. "Look what they've done to you!"

Henry begins to question the woman's credibility. Sometimes, he thinks, there's a fine line between perps and complainants. Indeed, a complainant can be just as bad.

Henry is amazed that a seven-month-pregnant woman would put herself in such a threatening situation. His frustration turns to anger when the woman refuses medical aid. He brings her back to the 46th Precinct. The two women prisoners are there. Henry has to print them and complete an On-Line Booking Sheet and other paperwork.

Soon the pregnant woman complains she doesn't feel well and wants to leave the station house.

"All right," Henry says, now sympathizing with her. The temperature has soared to the nineties, and everyone is uncomfortable. "Give me your address and phone number."

"I don't have a phone."

If she walks out, Henry thinks, this may be the last I'll see of her, and the arrests will be for naught.

"I'll let you go home, but you better not cross me. At six o'clock, you're to meet me on 161st Street at the courthouse. You know where it is, 215 East 161st?"

"Yeah."

"Don't screw me. Be there!"

The woman leaves, and Henry begins fingerprinting the two prisoners. Both have a rank body odor. One woman's fingers are swollen, and there are pieces of skin missing. They may be unprintable. He takes them to the bathroom so they may wash their hands. He has a female officer do a strip search on them. After they wash, the prints still are not coming out, so he sends them to the bathroom to wash again. He finally gets them printed, then takes them to Central Booking, where their photos are taken and they're lodged. He leaves, and to his surprise sees the complainant. When a complainant is present, instead of waiting for the arrest to be processed in turn and then to see the A.D.A., you go before everybody else. The pregnant woman is with a friend, one who was in the crowd earlier and who had yelled that a cop was coming down the block.

Henry tells the story to the A.D.A., saying he has an assault-two, a felony. The A.D.A. asks to hear the complainant's story. The woman tells it, and produces from her pocket a ball of hair. She puts it down on the desk and says it's the hair the women pulled out of her head when they were beating her up.

"Did you get the rock they hit her with?" the A.D.A asks Henry.

Henry's jaw drops. "You forgot, you stupid rookie fuck!" he tells himself furiously.

"Did you get the broom?"

"No."

The A.D.A. continues his discussion with the woman, putting the hair in an envelope as evidence.

The assistant district attorney is new and aggressive. Probably trying to make a name for himself, Henry thinks. After hearing the story, the A.D.A. tacks on an additional charge: sexually aggravated abuse, another felony. He asks Henry to return to the scene and find the rock and the broomstick. Henry says he has to check with his FTU sergeant.

"Bear with me," the A.D.A. says. "Sit outside."

Outside, the pregnant woman complains she is nauseated and wants to go to the hospital. Henry again becomes vexed, thinking she shouldn't have refused medical treatment when it was offered in the ambulance. She should have gone to the hospital when he pleaded with her before.

Henry goes across the street to buy the pregnant woman and her friend sandwiches, soda, and fruit, paying for the food out of his own pocket. They eat outside the A.D.A.'s office, waiting patiently for the A.D.A. The A.D.A. calls the precinct and speaks with one of Henry's sergeants to arrange for a car to take Henry back to the crime scene to collect the evidence. Another cop, a rookie, soon arrives fresh from the new tour that came on.

Henry doesn't think he'll be able to locate the rock and broom at the building. It's almost midnight. He takes the woman to Bronx Lebanon Hospital, where a Vitullo Evidence Kit will be used to collect evidence so that blood or other physical evidence from the perp and victim may be compared. Henry can't imagine what they'd find, however. The perps used a broom.

The emergency room at Bronx Lebanon is filled with victims of the fire and their relatives. There are babies crying, people moaning in agony. The nurses see the two uniformed police officers and help take the pregnant woman upstairs. Henry tells a doctor what happened, then leaves with the other officer to return to the crime scene. The officer appears very nervous and Henry offers to drive, but the officer declines; the sergeant has told him he's responsible for the car.

The scenario is like a bad dream that keeps getting worse for Henry. By this time he's feeling hyper and impatient. He is annoyed by the other officer, whom he thinks drives like the old lady in the television commercial saying, "Where's the beef?"

On Tremont Avenue, Henry calls Central and asks what footposts are in the area. He asks that they "eighty-five me, no emergency." Cops arrive, and Henry dispenses assignments: one to watch the car, three to accompany him into the building.

They open the door and walk up a couple of stairs to a vestibule. Then they open a second door that leads to the main lobby. At the second door, behind the stairs where the broom was, there's a short staircase that leads down to a back alley. In the alley are a group of people shooting up. Henry opens the door and points his flashlight; they run quickly, reminding him of roaches scattering like you sometimes see when you turn on the kitchen light at night. On a step Henry sees several hypodermic needles. He breaks them all and kicks them. He looks around and spots a piece of concrete that fits the description given by the pregnant woman. But the broom can't be found. Henry thinks the superintendent must have it. The super isn't in, and he knocks on doors asking for his whereabouts. No one knows where he is. Henry is amused that almost everyone he speaks with claims to be the super's relative—his aunts, uncles, or nephews. Henry decides to end the treasure hunt. He puts the rock under the seat of the RMP.

It's after midnight and Henry's starved, but he and his partner don't know where to eat. Henry's last food was juice at two P.M. the day before. On Jerome Avenue they pass by the scene of the fire; Bronx Task Force is guarding a barricaded perimeter of the fire scene. One of the officers suggests a diner. Henry buys a cup of coffee and an apple turnover and brings them back to the car, and they head back to Bronx Lebanon. Henry doesn't want his partner to pull up to the emergency entrance lest the pregnant woman's friend see them eating and ask for Henry's pastry. The officer looks at Henry as if he's out of his mind.

Soon Henry enters the hospital and heads up to the seventh floor to see the pregnant woman. He's aghast to see she's treating the whole situation like a big joke. A doctor signs Henry's memo book. Henry takes the woman and her friend to Tremont Avenue, where the pregnant woman lives in a dilapidated building. He is disgusted. None of this would have happened, he thinks, if the pregnant woman weren't there buying crack in the first place. What bothers him more is her apparent lack of concern for the baby she's carrying. He remembers her complaining at Central Booking that she wanted to go home. But he was thinking, "You're full of shit. You can't wait to get your next vial."

"Ladies," Henry says to the women when the RMP arrives at the women's home, "I highly recommend your avoiding 1911 Anthony. It's bad news."

"Oh, but my cousin lives there," the pregnant woman says.

The women leave, and the officers watch them go into the building. "She can't wait to get her next vial of crack," Henry says to his partner.

Henry returns to the 46th Precinct to voucher the rock. The desk sergeant, who somehow knows about the case, asks Henry for the hair.

Henry didn't get the hair from the A.D.A.

The desk sergeant is called away, and an old-timer looks at Henry. "You get a major rip for losing a piece of evidence. That hair is evidence."

"What am I going to do?" Henry asks.

Another cop says to go back to the woman's home and cut some hair off; no one will be the wiser. Henry thinks the idea is crazy.

The desk sergeant returns, and Henry tells him he left the hair at Central Booking.

"You'd better go back and get it," the sergeant growls.

It's three A.M. Henry is exhausted and uncomfortable in his uniform, which is stale with dried sweat. "I'm going around the clock on this one," he observes.

At Central Booking, Henry tells his story to a police officer, who manages to find the folder with the bag of hair attached. A note says the bag is for Officer Ramirez to voucher.

When overtime ends, vacation will begin for Henry; he can't

wait. He vouchers the hair and is preparing to finish up when his squad arrives at seven A.M. A sergeant tells Henry not to worry about filing his paperwork or signing his radio in. "I'll take care of it. Just change and get out of here."

After working almost twenty-four consecutive hours, vacation couldn't have arrived at a better time for Henry.

Cynicism is like a virus that infects the cop after repeated exposure to people in his precinct. They can be deceitful, argumentative, selfish, or hopeless, yet they are the ones he is supposed to be helping. The condition, further exacerbated by frustrations with the police department and criminal justice system, creates an outlook so corrosive that it can cause the cop to treat others with contempt, silent or not. Indeed, in big cities like New York, the cop doesn't make the city; the city makes the cop. Hopefully, the ideals of young rookies survive the bleaker aspects of the environment and the influence of some of their older, more negative colleagues.

Among Transit cops, the degree of cynicism that Lissette Sierra-Solis has witnessed runs high. These are officers who interact every day with subway commuters and transients, including the homeless and young teenagers who commit robberies. Lissette herself can empathize. She's had people approach her at a gate and tearfully plead for a free ride because they have to pick up their welfare check or have some other emergency, only to forget her face and come back the next day or week and put on the same act. She can see how after a while hard-luck stories don't faze cops, how too many people look and sound like liars, how cops can take little pity.

Even after only a short time on the job, Lissette struggles to ignore the cynicism that pervades her environment. There are a few extremely captious cops in her district, she says. "Everybody's like trash to them, regardless. They have the kind of personality where the minute they walk through the door, it's

'This goddamn job sucks, I hate the post I'm on, the people make me sick, I can't deal with these fuckin' mopes.' These people never have anything nice to say. They're always moaning, groaning, and griping. They rarely use discretion in making arrests; even with juveniles they won't hesitate to bring them in, knowing full well there are instances in which they could really give them a break."

A father and his fifteen-year-old daughter are riding the subway in the Bronx when the teenager, pointing indiscreetly to a disheveled man in his midtwenties, softly says, "That's him, that's the man." The train stops at the 161st Street station and the father approaches the man, his daughter a step behind him. The young man starts to run with the father and daughter in pursuit. Just then a cop comes out of the District 11 station house. The father spots him and shouts, "Officer, get that guy. He tried to rape my daughter."

The officer catches the man and brings him back with the victim and her father to the station house for the incident to be processed. Because the teenager is embarrassed to talk with any of the male officers there, the arrest is assigned to Lissette Sierra-Solis.

As Lissette begins talking with the girl alone in the Juvenile Room, she is struck by how fragile, thin, and young she looks, more like twelve than fifteen years old. The girl, an Indian like her accused attacker, is quiet and gives only one-word answers, like "yes" or "no." She seems inhibited and isn't contributing anything.

The situation reminds Lissette of the role play at the academy about the young girl who ran away from home and was found by two Transit cops early in the morning at a subway station.

As in the role play, the victim is shy and the situation painful to talk about. Lissette has to convince the real-life victim that this isn't a hopeless situation, that the police can do something for her. Lissette says she knows it's unpleasant to talk about,

271

but convinces the girl that it's the right thing to do. The man should be sent to jail because he could rape other girls. Feeling the genuineness of Lissette's concern, the girl opens up.

The victim tells how she walked her little brother to a school bus a few weeks previously and was returning to her apartment when she encountered her attacker blocking a stairway. He told her he had been following her for four months, then grabbed her by the waist and dragged her into his apartment. He threw her onto a bed and felt her body. She was terrified; as he tried to pull down her underpants, she got free and bolted out of the apartment.

For a couple of weeks she was too ashamed to tell her father, but then a friend convinced her to do so. Lissette understands the victim's reticence but wonders about her initial unwillingness to discuss what happened with her father. Later, the girl reveals that a friend of her father's had once raped her.

Lissette realizes that with a less empathetic cop, the young victim might have refused to cooperate. From her past experience as a social worker, Lissette knows that children and young teenagers have to be spoken to with sensitivity, especially when they are embarrassed about something. Lissette is happy with how she handled the situation. The girl has responded well, and even gives her a kiss before she leaves.

Authoritativeness, sharpness, and honesty are all qualities a cop should have. Compassion is another, for, without a sense of humanity, a cop can become as heartless as some of the people he arrests. The unkempt, wild-eyed emotionally disturbed person who frightens people is often more pitiful than dangerous and is usually in need of attention and human warmth rather than a jail cell. Overcoming the distaste and frustration of dealing with such people every day and keeping his compassion from eroding is a challenge from the start for the beat cop.

* * *

Tom Ramos is on his footpost in the 71st Precinct in Brooklyn when a woman dashes up to him. "A man around the corner with a knife is trying to cut up some kids!" she reports excitedly. Tom radios for backup and then runs to the corner, where he peeks out from the edge of a building. He sees a man standing in the middle of the block swinging a knife wildly and mumbling to himself. The man appears to be in his thirties. He looks like he could be a homeless person, perhaps emotionally disturbed, Tom thinks.

With his gun in his hand, Tom approaches the man and tells him to put the knife down. He hopes the man complies; he doesn't want to be in a confrontation with someone who obviously has had a heartbreaking life. The man drops the knife without argument. A backup unit arrives; officers question the bystanders and learn that the man has been living out of a shopping cart in the alleyway between the buildings, by the garbage cans. When some neighborhood kids taunted him, he went into a frenzy, took out a knife, and began swinging.

Tom puts the man against a car and does a quick pat-down. He doesn't find any weapons but observes a bulge in the man's crotch area.

"What's that?" he asks.

"A hanna."

"A what?"

"A hanna."

"What's a hanna?"

From the South, the man has an accent, and Tom has difficulty understanding his explanation.

Although the bulge is soft, Tom wants to make sure a weapon is not secreted in the man's pants and brings him to the station house. In a holding pen the man takes off his pants and reveals a huge left testicle, which Tom estimates to be fully seven inches long. Now he realizes what the man was trying to say: he has a hernia.

273

Because the man's identity cannot be verified, Tom, somewhat regretfully, has to put him through the system. Despite his knife-wielding fit, he appears basically gentle, more pathetic than dangerous. He's also drunk. Tom charges him with disorderly conduct.

There are some perps Tom wouldn't want to talk to, but this unfortunate man seems warm and eager to communicate. On the way to Central Booking in Brooklyn, the prisoner tells Tom he's had the hernia for three years and has to sleep with his left leg raised.

The A.D.A. later tells Tom that the prisoner is complaining of pain and needs to be brought to a hospital. At Woodhull Hospital in Williamsburg, a doctor examines the man. As he works, the doctor gives Tom and the prisoner a running commentary, a mini-medical lecture on hernias; Tom is fascinated. He is a little uneasy, however, as he watches the doctor work the man's protruding intestine back into the abdominal cavity until it is out of sight. The doctor warns his patient about the seriousness of his condition, telling him he could develop gangrene, but Tom doubts the man will heed the doctor's advice. He is released, and Tom brings him back to Central Booking, where he is lodged.

Getting help for this homeless man is the kind of thing that makes Tom Ramos feel good to be a cop. Most police work is enjoyable for him, the fulfillment of a dream. But with all the departmental restrictions and the fear of civil liability, he sometimes wonders how cops ever manage to get the job done. He understands the reasons for the NYPD's stringent policies, yet he feels the regulations send a subliminal message telling officers not to pursue every crime vigorously, so they won't make too many mistakes. But, he believes, being passive could itself be an even worse mistake.

As a rookie, Tom knows he's going to make some errors; everyone does. He just hopes they are not serious enough to jeopardize his job. Sometimes, Tom suspects, survival on the force is a matter of luck—not being at the wrong place at the wrong time.

After an incident, people are often vocal about police action, pointing out what they think the cops did wrong and what they should have done. Cops call these people Monday-morning quarterbacks. "But unless you're there," Tom says, "there's no way you can make that kind of judgment. That's why cops try not to second-guess other cops' actions. Because at that point the cop decided the action he took was what had to be done."

Although not denying that corruption may exist in the department, Tom believes the NYPD is probably less tainted than most police departments in the country. There's a great deal of paranoia, Tom notes: "The safeguards they put into the system put so much pressure on everybody that no one can trust anyone else." If a twenty-dollar bill is found under the seat by a cop making a routine inspection of his radio car, he can't be sure that it wasn't planted by IAD. If an off-duty cop in an unlicensed bar pleads to a uniformed officer not to report him, the on-duty cop cannot be sure the supplication isn't coming from an incognito IAD officer. Corruption in years past set the rigid standards of internal probing that exist today. "That's the price we have to pay for it," Tom says. "It's based on other people's mistakes."

After nearly six months in the Field Training Units, the July academy graduates have strong opinions about what it's like to be a cop in New York City and about the training that brought them to the streets. For most the job is satisfying, in good part because of the people they work with. But there are many frustrations. These usually boil down to disenchantment with three things: the criminal justice system, police administration, and civilians.

"In today, out tomorrow," runs the old saw about prisoners in the criminal justice system. A.D.A.'s who plea-bargain with prisoners, and judges who impose ridiculously light sentences, create a system in which criminal offenders are soon back on the streets, leaving the cops to deal with them all over again.

As to police administration, "the commanding officer of the precinct couldn't care less about what you do out there, as long as you have your three red lights, seven movers, and twenty-five parkers, and you're making the city some money," complains one graduate about writing so many tickets every day. "So the only people you have to depend on are your sergeant, if he's a good guy, and the other cops you work with." Others complain that administration doesn't back them up if there's a civilian complaint, and that civilian complaints prevent officers from getting into special details.

The police are supposed to protect and help civilians, but all too often the civilians are antagonistic or won't cooperate. A rookie remarks on a particular type of macho male: "Once they start getting their load on, forget it. 'I am a man,' they say, pounding their chest, prepared not to take any shit from the cop. It's so delicate how you deal with people. You could create a situation out of absolutely nothing, with the best will in the world. And that's what's frustrating."

"Being a super-active cop," says one officer, "will get you either one of two things: killed or jammed up."

Some rookies say the academy training just doesn't apply. "A lot of guys on the street don't show fear or respect for cops," one asserts. "Tell them to move off a corner, for instance, and they won't listen. They know the cops won't shoot them."

Another says, "Just try using Transactional Analysis on some of the people you come across. 'Excuse me, sir, you can't stand on this corner and drink an alcoholic beverage' won't work. If you want to get the point across, you say, 'Hey, look. I'll tell you once and tell you nicely. Get off the corner. If I come back here and you're still drinking, it'll be bad news for you.' It's not the winos or bums who are bothersome, or who are the problems. I'm talking about the people who hang out with Rambo and his four brothers—who look like they've been lifting weights all their lives, have gold chains around their necks, and carry a radio the size of a car. They're laughing at you as they watch you coming up the block, saying, 'Look at this dick.' It's a different world out there, a lot different than the way most people know it."

It seems to be a normal evolutionary process for academy graduates in their first year out on the streets to tell themselves, after witnessing the depraved conditions and being in constant contact with the worst people of society, "We can just forget all that bullshit we learned at the academy." This is somewhat demoralizing when they think back at how earnestly they applied themselves, only to find out that that's not what real life as a cop is about. Yet they would do better to consider the academy, in Captain DeRienzo's words, as "the beginning of training, not the end." The course work may be idealistic in today's world, but it does establish a critically important perspective: the need to treat others as human beings—respectable, decent, and innocent until proven guilty. Anything less would risk turning the law enforcement system into a farce and the society it protects into a police state.

On January 1, Andy Varga returns from vacation. The next day is his last of FTU; after almost six months of post-academy field training, he will begin working in his permanent command, the 9th Precinct. On his mind at present, however, are the seventeen summonses he has left in his book. He wants to finish them up before transferring.

It is easy for New York City cops to issue summonses for vehicle violations. They could spend their time just going up and down streets writing up parked cars. On the first day of the new year, Andy issues five summonses; the second day, twelve. On his pair of four-to-twelve tours, he enriches the city by casting paper penalties for expired registrations and inspections, missing front plates, mismatches between plates and registration stickers, and double parking.

At 11:45 P.M. on January 2, Andy Varga enters the 13th Precinct on 21st Street between Second and Third avenues. His tour officially ends in five minutes. He goes to the FTU office on the fourth floor to sign out. Seven other officers from his squad and a sergeant are there. The sergeant wishes them all good luck, and Andy goes to an adjacent locker room. He takes off his gun belt and uniform and puts them neatly into a green duffel bag. His shield goes in his wallet. He puts on blue jeans, a white sweatshirt with the word "navy" emblazoned across the front, white Reeboks, and a blue army jacket. At 12:15 A.M. he walks down to the first floor with three FTU friends and out the front door. They bid one another good-bye and urge each other to stay in touch as they part to different precincts.

Andy walks to his car parked a block away. He is tired and aware he has to report for roll call at the 9th Precinct at seven A.M. But his concern over the few hours' sleep he will get is overshadowed by the realization that he has just passed another milestone in his career: He has successfully completed the Field Training Unit program of the NYPD. For a fleeting moment he thinks back to that blustery first day of academy orientation in Brooklyn. It seems light-years away. He feels a little sad, as he did at the police academy graduation. He has enjoyed the past several months and will miss it. But he also looks forward to the future with both the exuberant pride of a person moving up in his career and nervous anticipation for what it will bring.

Andy gets into his car and lets it warm up for a minute. He drives west on 21st Street and turns right onto Park Avenue. It is drizzling out and mild for early January. As usual, even though it is early morning, the streets are filled with traffic.

Past 34th Street, past 42nd, there is an incessant flow of energy. Although weary and anxious about the job, Andy is vibrant. He's not just an ordinary person anymore; he's a crusader for law and order.

He soaks up the excitement of the city as he slowly proceeds north, feeling like a cop.

AFTERWORD

"Man with a gun. Man with a gun." The call came in from Central, with the address of an apartment in the Bronx. It wasn't a 10-85 or a 10-13, so the area wouldn't be flooded with cops unless something happened. For now this was just a routine gun run—if a gun run can ever be considered routine.

Tom Ramos received the call over his radio, and I followed him and two other officers as they went to investigate. When we arrived at the floor, the scene was murky and grim, threatening and depressing all at once. The hall was dimly lit, barren, the walls of chipped plaster. An oppressive stillness hung in the air as we pondered the prospect of some monster lying behind the closed door at the end of the hallway. A plan was whispered.

The officers drew their guns. Two of them began walking slowly down the corridor, and one stayed behind; he would be the line of defense should there be an assault from the other direction.

With their heavy-duty flashlights beaming a path, Tom and the other officers moved slowly and deliberately. I was right behind them. Having come this far, I wasn't going to pass up

281

this opportunity. But I was terrified, the stress almost unbearable. My mouth was dry and my heart was racing. When we were halfway down the hall, the door flew open and a man dashed out of the apartment. He stood facing us, a peculiar grin on his face. "Hey, man," he bellowed, "what's going on?" The officers ordered him not to move and approached him cautiously. Suddenly a hand and face protruded slightly from the open door. Deafening shots rang out before anyone could react.

For the first time I knew what it felt like to be a cop. To be on a job with the unknown lurking menacingly, the advantage always on the bad guy's side; to walk off a sunny busy city street and be thrust into a life-or-death situation with adrenaline flowing and fear gripping the heart. This time everyone involved walked away unhurt—the confrontation was staged at the NYPD's Tactics House as a learning experience for the recruits.

Looking back, I learned an enormous amount at the police academy, not only about the nuts-and-bolts aspect of police work, but also about what it takes mentally, about the psyche of cops. Some of my preconceived notions were confirmed; some fell to dust. I came away with definite opinions.

The search for good men and women police officers is indeed difficult, but the city of New York is a bit too liberal in its admissions policy. Background checks are about as thorough as can be expected with the restraints of time and money, but the department does admit occasional miscreants, not the type of people we usually think of as paragons of law and order and, perhaps, candidates for future corruption.

For example, a person can be appointed to the NYPD with certain types of misdemeanors on his record, such as petty thefts. This is not to say that such an applicant will definitely get on if he meets all the other requirements, but that he could. Cases with applicants of questionable background are decided on an individual basis.

Now the question that naturally arises is, should people who committed a peccadillo in their youth be allowed on the force? Should a young man who was caught hopping a turnstile at fourteen or stealing baseball cards at eleven be denied appointment to the police force? In reality, if someone had these crimes on his record, but went on to college, a respectable job, the military, or worked for Con Ed for a number of years, in each case without a blemish on his record, there's a good chance he might be hired. The case might be reviewed by the Applicant Review Board, the First Deputy Commissioner, and by New York City's Department of Personnel and an affirmative decision ultimately rendered. As a believer in people being able to reform, I think such a person could make a good cop.

But the department's policy does potentially open a can of worms. An applicant who was arrested for burglary or robbery but never prosecuted or convicted, for whatever reason, could also be hired. Consider a group of young men arrested in a stolen car. The D.A. decides not to prosecute Bob, a passenger in the back seat, because the lock was not "punched," that is, the car's ignition was not ripped out. Did Bob know the car was stolen? Bob didn't make any incriminating statements, nor did his friend, who was the driver. So while it is not known whether Bob actually knew the car was stolen, and he had been initially arrested and charged with a felony, he might later be hired by the police force. Do many "Bobs" make it onto the NYPD? Inevitably, I think, some bad apples pass through.

Some veteran police officers I spoke with say they resent kids coming into the department with a "criminal record." As an example of how liberal the department is today in hiring, it would be pointed out that if thirty years ago someone hadn't paid federal taxes, he wouldn't have been hired. Today, if an applicant hadn't paid taxes for a couple of years, he'd be told to pay them. If nothing else was held against him, he'd be hired.

Afterword

It should be pointed out that New York City does strive to recruit students of high caliber—its Cadet Corps program, for instance, provides patrol experience and other law enforcement training for college students interested in becoming police officers when they graduate.

Of course, persons with untarnished backgrounds but who aren't cut out to be cops in other ways also slip through the screening process. These people probably aren't candidates for corruption; they're just not up to the justifiably high standards of the NYPD and the impeccable image it wants to project. Police academy staffers can spot these recruits and are able to predict with startling accuracy who will eventually end up on the inside at a desk job.

One thing which I don't think is unreasonable to expect in a New York City police officer is the facile command of the English language. Verbal communication is the medium of most police work. Yet I observed some recruits who could barely speak English. There is nothing wrong with a person having an accent if he or she is otherwise competent in the language. But when sentences are choppy or fragmented, what force and authority do they convey on the street? What kind of image will that cop project to the people with whom he or she interacts? In my opinion, the department's sensitivity to charges of racism may continue to result in some overcompensation in this regard at the expense of a uniformly high level of skills, communication and otherwise, in their recruits.

A person could meet all the academic and medical requirements and still not be cop material. One recruit in a company whose classes I attended was painfully shy. When the instructor called on him, it was nerve-racking to watch him stammer through his answer. One wonders how authoritative or effective he'd be in various jobs he might handle, from a traffic summons or family dispute to a riot or a bank robbery. Because of the large classes, the instructors don't have an opportunity to observe every student in a role play.

NYPD cops themselves are opinionated about who shouldn't be on the force. Depending on whom you speak with, you might hear any of the following: small women, all women, short men, any person who hasn't served in the military, anyone who has committed a misdemeanor, anyone under the age of twenty-five.

On the other hand, I spoke to many recruits who found the selection process overbearing. "They know you better than you know yourself," one said.

One recruit had a slight hearing loss and failed his hearing test. He was put on medical review and given a makeup date. His job prevented him from taking the test, and he was put on freeze. A new class started; his background investigation began all over again. He had to go through another set of medical exams, and his own physician certified he wasn't hearing impaired. Another student officer who couldn't find a job had been working off the books for a while and had not paid his taxes. Accounting for this period was difficult. Another applicant was caught DWI during his investigation and was rejected.

Of course, once appointed to the force, recruits are on probation, and most of those who are not really fit to be cops are weeded out. The academy is a quasi-military environment with a rigid set of disciplinary rules, and insubordination or noncompliance will result in termination. The training is arduous, with long days of classes at both the academy and at remote sites in the city, and with ample homework. It requires seriousness and diligence on the student's behalf.

Indeed, the students constantly complained about discipline at the academy. I think it is absolutely necessary, not only to instill responsibility, but to initiate the recruits into a regimen that exists on the precinct level and that safeguards the public. Without the framework of such a strict disciplinary code, cops might become lackadaisical or abuse their power.

If from the beginning of their careers on the force, police

officers are allowed to develop a casual approach to their work, the city might one day find itself in trouble. If a city's police force can't be depended on for absolute responsibility and integrity, the very structure of society and life in the city could rest on a shaky foundation, leading to more crime and violence. There is a reason for every rule at the academy. The discipline—arriving on time, complying with dress and hygiene requirements, addressing superior officers properly, and much more—is all designed to help the students avoid trouble later in their careers. I got the feeling that if the rules weren't so austere, some recruits as well as experienced police officers would take advantage, with the result being some anarchy in the police department.

About the only unethical behavior I was aware of at the academy was that some recruits copied others' homework. Whether this transgression is a significant measure of future integrity on the streets I think is dubious, for it seemed to reflect not so much a lack of honesty as a lack of time. After an exhausting eight hours at the academy, then getting home at two A.M., a recruit might not always be able to read lessons in the three academic subjects and then do the written work.

I was very impressed with the instructors. All knew their subject cold, and they taught cogently and inspiringly. Many were not much older than their students, but they kept the necessary distance throughout the training period to be effective and set a good example.

Perhaps because of the substantial investment the city has in each of the recruits, and the political consequences of not graduating enough new cops, the academy does its best to get each student through. It may be going overboard. When recruits flunk a test in driver training or shooting or in gym, they may retake the test. And if they flunk again, they may take another test. This continues until they finally pass. But if a recruit is able to get through the driving course only once in five times, what will happen when he or she is speeding to an emergency on city streets crowded with pedestrians and other vehicles?

Anyone can pass a test given enough opportunities, but the difference between competent and accident-prone cops is that one performs well under stress while the other doesn't. In the street, cops have only one chance to get it right. After I left the academy, I was told that this problem was being addressed. It has been hypothesized that recruits who don't do well in driver training also don't do well in firearms or gym. But this is only a conjecture and is being studied.

Even with good students, the city can end up a loser. After six months or a year or two on patrol, cops can decide the job isn't for them and quit. A member of the force is free to resign at any time. What is most disheartening is students who take the training with less than honorable intentions. One instructor told me of a recruit who went through the academy only to resign the day after he graduated. He wanted to become a priest, but it had always been his fantasy to go through the police academy as if he were going to become a cop.

Another way the city loses money is when police officers quit the force to become firefighters. I was at the academy when the firefighters' civil service test was given, and I was shocked by the number of recruits who took the exam, including one of the student officers I followed. The recruits told me that in the fire department they would work fewer hours, make more money, and have less stress. Fine, but if that's their intention, they should not waste $26,000 of taxpayers' money and in the process rob a person who really wants the job of a place in the academy.

Other recruits told me that they had taken the police civil service tests for neighboring counties, like Nassau or Suffolk. If they were called anytime after graduation, they said, they would quit the NYPD. Would they mind going through academy training all over again? Not at all, if it meant becoming a suburban cop. The incidence of crime is minuscule compared to the city. The surroundings are more placid. There is less stress on the job, and in Nassau County, the pay is even higher.

New York City should require that cops be contractually forbidden from "rolling over" to the fire department until they've served on the NYPD for at least five years. The city should have a reciprocal agreement with police departments in neighboring counties not to hire away each other's graduates before a certain period of service is fulfilled. That way the city can recoup some of its expenses for training these officers.

During intervals between classes, it is costly to maintain the police academy staff. The instructors update the curriculum, but a long period could find them essentially just waiting for new students to come in. Some instructors get bored and return to precincts, in which case new instructors have to be recruited and trained. Perhaps the city should have regular classes of minimum sizes, with increases in the number of recruits as circumstances dictate. There may have to be more instructors hired periodically, but at least the academy would have a core of officers who are always training new cops.

Training and discipline at the academy seemed to me to be fair and even-handed. The instructors tried to instill a sense of authority, but there was no hint of machismo or cold-bloodedness. Rather, they tried to convey the sense of the humanity every good cop should have. They taught the recruits that they were people first, cops second. In a Social Science sensitivity lesson on homosexuality that I attended, the instructors told the class that if anyone was prejudiced toward gay men or women, the job wasn't for them, and they should walk out the door right then.

After this session, my last for the day, I left the academy and walked down the block. It was a balmy spring evening. A gym door was open to let in fresh air; only a wire screen separated interior from exterior. I stopped by this door to watch the recruits practice falling to the ground when thrown. Two young men strolling by stopped to watch with me. They were

288

convinced, they told me, that the academy was instilling brutality. No, no, I said, they teach compassion. The men seemed
concerned about what the academy teaches recruits about gays.
I told them about the class I had just attended, and they seemed
happily surprised. They barraged me with other questions
about the training as reverberations of falls on the mats and
the subsequent groans provided appropriate sound effects. I
felt as though I was doing public relations for the NYPD, but
I also was certain everything I was saying was the truth. As
they left, the two men shook my hand in gratitude for giving
them some new insights about the police.

I found my own attitudes toward cops changing too. Before
I entered the academy, I had variously thought of them as
supermen and superwomen, models of law and righteousness,
hard-nosed bullies, and corrupt brutes who took advantage of
their power. Now I saw them as human beings, sensitive to
the same things as everyone else. But one thought nagged at
me. Do the cops hold on to the compassion the academy en-
courages and teaches once they're out on the streets?

I never witnessed any evidence of racism at the academy—
not between the recruits themselves or in interactions with
instructors. This is such a sensitive area that there wasn't even
the good-natured bantering that sometimes occurs between
friends of different races. I did not hear one negative remark
from a recruit or instructor about anyone's race, beliefs, or
color.

At least one lesson of Social Science is devoted to destroying
the media image of cops. It awakens student officers bent on
a career of adventure and derring-do to the reality of police
life. It is pointed out how the image of cops as portrayed on
television is fanciful and fictitious, and how on TV police
action often violates the U.S. Constitution and the tenets of
our legal system completely.

Although the instructors impressed on the students that police work can be rewarding, they never tried to deceive recruits

with promises of adventure. The student officers were awakened to the fact that street cops do not investigate crimes, which was initially a surprise to some. The patrol officer's job with respect to the investigation of crimes is more or less finished when the detectives show up, except for possible future court appearances.

I, too, had glamorized notions of what police work is about. If I were a police officer, I would be active, take the real bad guys off the street, be known as a tough and honest cop, have my stable of stoolies, and be the one the captain would rely on for help. Alas, this is a television image. A TV show whose episodes reproduced the experiences of a real cop on his footpost or riding in a sector car during his daily tours would quickly end up in the ratings cellar.

Cops are not supermen and superwomen. They're as fallible as everyone else, but their professional exterior is harder. It has to be; the public needs to have confidence in those who uphold and enforce the law. Cops can't be wishy-washy in dealing with people—havoc would result. They have to be tough, authoritative, and sometimes callous. But observe one at home, and you'll see a genuine human being, worried about the mortgage, the in-laws, and what to cook for dinner.

At the close of a meeting I had early on with Captain De-Rienzo, he said, "Cops are just human beings. I hope you'll make that point."

Very human. I made many friends throughout the nearly six months I was at the academy, including many who aren't mentioned in this book. Never once did I feel their amiability was part of a concerted public relations ploy; it was clear that theirs was the sincere expression of genuine people. I had a running game with one Law instructor—Officer Christopher Higgins (I called him "Professor Higgins"). He always tried to engage me in spontaneous exchanges of turgid prose, but I was no match for his keen wit.

In the beginning there was some confusion as to my exact purpose. I was writing a book, they knew, but what kind of book? A novel? A nonfiction work using pseudonyms? Many people expressed surprise that I would be using real names.

I understood this better after learning (with astonishment) how high the level of paranoia is in the NYPD. In conversation, I heard about cops who have been screwed by the administration, but I hadn't any idea of how deep the fear ran until one particular jarring experience.

One evening after an interdisciplinary role play, I walked back to the Social Science Department room to interview an instructor. I was talking with her when in walked a six-foot-five young man with thick jet-black hair and an extraordinarily muscular physique. Wearing jeans and a tight T-shirt with a gun strapped in his shoulder holster, he looked like a real-life Rambo. He listened for a while, and I could see his eyes bugging out. He grew increasingly agitated until he blurted out to the instructor, his friend, "Don't talk to him anymore!"

I turned around. "Why? What's the matter?"

"You're from IAD!"

I assured him I wasn't, that I was writing a book, that I had been at the academy for months, and most of the instructors knew me. I was just conducting interviews for the book, I explained.

"You're lying," he said. "You're an undercover cop looking to get other cops in trouble."

To invoke fear in a cop who seemed so intimidating himself gave me a fleeting feeling of power, but I continued to deny being from IAD. It was not until a veteran instructor heard the commotion and pulled my accuser aside to verify my identity that Rambo was convinced I was harmless. I was walking down the stairs of the academy when the officer came running after me to apologize. He implored me to stop by his station house in the Bronx so he could give me a tour of his precinct.

When a cop knows he can trust you, he opens up and shares all sorts of personal experiences and thoughts. Until that time, however, you are assumed to be working for IAD or FIAU.

After a while I began to feel paranoid myself.

As I continued to observe the training and assimilate police lore, I began to feel more and more like a cop. It can't be helped. You consort with them long enough, you begin to identify with them. There were some grim reminders, however, that I wasn't a cop at all.

During the training I attended a course at the NYPD's outdoor range at Rodman's Neck in the Bronx. I stayed late one day and was in a hurry to get home to take care of some business. I went about ten or fifteen miles over the speed limit. Sure enough, I got picked up by radar on the Bronx River Parkway and suddenly saw a flashing red light on top of an unmarked car behind me. I pulled over to the shoulder.

I had just spent over eight hours with police sergeants, lieutenants, and captains as a friend—an outsider maybe, but still a friend. I had felt relaxed with them.

Now, over to my window marched this imposing figure in a black leather jacket and boots, looking like a Gestapo officer—that's how NYPD Highway cops dress. He asked to see my license, registration, and insurance card, and I was so nervous I couldn't even get out an "okay." It occurred to me to drop a few names—the high-ranking officers I'd just been with at the range—to evade the ticket and higher insurance premiums I'd have to pay as a result. But the guy might be a real hard-nosed you-know-what, I reflected, and I could risk scuttling the book project or getting arrested for an attempt to bribe. Maybe, I hoped, he would notice the range target lying next to me on the front seat, decorated with so many bullet holes that it looked like Swiss cheese. He didn't. I took the ticket meekly, like any other civilian. As thrilling as my experiences had been up to this point, as much as I was vicariously feeling like a cop-in-the-making, I realized that no matter how much I learned, how close I grew to other cops, I wasn't one of them.

After being at the academy awhile, I think I began to suffer from what Dr. Jess Maghan, the Director of Training and the only civilian executive staff member, calls "penis envy." All the police staff carry guns. Throughout the day you talk with these people, joke with them, eat with them, work with them. But they've got something you don't, something powerful and conspicuous, and you want one!

Ah, power . . . I often asked both the instructors and the recruits what they thought about the "power" they have as police officers. Invariably, they responded that they didn't have that much power, and they could exert only what they had to, of course, within the law.

But how I coveted that power. How many times had I seen rude, dangerous drivers blatantly go through red lights or cut me off so that I almost had an accident? If only I were a cop, I'd pull them over and stick a ticket in their faces. But I can't do that. These people can; if they see something wrong, they can take action. I can only call 911. Of course, I could make a citizen's arrest if an offense were committed in my presence, but I'd probably be laughed at, if not beaten up. Not being a cop makes a big psychological difference.

After all the classes I felt I knew the law in general and felt confident about how to deal with people on the street. I had been through the training; I just didn't get a gun and shield like the real recruits. And to that extent, as close as I became to certain officers, I felt a barrier between us. It was always in the back of my mind that they were not civilians as I, but the law. No matter how friendly we could be, if I broke the law, it would be their job to issue me a summons or arrest me. The difference in status makes it impossible for civilians and cops to ever be on equal terms. Few officers I ever spoke with expressed exhilaration with their power, but power is theirs and it is indeed an awesome thing.

A question I thought about constantly near the end of training: After the recruits graduate, will they really be cops? I don't mean just people with guns and shields, but intuitive, effective enforcers of the law?

The answer is no. As in most other professions, the real learning is on the job. Information and theory from books and classroom discussions form the foundation of knowledge, but putting concepts into practice requires actual experience. Like the veteran surgeon who is able to sense when complications may arise and to respond to them effectively, so, too, does the police officer generally need years of patrol experience not only to respond correctly to crimes and accidents, but to be able to look at a street scene and sense that something is wrong, stopping a crime before it happens. Police work sometimes requires instant judgment, not only for safety but for the successful conviction of a criminal. Cops have to act within the law, crooks don't.

At the academy the students learn the legal elements involved in taking police action, the paperwork, and the ethics and psychology involved in dealing with people of diverse social, ethnic, and religious backgrounds. It is only through repeated application of these principles that they master the job, at least the mechanics of it. One student, about to graduate, said to his instructor, "We've covered so many legal aspects. How am I going to remember them all and put them together in the few brief moments I may have to make an arrest?" The instructor gave the recruit a rule of thumb: "If you sense your life is in danger, and you're not sure whether you have a sufficient level of proof to make an arrest, then toss the perp (turn him around), frisk him, and bring him to the station house as long as you are able to articulate a reason for your action later. The most important thing is not to become a statistic, a revision in the *Patrol Guide*."

During post-NYPD training at the Transit Police Academy, the whole issue of whether the separate Transit and Housing Police should merge with the NYPD came into focus for me.

The Transit Police Department seems to suffer from low morale. I didn't do any post-academy Housing Police training or follow any Housing officers, but it seemed to me that their problems were similar.

Many Transit officers, frustrated with what they perceive as limitations of the job, would themselves like the departments to fuse. They say that for the most part the Transit police aren't involved in complicated crimes, so there is little challenge in their work. Fare-beating is the crime most common in Transit work. "I didn't like being on patrol just for that," one officer said. "Harassing people for not paying a buck, that's petty stuff."

Some Transit cops are also sensitive to the public perception that they are somehow not "real" cops, but train guards. One afternoon in the instructors' room on the fifth floor of the Transit Police Academy, two instructors were arguing about the merits of their job. The one arguing against it, a very bright fellow, felt severely limited in career opportunities and frustrated by the nature of the job—working trains and stations and handing out endless summonses for fare-beaters. The other said he found the work challenging and gratifying, and that if the other didn't like it, he should roll over (transfer to City).

The new Transit cops were frustrated that so much of what they had to learn at the academy was irrelevant to their work. Car stops, vehicular summonses, certain accident cases—these and other lessons have no application in the subway.

The job of the Transit police officer is taxing. He spends some seven hours a day in the bowels of New York City, on subway platforms and in trains. Many of the people who would be issued tickets—the derelicts who urinate on the tracks for instance—either don't have an address (they *live* in the subway) or wouldn't show up for a court appearance anyway. Follow-through is constantly frustrated.

Instead of a varied landscape of buildings, a busy street alive with pedestrians, trees, playgrounds and parks, all under sun and sky, the Transit cop's world consists of trains, turnstiles, and people in a rush, all under a roof of filthy cement. The subways are crowded with good citizens, but also with beggars and the homeless, some emotionally disturbed, some badly in need of medical attention, young people blasting music from boom boxes. All this in the gloomy, stench-ridden confines of an underground tunnel. Patrolling this environment every day of a twenty-year career could drive a cop mad!

Transit cops generally work by themselves, and this is lamented not only for the loneliness but for the help a partner could bring. A rookie told me: "You're not going to remember everything you learned at the academy. When you're with a partner, what you don't remember, he might remember. You just put your heads together and think better. You react to certain situations better."

Although people frequently approach the Transit cop for directions or other minor matters, Transit officers long for real conversation on the job. The only person they can really talk to at a post is the token booth clerk, who isn't allowed to invite them into the booth. Adds the rookie: "So you're standing there, trying to talk through that little hole where they fit the money through. You can't hear each other half the time, so half the time you don't even bother to talk to them. You have to repeat yourself whenever a train comes by, so you just stand there and walk up and down, and it's quite boring. Once in a while you might get something. I've heard of cops walking into robberies, but that's quite rare."

There are some Transit cops who are content with their job. Their attitude is, "We've got it made. We don't have to do anything. We're not pressured to do summonses, we don't really have quotas. If you go to City, you have to work."

Most of the Transit officers I spoke with, however, were eager to work. They wanted to get into special units and complained there aren't any good ones in Transit, that they'd have to go to City for them. They seemed demoralized.

Another complaint of Transit cops is the radio. In certain locations and under certain conditions, like rainy weather, radios won't work. Any calls made on the radio won't be heard.

The overall solution to this dilemma is for the City, Transit, and Housing police departments to merge, and for officers to rotate in patrolling the city streets, subways, and housing projects. This way everyone shares the challenge and the less appealing aspects of the various patrols. A merger between the Transit and City police departments has been discussed for years but is still being studied—and hotly debated.

Although it may seem that my access to recruits and staff was unlimited, the office of the Deputy Commissioner of Public Information did impose restrictions on the number of classes I could attend in the academic areas. Some instructors told me confidentially that were it not for a *New York Times* reporter who had written a recent series about training at the academy, I probably would have had complete and unlimited access. The reporter, it seemed, had committed some minor sins that had bothered a few people, but the crowning offense involved an article she wrote in which she mentioned that a female recruit's motivation for working with abused children as a police officer originated from her and her siblings being abused by their father when they were children. I was told that this was how the reporter interpreted the recruit's mentioning that when she was a child her father occasionally spanked her, as many parents punish a child. The story caused a rift between the woman and her father, and she became intensely upset. Future articles were vetted line by line by academy officials. Though I was not permitted to attend every class, the possibility of approving my work was never even raised.

Under my mandate I could attend all instruction at the academy's firearms and driving ranges, and all special classes (including role plays) at the academy except, as it turned out, one. This was the series of classes given by the internal police machine, Internal Affairs. DCPI pulled back on this, and I think the decision says something about how paranoid most divisions are about the cops who watch over the cops. "Let sleeping dogs lie," my DCPI contact told me somewhat mysteriously. As far as the academic classes were concerned, I was permitted to attend four in each area. The instructors helped pick out the lessons they thought would be most valuable. With all the special classes, I was at the academy at least three days every week and sometimes every day.

With regard to the DCPI restriction on how I was to approach the recruits I wanted to follow, I must confess I didn't select any I saw in the street in the academy uniform. Two were recommended by their instructors, and the other two I chose at the firearms range. One of these was Tom Ramos, whom I picked because of his always serious countenance, the calm, confident way he carried himself. Something told me that one day he'd make a great cop. He seemed different—more mature, more independent, more serious than the other recruits I got to know, and I thought he would make an interesting study. During a break, some students from his company approached me to object to my choice. They said he was too much of a "company man," but were called back to muster before I could hear their other reasons. I never did find out what they were, but by the end of training Tom seemed to be much better liked than he had been earlier. I was glad I had chosen him.

After a few months I no longer felt like an outsider at the academy. I was always a bit nervous in front of any of the commanding officers, but never with the instructors. I think they accepted me as a friend, and trusted me to write about them truthfully.

The recruits, too, took me into their confidence. They voiced freely and candidly their opinions about what they liked and didn't like at the academy. They invited me to study sessions and to the company parties held before graduation.

After a few months, the entire class, I believe, knew me, or knew at least that somebody was writing something about the police academy. Since I was following the B Squad, I was visible to these recruits in large lectures or at special classes. Word filtered back to the A Squad. Some recruits eventually told me they had heard I was writing a book, but they weren't sure of its exact nature.

Only once was I ever embarrassed at the academy. This was during the week before graduation, when guest speakers from various NYPD units made presentations. Someone from DCPI was talking about the media before the entire B Squad in the auditorium. The speaker asked who didn't trust writers and the media. There I was, conspicuously sitting in an aisle wearing a jacket and a tie in a room full of uniforms. As nearly every hand went up, some 400 pairs of eyes glanced over at me. I slouched in my seat and smiled with my lips pressed tightly together.

The recruits entered the police academy as civilians and exited as cops. This is certainly a heady prospect, especially for those in their early twenties, a relatively young age. As one twenty-year-old female recruit who had never driven a car until preparing to enter the academy put it, "The NYPD gives you a gun, a shield, and a car, and tells you to be responsible for eight hours a day—to protect the public and make arrests when necessary. That's a lot of responsibility for someone who just got a driver's license." Indeed, in the course of six months, their lives had charted a drastically different course.

There was no one point during the training at which a recruit seemed to suddenly metamorphose from civilian to cop. It seemed to me a gradual transformation far from complete even at graduation.

But I did see changes, and these were fascinating. In the beginning the recruits were timid. I was constantly saluted by recruits in the hall. They didn't know who I was; dressed in a business suit, I could have been a superior officer. It was funny to see the recruits lined up outside Room 610, still as statues, afraid to so much as twitch an eyebrow. By the end of training at the academy, I saw just about everyone relax under the discipline, and some acquired an air of cockiness.

What was most startling was that only a few months into Field Training the recruits were already speaking and acting like "hairbags," old-timers. Most of the academy graduates were placed in run-down neighborhoods, usually drug-prone locations, for their field training, so stress and burnout began eating away at the new officers right from the start. It was only natural for them to develop attitudes. By this time they had completed a rigorous training program, had made friends with experienced, salty cops, and had seen some of the uglier sides of our society.

The idealism that I had admired earlier quickly dissipated, giving way to cynicism. I saw their tolerance for underprivileged people begin to crumble. Gone was the wide-eyed eagerness to help other people so strong only a short time earlier. No longer were they the diffident, restrained individuals expressing measured opinions at the academy. The rookies were out in the real world now, dealing with desperate people living desperate lives under dehumanizing conditions. A sense of hopelessness overshadowed the previous "I want to change the world" attitude. I was told the change in outlook would be even more dramatic after only three years.

"When you first get on the job," one cop told me, "you look for ways to help. But then you grow weary. After a few years, when you see an old lady with a flat tire, you turn your head the other way when you ride by, and hope you don't get caught."

For some recruits, becoming a cop is a rude awakening to certain realities of society. The kid from a comfortable Long Island home with a manicured lawn is amazed to see twelve people living together in a single room in Brooklyn. She has to put up a front to accept this, and pretty soon she becomes a little cold, a little heartless.

The academy can't train an officer to be inured to tragedy yet still be compassionate and sympathetic. Though in time most do become hardened to the results of violence and poverty, often young cops seem to lose in compassion what they gain in steadfastness. New cops do have to begin building walls around themselves right away to survive on the street, and often this takes a toll on their humanity.

Much is made about the NYPD being young and inexperienced. While these two factors do characterize the force, there are some inherent benefits for both the department and the public in what the new officers receive—modern police training with an emphasis on human awareness and sensitivity to the human condition. As the veterans retire, I suspect the problems traditionally associated with police, such as brutality and corruption, will decline. Already, the NYPD is moving toward a more educated force.

The academy has a tough job in preparing cops to patrol the streets of New York. It's a difficult task to teach students within the short span of twenty-three weeks about the law, police procedure, tactics, human psychology, the city's ethnic groups and their cultural practices, and much more.

If a member of the force is found guilty of corruption, I do not think blame can be laid on the police academy. Bad eggs do seep into the applicant pool, as I've mentioned, even if they are intelligent enough to do all the right things throughout training. And whether the academy can be blamed for a bad decision made by a cop is questionable. Police work is based on contingencies. Human beings are unpredictable, and real life reactions are different from those elicited by the conditions of training. An institution can lay the groundwork, but textbook responses to life-or-death situations are the stuff of which heroes are made.

The instructors constantly challenged the students in a way that showed they genuinely cared. Dry subject material came alive in their hands. Classroom discussions were animated events in which recruits participated eagerly. I believe, after all my experience, that the academy, although constantly refining its program, does virtually all that is humanly possible to produce first-rate rookies.

After graduation I did three weeks of additional training at the Transit Police Academy. When this was over, it was difficult adjusting to "reality." I went home and took out a blank pad of paper to begin writing this book. After half a year of interacting with cops and living in an unfamiliar world, I found it difficult to work. I felt depressed, lethargic, sullen. Instead of beginning the first chapter, on the blank sheet I jotted down the following:

Now that my time at the police academy has come to an end, I feel empty. With the recruits leaving the academy to take their place on the streets, I feel like I'm watching my ship sail out to sea without me. I don't think I'll ever forget my excitement: driving a radio car at top speed on the driving range; shooting "perps" at Rodman's Neck; sitting in a classroom with eager, future cops and watching them sort out the problems that even now they are dealing with on the street.

People are sometimes fortunate in life to take a flight from reality that lands them on some fantasy island where dreams are cultivated, where a glimpse is afforded into an alien world, a special world. As brief a journey as it may be, it's one they remember for the rest of their lives. That's how I feel after training with the world's greatest police force.